The Writer's
Harbrace
Handbook

brief edition

John C. Hodges

Robert Keith Miller
University of St. Thomas

Suzanne Strobeck Webb
Texas Woman's University

Winifred Bryan Horner
Texas Christian University

HEINLE & HEINLE

THOMSON LEARNING

Australia • Canada • Mexico • Singapore • Spain
United Kingdom • United States

HEINLE & HEINLE

TM

THOMSON LEARNING

Publisher: **Earl McPeek**
Acquisitions Editor: **Julie McBurney**
Market Strategist: **Katrina Byrd**
Developmental Editor: **Michell Phifer**
Project Editor: **Jon Davies**
Art Director: **Garry Harman**
Production Manager: **Suzie Wurzer**
Compositor: **TechBooks**
Printer: **R.R. Donnelley, Crawfordsville**

Cover image: Copyright © Photodisc

Printed in the United States of America

3 4 5 6 7 05 04 03 02

For more information about our products,
contact us at:
Thomson Learning Academic
Resource Center
1-800-423-0563

For permission to use material from this
text, contact us by: Phone: 1-800-730-2215
Fax: 1-800-730-2215
Web: http://www.thomsonrights.com

Library of Congress Catalog Card Number:
00-111781

ISBN: 0-15-506830-x

Asia
Thomson Learning
60 Albert Street, #15-01
Albert Complex
Singapore 189969

Australia
Nelson Thomson Learning
102 Dodds Street
South Melbourne,
Victoria 3205
Australia

Canada
Nelson Thomson Learning
1120 Birchmount Road
Toronto, Ontario M1K 5G4
Canada

Europe/Middle East/Africa
Thomson Learning
Berkshire House
168-173 High Holborn
London WC1 V7AA
United Kingdom

Latin America
Thomson Learning
Seneca, 53
Colonia Polanco
11560 Mexico D.F.
Mexico

Spain
Paraninfo Thomson Learning
Calle/Magallanes, 25
28015 Madrid, Spain

Preface

Emphasizing the importance of the writing process, *The Writer's Harbrace Handbook,* Brief Edition, offers the clarity and accuracy that have made the *Harbrace Handbook* a standard of reliability since 1941—doing so in a compact format ideally suited for writers who want easy reference to key principles.

The first ten chapters focus on writing—with a purpose, for an audience, in a specific context—providing useful advice for the development of an effective writing process and for successful communication with readers.

Chapter 1, "Reading and Writing Critically," demonstrates the close relationship between reading and writing. It offers practical advice on such topics as how to read a writing assignment and how to benefit from visiting a writing center. It also discusses how the process of writing involves assessing the rhetorical situation: purpose, audience, and context.

Chapter 2, "Planning and Drafting Essays," discusses strategies for discovering and focusing a subject: journaling, freewriting, listing, and questioning. The importance of a clearly defined thesis is explained and illustrated. This chapter also discusses how to outline an essay and how to use details and examples to develop ideas.

Chapter 3, "Revising and Editing Essays," includes a detailed discussion of how to benefit from peer review as well as advice on writing introductions and conclusions. This chapter explains the difference between revising and editing, emphasizing the importance of both. To illustrate how revision can improve a draft, two versions of a student essay are included.

Because formatting an essay for submission is closely related to editing it, chapter 4, "Document Design," discusses MLA standards for headings, margins, and spacing. It also discusses how computers help writers add such elements as charts and photographs to papers. In addition, this chapter includes advice on how to construct a Web page.

Chapter 5, "Writing Arguments," will help students distinguish between fact and opinion, evaluate a writer's credibility, determine the nature of a claim or proposition, and understand how to reason logically.

Chapter 6, "Research: Finding and Evaluating Sources," discusses how to search the World Wide Web and other electronic sources as well as how to find and benefit from sources that are available only in print (such as the texts of most books). In addition, this chapter explains how to evaluate the credibility of sources. It also explains how to conduct interviews and surveys.

Chapter 7, "Research: Using and Citing Sources," includes an extensive treatment of MLA- and APA-style documentation, including the current standards for citing sources accessed by computer. It also includes advice on taking notes, paraphrasing and summarizing, and avoiding plagiarism. Two student essays, with commentary, illustrate MLA- and APA-style papers and demonstrate how research supports a thesis.

Advice on how to overcome writer's block, as well as how to prepare and respond to essay exams, can be found in chapter 8, "Writing under Pressure."

Chapter 9, "Writing about Literature," includes definitions of terms used to discuss fiction, drama, and poetry. It also shows how understanding these terms helps writers to plan and develop essays about literature.

In addition to discussing how to use electronic mail effectively and how to write good memos and letters, chapter 10, "Writing for Work," also shows how to write a résumé.

The chapters devoted to writing essays and other texts are followed by seven devoted to **grammar,** demonstrating that attention to grammar is part of the rhetorical process rather than a separate subject that must be mastered before writing. The grammar chapters are followed by five on **style**, because understanding grammar helps writers make informed rhetorical choices, which, in turn, can lead to the writing of sentences that are more complex, emphatic, and varied. Four chapters on **diction** also address rhetorical choices, since diction is closely related to style. These chapters are followed by several on **punctuation** and **mechanics**, signaling that even details such as these often have a rhetorical dimension, although editing for them can be addressed toward the end of the writing process.

Within these chapters:

- Clear explanations give the reasons for specific rules and advice. Students make better choices when they understand this background.

- In the same spirit, grammatical and rhetorical terms are defined when they are first introduced, reducing the extent to which students will need to consult the glossary.

- In addition, sample sentences with handwritten revisions illustrate the principles being taught.

About the book as a whole

- Bulleted lists begin each chapter, providing users with a quick reference to what follows.

- Specific examples throughout the book demonstrate the principles of writing that are applicable to both course work and professional tasks, and frequent cross-references establish how these principles inform each other.

- Advice on using the computer as a learning tool is integrated throughout the book. Computer boxes and icons highlight discussions involving electronic composition in almost every chapter.

- Similarly, discussion of writing difficulties common to dialect and to English as a Second Language are integrated throughout the book and identified by a globe icon. This integration recognizes that these difficulties are often faced by students for whom English is their first language.

- A four-color design offers a clear and varied palette for the various boxes, screens, and annotations and facilitates ease of reference, as does the comb binding, which allows the book to lay flat. Color-coded tabs clearly demarcate the six major sections of the handbook as well as highlight the chapter on MLA and APA documentation and the glossaries at the end of the text.

The following supplements accompany *The Writer's Harbrace Handbook.*

Instructor Supplements

Instructor's Manual
Harcourt Brace Guide to Teaching First-Year Composition
Harcourt Brace Guide to Teaching Writing with Computers
Harcourt Brace Guide to Writing across the Curriculum
Harcourt Brace Guide to Peer Tutoring
Harcourt Brace Sourcebook for Teachers of Writing
Diagnostic Test Package
Transparency Masters
Instructor's Correction Chart
Exercise Bank (available in print and on disk for PC or Mac)

Student Supplements

College Workbook
Basic Writer's Workbook
ESL Workbook
Working Together: A Collaborative Writing Guide
The Resourceful Reader
Writer's Harbrace CD-ROM
Writer's Harbrace WebCT (course management software with exercises)

For additional information on these and other supplemental materials for *The Writer's Harbrace Handbook,* please visit the Harbrace Web site at http://www.harcourtcollege.com/english.

Acknowledgments

We continue to be grateful for the many reviewers who contributed to the full edition of the *Writer's Harbrace Handbook* as well as the instructors who participated in focus groups and surveys.

For the material on English as a Second Language, we are indebted to Kelly Kennedy-Isern of Miami Dade Community College. Her special expertise added much to the handbook.

Specialty Reviewers

For *argumentation:* Marie J. Secor, Pennsylvania State University. For *research:* Helen J. Schwartz, Indiana/Purdue University; James Lester, Austin Peay State University; Jan Malcheski, University of St. Thomas. For *composition:* Christine Farris, Indiana University at Bloomington; Erika Scheurer, University of St. Thomas; and Victor Villanueva, Washington State University. For *grammar:* Dennis Baron, University of Illinois at Urbana at Champaign; Chris Collins, Cornell University; John Peters, California State University at Northridge; Mary Ramsey, Georgia State University; and Gilbert Youmans, University of Missouri at Columbia. For *literary theory:* Michael C. Jordan, University of St. Thomas.

Class Testers

Vicky Anderson, Loyola University of Chicago; Nancy Ellis, Mississippi State University; and Cecile Anne de Rocher and Tammy Cole of Georgia State University.

Handbook Reviewers

Adrienne Acra, Old Dominion University; Brian Anderson, Central Piedmont Community College; Brenda Ayres, Middle Georgia College; Kirsten Benson, University of Tennessee at Knoxville; Anne Bliss, University of Colorado at Boulder;

Mona Choucair, Baylor University; Kurtis Clements, University of New Orleans; Karen Weaver Coleman, Reading Area Community College; Margaret DeHart, Trinity Valley Community College; Cynthia Denham, Snead State Community College; Brenda Dillard, Brazosport College; Janet Eber, County College of Morris; Patrick Enright, Northeastern State University; Karen Grossaint, Regis University; Kim Haimes-Korn, Southern Polytechnic State University; Nels Highberg, University of Illinois at Chicago; Mary Hurst, Cuyahoga Community College; Wendell Jackson, Morgan State University; Maggie Jenkins, Pellissippi State Technical Community College; Peggy Jolly, University of Alabama at Birmingham; Yvonne McDonald, Milwaukee Area Technical College; Susan McKay, Weber State University; Gwendolyn Morgan, Clark Atlanta University; Sue Munn, Floyd College; Deborah Normand, Louisiana State University; Sue Pine, Florida Community College at Jacksonville; Zaide Pixley, Kalamazoo College; Katherine Raign, University of North Texas; Porter Raper, Portland Community College at Cascade; Denise Rogers, University of Southwestern Louisiana; Paula Ross, Gadsden State Community College; Donna Schouman, Macomb College; Brian Shelley, Campbell University; Sylvia Shurbutt, Shepherd College; Terry Spaise, University of California at Riverside; Rebecca Stout, Texas A&M University; Tracy Thornton, Old Dominion University; Richard Viti, Southern Illinois University; Mike Williams, New Mexico Junior College; and Wanda Williams, Jefferson State Community College.

Focus Group Participants

Linda Hill, Sheila Fox Miller, Mary Ann Robinson, Rosia Wade, Celia Wood, and Stephanie Brook Woods of Hinds Community College; Michalle Barnett, University of Alabama at Birmingham; Tim Barnett, Northeastern Illinois University; Donna Gessell, North Georgia College and State University;

Fred Green, Floyd College; Kirsten Komara, University of Evansville; Jack O'Keefe, Daley College; Donna Singleton, Reading Area Community College; Julie Hagemann, Purdue University-Calumet; Sylvia Stacey and Richard F. Tracz of Oakton Community College; Susan Giesemann North, University of Tennessee; and Jane Wagoner, Wilbur Wright College.

For the preparation of this brief edition of *The Writer's Harbrace Handbook,* we thank our copy editor—Mike Nichols—and the talented staff at Harcourt College Publishers: Julie McBurney, acquisitions editor; Michell Phifer, senior developmental editor; Jon Davies, senior project editor; Suzie Wurzer, production manager; and Sue Hart and Garry Harman, art directors.

Contents

 Writing

Grammar

xx   **Contents**

Effective Sentences

Diction

 Punctuation

Mechanics

The Writer's
Harbrace
Handbook

brief edition

Writing

Writing

Chapter 1

Reading and Writing Critically

Because the volume of information in the world is rapidly increasing—in many media and especially on the Internet—the ability to read and write critically is central to your education. By reading critically, you can make good choices, evaluate what you choose to read, and understand key points. By writing critically, you can improve your understanding of what you read, generate new ideas, and communicate successfully with other readers.

Critical writing can take many forms. Among those discussed in this handbook are

- an essay from personal experience (**3h**),
- an argument from personal experience (**5j**),
- an argument based on research (**7f(2)** and **7i**),
- a memo or letter (**10b–c**), and
- a résumé (**10e**).

But whatever form it takes, critical writing—like critical reading—involves active engagement, the curiosity and discipline to figure something out.

This chapter will help you see that reading and writing involve a series of components (**1a**). It will also help you understand

- how to take an active role in your education (**1b**),
- how to read syllabi and writing assignments (**1c**),
- how to preview reading assignments (**1d**),
- how to distinguish between content and your personal response to reading (**1e**),
- how to evaluate and establish credibility (**1f**), and
- how to assess the situation in which you must complete a writing assignment (**1g**).

1a Both reading and writing are best approached as processes.

When reading critically, you might begin by looking over the text to get a rough sense of it (**1d**); then read for content (**1e(1)**), noting personal responses (**1e(2)**) and evaluating credibility (**1f**). Finally, go back and reread the whole work so that you understand it more fully.

An Outline of the Reading Process

Previewing	Skim what you are planning to read, getting a sense of how the material is organized and what it contains (**1d**).
Reading for content	Determine what the writer of the piece is trying to communicate. Note the major points. Underline, highlight, or annotate key passages whenever possible (**1e(1)**).
Noting your personal response	Consider what you like or dislike about what you have just read, what interested you the most, and whether any parts of this material made you think about your own experience (**1e(2)**).
Rereading	Check your understanding of the content. Consider how the material has been presented by appraising how the writer has focused, organized, and developed ideas (**1f, 5e, 6c**).

Experienced writers also recognize that they cannot be expected to do everything at once. They do not feel compelled to always follow the same procedures; nor do they expect that other writers will always complete the same steps in the same order. Nevertheless, writing usually involves four stages.

An Outline of the Writing Process

Prewriting	Read critically. Think about what you want to write about, take notes, make lists, raise questions, make an outline.
Drafting	Get your ideas down quickly. Write as much as you can. If unexpected ideas come up as you draft, get those down too. Do not worry about being perfect.
Revising	Make cuts and additions to improve focus and development. Improve the structure of paragraphs and the organization of the work as a whole. Reconsider your introduction and conclusion.
Editing	Tighten and clarify sentences. Improve word choice. Eliminate mistakes in spelling, punctuation, and mechanics.

Chapters 2 and 3 discuss writing processes in detail, and additional information about process can be found in chapters 5 through 10.

1b You can become a better reader and writer by being actively engaged in your education.

Although you will frequently benefit from working in collaboration with others (see 1b(3) and 3e), you are most likely to grow if you take responsibility for your own learning. Others can be guides, mentors, coaches, teammates, or judges, but you still have to decide what to do and then do it.

(1) Inventories

Inventories are lists in which people record what they have so they can assess where they are and plan for where they want to go. Keeping an inventory can help you monitor your own growth and learn how to distinguish the kinds of advice that are the most helpful to you. Experiment with inventories by taking one each college term or at least one each academic year.

Begin by considering what good writing involves:

- understanding your rhetorical situation (1g),
- establishing a clear focus (2b),
- developing a main idea (2e),
- writing in unified and coherent paragraphs (3c),
- arranging paragraphs in a meaningful sequence (2d),
- observing the rules of grammar (chapters 11–17),
- using a clear and engaging style (chapters 18–26), and
- mastering the conventions of punctuation and mechanics (chapters 27–35).

Then consider your own priorities. Which of these areas are of greatest concern to you? Which can be safely deferred until you have met your most important goals? What are you already doing well?

Using a simple chart, you can then take stock. The following form can help.

A Writing Inventory

What I have been told by readers:

	Strengths	*Weaknesses*
Content		
Organization		
Style		
Surface Errors		

What I think my strengths are:

What I want to improve:

This form can be modified for other purposes, such as improving your skills as a critical reader or your overall study skills. Whatever the focus of your inventory, preserve each one and as you write new ones, compare the results so you can monitor your progress.

Keeping an inventory involves keeping track of what others have told you about your work and distinguishing their comments from your own sense of how you are doing. This exercise sometimes shows that a writer has been overly influenced by a single reader or, at the other extreme, has chosen to ignore what several readers have reported. Writers need to see themselves as others see them, as well as reflect on how they see themselves.

(2) Reading journals

Like a personal journal (pages 30–31), a reading journal provides an opportunity for using daily writing as a way to improve your understanding of experience. In this case, however, you focus exclusively on responses to your reading. You are much more likely to remember what you have learned from reading when you write about it. Moreover, writing regularly about your reading can also increase your comprehension of content and help you identify ideas for papers.

You are especially likely to benefit from keeping a journal that is structured to improve both comprehension and creativity. One way to do this is to keep what is called a **double-entry journal,** or a journal with two parts for each entry. Use the left side of each page to summarize what you read (see 7c(4)) and the right side to record your personal responses to this material (see 1e(2)). Or you could write two paragraphs a day: a paragraph summarizing what you learned from something you read followed by a paragraph reflecting on this material. You could also keep entries in different computer files.

Keeping entries devoted to summarizing content separate from those devoted to recording personal responses will help you when you review what you have written. When preparing for an examination (see **8c**), for example, you will be able to easily identify the entries that will help you remember content. And when preparing to draft an essay (see chapter **2**), you can turn to those entries in which you recorded your own ideas.

(3) College resources

One of the advantages of studying at a college or university is that you can get academic support. Everyone needs help at some point, but you need to become aware of the resources available.

(a) Instructors

For most questions about the work you are doing in a course, your instructor should be able to help. Although you can get answers to many questions in class, here are some tips for making a conference with your instructor productive.

CHECKLIST for Getting Help from Your Instructor

- Learn the instructor's office hours and location.

- Ask if it is possible to make an appointment.

- Identify the goals you have for this visit. What information do you need most? What do you need to take away with you if this meeting is going to be productive?

- If you are planning to discuss a specific reading or writing assignment, bring a copy of it to the meeting.

- Tell your instructor what you need. Do not expect your instructor to read your mind.

In addition to conferring with instructors in their offices, you may be able to consult with them through e-mail (see **10a**) or through a Web site (see **6d(2)**) created for your class. If an e-mail or other electronic address does not appear on the syllabus, ask whether electronic communication is possible.

(b) Writing centers

Many students find that they benefit from discussing work in progress with tutors who have recently completed similar kinds of assignments. Your college is likely to have a writing center where this kind of consultation can take place.

CHECKLIST for Visiting a Writing Center

- Learn when the center is open and how long you can expect a tutorial session to last.

- Find out whether you can get help whenever you stop by or whether it is best to make an appointment.

- If you are working on a specific assignment, bring the material with you: your assignment sheet, books or articles, and, most important, anything you have already written.

- Be prepared to explain your assignment to your tutor and to indicate the kind of help you need.

- Recognize that tutors are ready to help you with your *writing;* they will not simply check something over for errors. Make your visit at least a day before your assignment is due.

- If you have a good session with a tutor, learn his or her name so that you can develop a working relationship.

- If you have a frustrating experience with a tutor, ask for someone else on your next visit, and do not judge the entire staff by a single bad experience.

(c) Libraries

The staff of your college or university library are ready to help you find the material you need for writing from research. (See chapters 6 and 7.) You can expect to find this help by stating your needs at the reference desk. Moreover, many libraries now offer workshops and other training sessions for finding information on the World Wide Web (see 6d(2)).

1c Reading syllabi and assignment sheets carefully can help your academic performance.

Critical readers pay close attention to any text that establishes their rights or responsibilities.

(1) Syllabi

Reading a syllabus carefully can help you avoid misunderstanding what is required of you.

CHECKLIST for Reading a Syllabus

- Note your instructor's name, office number, and office hours.

- Note the texts required for the course.

- Look closely at what the syllabus says about writing assignments. When will papers be due? Are there penalties for turning papers in late?

- Will there be quizzes or exams? (See chapter 8.)

- How will your final grade be determined?

- Does the syllabus include an attendance policy?

Hold on to your syllabus so that you can review it regularly. Clearly defined policies and expectations can be overlooked when you have many demands on your time.

(2) Assignment sheets

An assignment sheet explaining what an instructor expects you to accomplish deserves close attention. If you read quickly, you may end up responding to one aspect of the assignment and overlooking another. Or you may focus on one aspect of your writing when the assignment directs you to focus on another. If you have questions after you have studied the assignment, be sure to ask your instructor.

CHECKLIST for Reading an Assignment Sheet

- How much flexibility does this assignment allow? To what extent does it leave you free to make choices? What guidelines does it provide for helping you make those choices?

- What does this assignment definitely require you to do?

- What are your purpose, audience, and context? (See **1g**.)

- What strengths can you bring to this assignment?

- What do you still need to learn if you are going to complete this assignment successfully?

- How much writing is expected of you?

- How much time should you devote to this assignment? When should you get started?

- Should you consult with your instructor or visit a writing center? (See **1b(1–2)**.)

1d Previewing can help you read a text critically.

To **preview** reading means to assess how difficult a text will be and what you are likely to learn from it. Comprehending what you read is the first step toward reading critically.

When you page through a magazine looking for articles that seem interesting, you are, in a sense, previewing it. A more systematic preview can give you better results, especially when you are undertaking college reading assignments. Look for the following features.

Title	Titles and subtitles often reveal the focus of a work and sometimes even its thesis, so they are usually worth noting. (See **3b(3)**.)
Directories	A *table of contents* identifies the chapters within a book; an *index,* at the back, lists the specific topics covered. Checking these directories can help you determine whether the book will have the kind of information you are looking for and, if so, exactly where you can find it. A *bibliography,* or a list of works cited, indicates how much research is involved; it can also direct you to other useful sources.
Length	When you consider length, you can estimate how much time you should set aside for reading. By checking length, you can also estimate whether a work is long enough to include useful content.
Visual aids	The extent to which visual aids are useful varies, because different readers have different learning styles. Nevertheless, graphs and illustrations break up what might otherwise be large blocks of densely written text and signal points where you might pause.

Summaries   A summary can help you decide whether the work as a whole will be helpful. It can also help you follow a difficult text because you will know its major points in advance. Summaries can often be found in the *preface* of a book, as well as in introductory and concluding chapters. Scholarly articles often begin with a summary identified as an *abstract* (see pages 220–21). Within articles, the introductory and concluding paragraphs often include summaries (see **6d(1)c**).

In addition to looking for these features within the work you are previewing, assess how much you already know about the subject. If the work looks difficult and you are unfamiliar with the subject matter, you might benefit from doing some preliminary reading by downloading a less demanding work from an electronic indexing service or the World Wide Web (see **6d**). You can also increase your capacity for critical reading by being alert for occasions when you are tempted to dismiss new ideas prematurely.

To preview college reading assignments, ask the questions in the following checklist.

CHECKLIST for Previewing a Reading Assignment

- How long is this work, and how long are different sections of it? Does the organization seem straightforward or complex? How much time will you need to read this piece carefully?

- What do you already know about this subject? Can you keep this knowledge in mind as you read so you can establish some immediate connection with the text?

- Do you have any strong feelings about this subject that could interfere with your ability to understand how it is treated in this text? (See **1e**.)

- Do you know anything about this author, and if so, can you trust what he or she writes? If the author is unfamiliar to you, is there any biographical information in the source that will help you assess his or her credibility? (See **1f** and **6c**.)

- What can you learn from the title? Is there a subtitle? If there are subheadings in the text, what do they reveal about the organization?

- What do the table of contents and index indicate about what is in the book? Does this article include an abstract?

- Are there graphs, figures, or other visual aids? If so, how can this material be useful to you?

- Is there a bibliography that will indicate how extensive and current the research is?

- Does the introduction or conclusion reveal the author's thesis? (See **2b**.)

- Has the author included a summary near the conclusion or at the end of any of the subsections?

- Would it be easier for you to understand this text if you read something else first?

In addition to asking yourself these questions, you can benefit from scanning specific sentences and phrases. Although the central idea can occur anywhere within a paragraph (see **3c(1)**), it often appears in the first or last sentence. By reading these sentences, you can get a sense of a work's content and organization.

The main outline of a text can also be determined by words that indicate sequencing, such as "There are *three* advantages to this proposal. . . . The *first* is. . . . The *second* is. . . ."

In addition, you can scan for key phrases that writers use to signal important points. The phrase *in other words,* for example, signals that a writer is about to paraphrase a point just made—probably because it is important (see 7c(3)). Other key phrases include *in the following article* (or chapter), which can signal a statement of the author's focus or purpose; and *in summary, in conclusion,* and *the point I am making,* which signal that a point is being made about the information just presented.

Although previewing is a way to make reading easier and more meaningful, it is not the same as reading a text closely.

1e Critical readers can distinguish between the content of what they read and their personal response to that material.

Reading is a transaction between writers and readers. Writers choose words to express themselves and make these words available to others. Readers then try to understand these words.

Sometimes, however, communication between writers and readers breaks down. Writers may have used language carelessly, or readers may have read in haste. Moreover, even language that is well chosen can be misleading because words have different meanings (or denotations) as well as strong associations (or connotations) that vary from reader to reader (see 24a). By becoming a critical reader and writer, you become a better communicator and develop strategies for resolving misunderstandings.

To read a text critically, you need to ask at least three questions of it:

- What exactly is this writer trying to tell me?
- How did the writer try to communicate this content?
- What does this text make me think or feel?

(1) Content

Because meaning depends on how and where words are used, reading for content involves constructing knowledge from groups of words—sentences, paragraphs, sections, and chapters—and building on this knowledge as you acquire new blocks. For example, you may understand a sentence when you first read it, then understand it better after finishing the paragraph in which it appears. The challenge is to understand as much as you can but to keep that understanding flexible enough to accommodate what will come. Critical readers usually reread texts that are important to them.

When reading for content, make sure you understand the words on the page. You are likely to encounter words that are new to you. The meaning of such words may be defined in the text itself, or you might be able to infer their meaning from the way they have been used. Whenever a new term appears in a critically important position such as a thesis statement (**2b**) or a conclusion (**3b(2)**), you should take the trouble to learn its meaning. Similarly, you should consult a dictionary (**23a**) when an unfamiliar term appears repeatedly.

(2) Personal responses

Because we sometimes judge others prematurely, we misunderstand what they say or write. Critical readers pay attention and do not allow their personal responses to interfere with their ability to understand. But in addition to reading for content (see **1e(1)**), they also note what they think about this content; they consider where they agree or disagree, become frustrated or intrigued. They then determine exactly what triggered this response. Is it the writer's tone (**3a(3)**), an example that evoked a personal memory, a lapse in the organization (**2c**), the subject itself (**2a**), or something altogether separate from the text?

By noting personal responses and recognizing that they are independent of a work's content even if they are inspired by it, critical readers increase their understanding of the choices writers make. Such responses can also generate ideas that can lead to new pieces of writing. (See 2a, 5b, 6b, and 9c.)

CHECKLIST for Recording Personal Responses

- Note passages that capture your attention.

- Put a question mark in the margin when you do not understand a passage—or understand it but question its accuracy.

- Put an exclamation point in the margin when a statement or example surprises you.

- Write *yes* or *no* in the margin when you agree or disagree. When a passage reminds you of something else you have read, note that comparison in the margin.

- Keep a reading journal (1b(2)). Include at least one question, compliment, or reservation about what you read each day.

- Correspond by e-mail with other people who are reading the same material (10a).

- Talk with friends and family members about any texts you have enjoyed reading.

1f Good writing conveys credibility.

In addition to reading to gain comprehension and to determine a personal response, critical readers look for signs that help them determine whether an author is well informed and fair minded. To determine how credible a writer is, ask yourself the questions in the following checklist.

CHECKLIST for Evaluating Credibility

- Does the writer sound committed to communicating with readers? As a reader, do you feel that you are being addressed respectfully?

- Does the writer seem knowledgeable about the topic?

- Does the writer support claims with evidence? (See **5d** and **5e**.)

- Does the writer reveal how and where evidence was obtained?

- Does the writer recognize that other points of view may be legitimate? (See **5e(2)**.)

- Does the writer reach a conclusion that is in proportion to the amount of evidence produced? (See **5d**.)

If you are uncertain about a writer's credibility or simply want to learn more about this person's professional standing, you can often obtain additional information by searching an electronic indexing service or the World Wide Web (see **6d**).

Similarly, when you revise your own writing (see chapter **3**), consider your own credibility by asking yourself what you would ask of others. Doing so can help you see where you need to develop a point, moderate a claim, or adjust your language.

1g Writers must understand their purpose, audience, and context.

Critical writers have a clear sense of purpose, audience, and context.

Purpose   What a writer hopes to achieve in a piece of writing

Audience   Who will read the piece in question

Context   Where and when the exchange between writer and
audience takes place

Your purpose should be appropriate for both the audience and
the context. For example, you would not convince a prospective employer to hire you if you spoke the same way you talk
to your closest friend. Nor would you speak the same way to
your friend regardless of the context: where and when the conversation takes place, as well as social factors can influence it.
You should demonstrate similar flexibility when writing. The
combination of purpose, audience, and context is called your
rhetorical situation. Assess your rhetorical situation when you
are planning to write (see chapter 2), and remember it when
you are revising your work (see chapter 3).

(1) Purpose

The clearer your purpose, the better your writing is likely to
be. To clarify your purpose, it helps to ask yourself whether
you want to

- express how you feel about something,
- amuse or entertain readers,
- report information to readers,
- explain the significance of information,
- persuade readers to agree with you, or
- convince readers to undertake a specific action.

When classified according to purpose, nonfiction writing is often described as **expressive, expository,** or **persuasive.**

    Expressive writing emphasizes the writer's feelings and reactions to people, objects, events, and ideas. The following example comes from an essay designed to convey how the author
feels about the relationship he had with his father.

At just about the hour when my father died, soon after dawn one February morning when ice coated the windows like cataracts, I banged my thumb with a hammer. Naturally I swore at the hammer, the reckless thing, and in the moment of swearing I thought of what my father would say: "If you'd try hitting the nail it would go in a whole lot faster. Don't you know your thumb's not as hard as that hammer?" We were both doing carpentry that day, but far apart. He was building cupboards at my brother's place in Oklahoma; I was at home in Indiana putting up a wall in the basement to make a bedroom for my daughter. By the time my mother called with the news of his death—the long distance wires whittling her voice until it seemed too thin to bear the weight of what she had to say—my thumb was swollen. A week or two later a white scar in the shape of a crescent moon began to show above the cuticle, and month by month it rose across the pink sky of my thumbnail. It took the better part of a year for the scar to disappear, and every time I noticed it I thought of my father.

—SCOTT RUSSELL SANDERS, "The Inheritance of Tools"

Expository writing focuses on objects, events, and ideas, rather than on the writer's feelings about them. Textbooks, news accounts, scientific reports, and encyclopedia articles are usually expository, as are many of the essays students are expected to write in college. When you report or explain, you are practicing exposition. The following paragraph comes from an article that explains what happens to people when exposed to severe cold.

But those who understand the cold know that even as it deadens, it offers perverse salvation. Heat is a presence: the rapid vibrating of molecules. Cold is an absence: the dampening of the vibrations. At absolute zero, minus 459.67 Fahrenheit, molecular action ceases altogether. It is this slowing that converts gases to liquids, liquids to solids, and renders solids harder. It slows bacterial growth and chemical reactions. In the human body, cold shuts down metabolism. The lungs take in less oxygen, the heart pumps less blood. Under normal temperatures, this would produce brain damage. But the chilled brain, having slowed its own metabolism, needs far less oxygen-rich blood and can, under the right circumstances, survive intact.

—**PETER STARK,** "As Freezing Persons Recollect the Snow"

Persuasive writing is intended to influence the reader's attitudes and actions. Most writing is to some extent persuasive; through the choice and arrangement of material, even something as apparently straightforward as a résumé can be persuasive. However, writing is usually called persuasive if it is clearly arguing for or against a specific position (see chapter 5). Note how the author of the following paragraph calls for better management of national parks.

We must protect our national parks, for our families and for our future. The only way that we can ensure that our priceless heritage of national parks and other public lands is still here for our grandchildren is through responsible federal management. We must not abandon the guiding principles set down in 1916: Our parks must remain "dedicated to conserving unimpaired . . . natural and cultural resources and values . . . for the enjoyment, education and inspiration of this and future generations."

—**MELANIE GRIFFIN,** "They're Not for Sale"

Writers frequently have more than one purpose. For example, it is often necessary to report information when you are trying to persuade. There is nothing wrong with having more than one purpose. If you do, you should be using one to help you achieve the other—which is very different from writing without a purpose or simply losing sight of your original purpose.

CHECKLIST for Assessing Purpose

- If you are writing in response to a specific assignment, what is your instructor's purpose in giving it? Check your assignment sheet (**1c(2)**) to see what goals your instructor has set for you.

- Are you expected to fulfill a given purpose, or can you define your own?

- Are you trying primarily to express how you feel? Are you writing to improve how well you understand yourself or trying to help others understand you better?

- Are you trying to be entertaining? What do you hope to accomplish by treating your subject humorously?

- Are you writing primarily to convey information? Are you trying to teach others something that they do not know already or to demonstrate that you have knowledge in common?

- Are you writing primarily to persuade your readers? Do you want them to undertake a specific action?

- Do you have more than one purpose in writing? Can you achieve all of them? Are any in conflict?

---

(2) Audience

Understanding your audience will help you decide on the length and depth of what you write, the kind of language to use, and the examples that will be the most effective. Some writers like to plan and draft with a clear sense of audience in mind; others like to focus on the audience primarily when they are revising. (See chapters 2 and 3.) At some point, however, you must think clearly about who will be reading what you write and ask yourself whether your choices are appropriate for this audience.

(a) Specialized audiences

A **specialized audience** has a demonstrated interest in your subject. If you are writing about the harm done through alcohol abuse, members of organizations such as Alcoholics Anonymous or Mothers Against Drunk Driving would constitute a specialized audience. These audiences would have different kinds of expertise and possibly different agendas, so it would be unwise to address each of them the same way. In each case, however, you could assume that your audience has a special interest in your subject and some knowledge of it.

When writing for specialized audiences, you need to consider how much and what sort of information, as well as what methods of presentation, are called for. You can adjust your tone and diction as you tailor your presentation. (See 3a(3) and chapter 23.) If you provide a detailed explanation of basic terms or procedures, an audience of experts might decide that your work is too simple to be helpful and choose to read something else instead. But if you can provide the same audience with new information—or a new way of understanding information with which it is already familiar—the attention you receive is likely to be favorable.

When you write a paper for a college course, you can usually assume that your instructor is a specialized audience. If you are writing an essay about a novel assigned by your English instructor, for example, it is not necessary to summarize the plot unless you have been specifically asked to do so. You can assume that your audience already knows what takes place. Instead of reporting what happens, use your essay to communicate your interpretation of the material you have both read. (See chapter 9.)

Writing for members of a specialized audience does not necessarily demand that you know more than they do. At times it may be sufficient to demonstrate that you understand the material and can discuss it appropriately.

(b) Diverse audiences

A **diverse audience** consists of readers with different levels of expertise and interest in your subject. When writing for a diverse audience, you can usually assume that your readers have interests different from yours and many demands on their time but share a willingness to learn about new material if it is presented clearly and respectfully by someone who is taking the trouble to identify with them. The key to communicating successfully with diverse readers is to find some way to draw them together on common ground and to join them there.

One way to envision a diverse audience is to think in terms of educational level. Instead of writing for students in general, you could ask yourself whether the audience you most want to reach is composed primarily of students in their first or fourth year of college. By considering the educational level of your audience, you will find it easier to make appropriate choices in diction (see chapters 23 and 24) and detail (see 2e).

You could also envision a diverse audience defined by some other common ground, such as gender. If you look through popular magazines, you can easily find articles written for either men or women. However, when writing for a gender-specific audience, do not make the mistake of assuming that all men or all women think the same way or share the same values. Further, there is a big difference between consciously choosing to write for a gender-specific audience and accidentally ignoring gender differences when writing for an audience that includes both men and women.

Sometimes you may not know much about your audience. When this is the case, you can often benefit from imagining a thoughtful audience of educated adults. Such an audience is likely to include people with different backgrounds and cultural values (see 9b(2)), so be careful not to assume that you are writing for readers who are exactly like you. To a considerable extent, the language you use will determine whether diverse readers feel included in or excluded from your work (see **23d**). Be careful to avoid jargon or technical terms that would be understood only by a specialized audience. If you must use a specialized term, explain what you mean by it. (See **23b(6)**.)

(c) Multiple audiences

Writers often need to address multiple audiences. At work, for example, you might write a memo that will be read not only by the person to whom it is addressed but also by people who receive copies (see **10b**). The readers in a multiple audience can have different expectations. If, for example, you are asked to evaluate the performance of an employee you supervise and send copies to both that person and your boss, one part of your audience is probably looking for praise whereas the other is looking to see whether you are a competent supervisor.

The use of electronic communication (see **10a**) has increased the likelihood of writing for multiple audiences because messages can be easily forwarded or viewed— and not always with the writer's permission. When writing texts for electronic submission, consider whether anyone outside your immediate audience may read your work.

When writing essays in college, you may also find yourself writing for multiple audiences. The most common example is drafting an essay that will be discussed in a small group of fellow students and read by your instructor. If you choose to write an essay for a diverse audience and submit it to an instructor who is a specialist on your subject, you are actually writing for multiple audiences. Considering a variety of positions (see **5e(2)**) is helpful when planning, drafting, and revising your essay (see chapters **2** and **3**).

CHECKLIST for Assessing Audience

- Who is going to be reading what you write?

- What do you know about the members of this audience? What characteristics can you safely assume about them?

- What values do you share with them?

- How do you differ from them?

- How much do they already know about your topic?

- What kind of language is appropriate for them?

- How open are they to views that may be different from theirs? Are they likely to prefer hearing you restate what they already know or learning something new?

- What do you *not* know about your audience? What assumptions would be risky?

- Are you writing with one audience in mind and then expecting a different audience to read what you have written? If so, have you clearly indicated the audience you have in mind so your readers can imagine that they are part of it?

---

(3) Context

Context means the circumstances under which writers and readers communicate. It includes time and place. An essay written outside of class may be very different from one written in a classroom even if both are written for the same instructor and in response to the same question. What you are able to write has been influenced by time and place, and your audience is likely to take this into account. Similarly, an instructor may expect more from an essay written at the end of the course than from one written at the beginning.

Context is also influenced by social, political, religious, and other cultural factors (see 9b(2)). Your background and beliefs often shape the stance you take when writing. Writers can benefit by considering whether such factors have led them to make assumptions about their audience that may or may not be accurate.

When you read the work of other writers, you will sometimes find examples in which the context is specifically stated, as in the following passage.

> In the twenty-second month of the war against Nazism we meet here in this old Palace of St. James, itself not unscarred by the fire of the enemy, in order to proclaim the high purposes and resolves of the lawful constitutional Governments of Europe whose countries have been overrun; and we meet here also to cheer the hopes of free men and free peoples throughout the world.
>
> —WINSTON CHURCHILL, "Until Victory Is Won"

Often, however, the context must be inferred. Whether or not you choose to state your context, considering it is essential.

CHECKLIST for Assessing Context

- Under what circumstances are you writing this essay? If you are free to choose the time and place in which you write, have you set aside sufficient time and found a site where you can work without distractions?

- Under what circumstances will your essay probably be read? If it is going to be one of many essays in a pile on someone's desk, can you help that person quickly see the purpose of your work and how it responds to your assignment?

- How has your response to this assignment been influenced by what else is going on in your life? Are you satisfied with this response, or does it put you at risk?

- Have you been asked to write an essay of a specific length? If length has not been specified, what seems appropriate for your audience?

- What document design (see chapter 4) is appropriate for this context?

Chapter 2
Planning and Drafting Essays

Experienced writers understand that writing is a process (see 1a). When you engage in this process, you must consider your purpose, audience, and context (see 1g). You must also be prepared to revise and edit what you write (see chapter 3).

This chapter will help you

- find good topics (2a(1)),
- focus your ideas (2a(2)),
- write a clear thesis statement (2b),
- organize your ideas (2c), and
- draft well-developed paragraphs (2d).

Try to focus on one activity at a time.

As you plan and draft an essay, you may need to return to a specific activity several times. For example, drafting may help you see that you need to go back and collect more ideas or change your thesis. Repeated effort provides opportunities to improve. (See chapter 3.) Working out your ideas and making them clear to readers will also help you gain new insights.

2a Writers find appropriate subjects and decide how to focus them.

Whether you are assigned a subject or are free to choose your own, you must consider what you know—or would like to learn about—and what is likely to interest your audience (see 1g(2)). You must also decide how to focus your subject so that you can develop it adequately within the time and space available to you.

Sometimes you might be asked to choose your own subject. In this case, you should consider your interests and your experience. The first step toward interesting an audience in your subject is to be interested in it yourself. Often the best subject is one drawn from your own experience, because experience has given you knowledge of the subject.

More often, however, you will be asked to write essays about subjects outside your personal experience but within your academic experience. For instance, if you are not limited to a specific question when assigned a paper in American history, you would be responsible for choosing your subject. Just as you do when you write about personal experience, you should make an effort to find material that interests you. Look in your textbook, particularly in the sections listing suggestions for further reading and study. Go through your lecture notes and examine the annotations you made in the works you read for the course. (See **7b.**) Ask yourself whether there are any aspects of your subject about which you would like to learn more. Writing about a subject is one of the best ways to learn about it, so use this assignment to satisfy both your audience and yourself.

(1) Subjects

If you have a hard time finding something to write about—or have so many ideas that you have trouble choosing among them—try **journaling, freewriting, listing,** or **questioning.** Discussing assignments with other people can also help you generate ideas and decide on those likely to yield good essays. Different methods may work best for different subjects; if you run out of ideas when using one method, switch to another.

(a) Journaling

Keeping a journal can generate subjects for essays. Although there are many kinds of journals, students often benefit from writing in a personal journal or a reading journal.

In a **personal journal,** you reflect on your experience. You use writing to explore how you feel about what is happening in your life. You might focus on external events, such as what you think about your job, or focus on your inner life by exploring changes in mood or attitude.

Like a personal journal, a **reading journal** includes responses to experience. In this case, however, the emphasis is on exploring the ideas generated by what you experience through reading. (See **1b(2)**.) In either case, feel free to write quickly without worrying about spelling or grammar.

(b) Freewriting

When freewriting, writers record without stopping whatever occurs to them during a limited period of time—often no more than ten minutes or so. They do not worry about whether they are repeating themselves or getting off the track. No matter how bad the writing may be, the process helps them discover ideas they did not realize they had. The entries in a journal are usually freewritten, but freewriting is not limited to journaling. You can take out a sheet of paper and freewrite whenever you have a few minutes to spare. In directed freewriting, writers begin with a general subject area and record whatever occurs to them about this subject during the time available.

(c) Listing

The advantage to listing, also known as **brainstorming,** is that it lets you see individual items at a glance rather than having to pick them out of a block of writing. It also encourages the establishment of relationships. Jot down any ideas that come to you while you are thinking about your subject. Do not worry if the ideas come without any kind of order. The point is to collect as many ideas as you can.

When preparing to write his essay (see pages 71–73), Peter Geske made the following list after he had decided to focus his essay on the quality of the education he received at his high school.

```
geometry with Kleinberg
sophomore English with Mrs. Sullivan
American history with Mr. Rodriguez
out-of-date books
a terrible library
out-of-control classes
failing chemistry
partying throughout senior year
overcrowding
useless computers
```

As you look through the list, you will find some ideas that are closely related and could be grouped together. For instance, "out-of-control classes" could be related to "overcrowding." After recording ideas as they occur, writers then decide what needs to be added, deleted, or rearranged. (See pages 37–38.)

For an example of a list written and revised under pressure, see page 238.

(d) Questioning

Explore a subject by asking yourself some questions. There are two structured questioning strategies you might use—journalists' questions and a similar approach known as the pentad, which encourages seeing relationships. **Journalists' questions** ask *Who?, What?, When?, Where?, Why?,* and *How?* Using journalists' questions to explore the subject of high school education could lead you to think about *who* goes to public high school and *who* teaches there, *what* courses are offered, *when* education improves or deteriorates, *where* funding comes from and *where* teachers get their training, *why* some classes get overcrowded and *why* funds are short, and *how* education stimulates or *how* it fails.

The **pentad** considers the five dramatic aspects of a subject.

Act	what happens
Actor	who does it
Scene	the time, place, and conditions under which the event occurred
Agency	the method or circumstances facilitating the act
Purpose	the intent or reasons surrounding the act

Using this method can help you discover relations among the various aspects of the subject.

(2) Focus

A simple analogy will help explain focus: when you want a picture of a landscape, you cannot photograph all that your eye can take in. As you aim your camera, you look through the viewfinder to make sure the subject is correctly framed and in focus. You may wish to move in closer and focus on one part of the scene, or you may decide to change your angle. You can think of your writing the same way—focusing and directing your ideas just as you focus and direct the lens of your camera, moving from a general subject to a more specific one.

For example, "high school" is too large and general a subject to make a good topic. However, some of the items that emerged when listing on this subject (page 32) can be grouped to form a manageable topic. Or a single item, if well chosen, could lead to a sharply focused essay of some depth.

In addition to reviewing the ideas you have generated through strategies such as freewriting and listing, you can discover a focus by thinking in terms of how strategies used for developing your ideas (see **2e**) can take you in different directions. Using "high school" as an example of a subject that needs focus, here are some questions inspired by considering development strategies.

a. *Narration.* What is the story of my high school education?
b. *Process.* How do teachers teach? What was my learning process like?
c. *Cause and effect.* Why did I hate high school? How was I influenced by peers? Would I have done better in a different school district?
d. *Description.* What did a typical class look like? What was it like to be in study hall, the cafeteria, or the gym?
e. *Definition.* What is education? What is a good school? How demanding should a high school education be?
f. *Classification and division.* How could I classify the students or teachers in my high school? What is the significance of dividing students by year rather than by accomplishment?
g. *Example.* What was a typical day like? Who was my best teacher, and who was my worst?
h. *Comparison and contrast.* How did my school compare with a rival school? What did my two best teachers have in common?

Although you might need to combine two or more strategies to develop your work (see **2d**), thinking initially in terms of a single one can help you clarify your focus.

Because writing is a form of thinking, your focus may also emerge from writing your first draft and then assessing it. When you compare the draft of Peter Geske's essay on high school education (pages 68–70) with the final version of it (pages 71–73), you will see how drafting and revising can sharpen a writer's focus.

Whatever method you use to focus your work, your choice should be determined by your interests, your purpose, the needs of your audience, and the time and space available.

CHECKLIST for Assessing a Topic

- Can you do justice to the topic in the space available to you? Should you narrow it?

- Do you know enough about it to be able to write about it at the length your instructor requires? Should you expand it?

- Are you interested in this topic?

- Could your audience be interested in it?

- Is it appropriate for the assignment?

- Are you willing to learn more about it?

2b   A clearly stated thesis conveys your main idea.

If you have limited and focused your subject, you have begun to develop an idea that controls the content and organization of your paper. In college, you will be expected to state your main idea succinctly. The **thesis statement** contains a single idea, clearly focused and specifically stated, that grows out of your exploration of a subject. A thesis statement can be thought of as a central idea phrased in the form of an assertion (see **5d**); that is, it indicates what you claim to be true, interesting, or valuable about your subject.

Rather than starting with a preconceived thesis that you must then struggle to support, let it develop out of your thinking process as you draft your paper. Your goal should be a claim that is neither self-evident nor too broad.

A clear, precise thesis statement will help unify what you write; it will guide many decisions about which details to keep and which to toss out. You can also use the thesis to guide your search for information to support your point. But it is important to allow your essay to remain flexible in the early stages. As you write, check your thesis statement frequently to see whether you have drifted away from it. Do not hesitate to change your thesis, however, if you find a more productive path or one you would rather pursue. When you revise, test everything you retain against the thesis you have finally decided on, and discard anything that does not contribute (see chapter 3).

A thesis is usually stated in a declarative sentence with a single main clause—that is, in either a simple or a complex sentence (see 12c). If your thesis statement announces two or more coordinate ideas, as a compound sentence does, be sure that you are not losing focus. If you wish to sharpen your thesis statement by adding information that qualifies or supports it, subordinate such material to the main idea.

The clearer your thesis, the more focused your essay is likely to be. The following examples show ways to focus and clarify vague thesis statements.

Vague   It is hard to make decisions.

Better   Making financial decisions is difficult for me because
I am confused by the number of investment choices
that are available today.

Vague   The media have a lot of influence on how people think.

Better   The frequent use of unusually thin models in television
and magazine advertisements has contributed to the
rise of eating disorders among adolescent girls in the
United States.

Thesis statements appear most often in the first or second paragraph, although you can put them anywhere that suits your purpose—occasionally even in the conclusion. The advantage of putting the thesis statement in the first paragraph, however, is that your reader knows from the beginning what you are writing about and where the essay is going. This technique also helps readers who are searching for specific information locate it easily.

> **CHECKLIST for Assessing Your Thesis**
>
> - Is your thesis clear?
>
> - Could it be more specific?
>
> - Is it likely to interest your audience?
>
> - Does it accurately reflect what you think?
>
> - Can you support it?
>
> - Will you be able to support it within the length specified for this essay?
>
> - Is it placed where readers will be able to find it easily?
>
> - Would your readers benefit from having it restated later in your essay?

2c Arranging ideas requires choosing appropriate methods.

Many writers need a working plan to direct their ideas and keep their writing on course. Some use informal written lists; others use formal outlines. Such plans are especially helpful for writing lengthy papers (see chapter 7) and for writing under pressure (see chapter 8). Whatever method you choose, remember that you can always change your plan to suit any new direction your writing takes.

(1) Informal working plans

An informal working plan need be little more than an ordered list that grows out of a collection of ideas (see page 32).

```
1. Physical description of my school
2. Textbooks, computers, and other supplies
```

3. Class size
4. Courses that were a waste of time
5. Bad teachers
6. A few bright spots

When you make such a list, ideas might overlap. For example, it may not be possible to separate "courses that were a waste of time" from "bad teachers." Some ideas may drop out, and others may occur to you as you draft. But you have the beginning of a plan that can guide you.

(2) Formal outlines

Writers sometimes find themselves required to follow a plan of organization that has been determined for them. Often, however, outlines grow out of the writing. Some writers can develop an excellent plan from listing or journaling; others discover that they need to rethink their original plan after they have actually written a draft. But whether an outline is written before or after the first draft, a formal outline is often helpful when analyzing a draft and preparing to revise it.

A structured outline uses indentation and numbers to indicate various levels of subordination. The main points form the major headings, and the supporting ideas form the subheadings. An outline of Peter Geske's essay (pages 71–73) might begin as follows.

THESIS: Academic facilities and standards
were so low at my high school that I learned
very little while I was there and became
discouraged about school.

   I. Description of the school
      A. The building itself
         1. Run-down

          a. Exterior
          b. Interior
       2. Overcrowded
          a. Hallways
          b. Classrooms
    B. Facilities
       1. Terrible library
          a. Few books
          b. Poor access to the Web
       2. Inadequate labs
          a. Chemistry lab
          b. Biology lab
II. Description of programs
    A. Typical courses
       1. Math
          a. Using poor teaching methods
          b. Harassing students
       2. Chemistry
          a. Reading from the textbook
          b. Giving unfair tests
    B. Bright spots
       1. American history
          a. Analyzing the news
          b. Getting extra help
       2. English
          a. Reading good stories
          b. Doing creative writing

The types of outlines most commonly used are topic and sentence outlines. The headings in a **topic outline** are expressed in grammatically parallel phrases, as in the example above, whereas a **sentence outline** presents headings in complete and usually parallel sentences. A topic outline has the advantage of brevity and highlights the logical flow of your paper; a sentence outline forces you to think through your ideas more thoroughly. Regardless of the type of outline you choose, you will need enough headings to develop your subject fully within the boundaries established by your thesis.

2d Draft your essay by writing well-developed paragraphs.

You develop a draft by developing the paragraphs you use to build the essay as a whole. If you are working from an outline, especially a topic or sentence outline (see **2c(2)**), you can anticipate the number of paragraphs you will probably write and what you hope to accomplish in each paragraph. If you are working from an informal working plan (see **2c(1)**), you will have a sense of where you want to take your ideas but may be uncertain about the nature and number of paragraphs you will need. In both cases, however, you need to develop each paragraph fully; then decide whether additional paragraphs would help your audience understand the main idea of your essay.

Typically, paragraphs range from 50 to 250 words. Paragraphs in books are usually longer than those in newspapers and magazines, and your own paragraphs are likely to vary.

Although long paragraphs that exhaust one point or combine too many points can be problematic for readers, do not worry about whether any of your paragraphs are getting too long when you are drafting. You can condense or split up an overly long paragraph when you revise (see chapter **3**). At this point, it is better to go on too long than to stop too soon, because your best sentences may be the last to appear.

Students sometimes fall into the habit of writing short paragraphs because they are afraid that they will be told to "break up" long ones. There are certainly times when a paragraph becomes so long that it is hard for readers to make their way through it, times when a writer has become repetitive or insisted on giving a dozen examples when half that number would do. These paragraphs often take up more than a page. But if you go to the other extreme and have four or five paragraphs on a single page, your writing is going to seem choppy. Experienced writers may write some paragraphs that are only three or four lines long and others that fill a page. But most of their pages will consist of two or three well-developed paragraphs, each of which is **unified** and **coherent** (see **3c**).

Although one-sentence paragraphs are occasionally used for emphasis (see chapter **21**) or to establish a transition (see **3d**), short paragraphs often indicate inadequate development. The most common reason for paragraphs that are too short to be satisfying is that a writer has become frustrated or distracted—abandoning a train of thought rather than developing it. Although there will be times when you can combine two short paragraphs as you revise (see chapter **3**), there will be more occasions when you need to make a short paragraph longer by developing it. Most short paragraphs need to be developed with specific details or examples (see **24a(3)**).

Instead of considering development a chore, think of it as an opportunity to have your say without anyone interrupting you or changing the subject.

(1) Details

A good paragraph gives readers something to think about. Consider the following paragraph.

> Father Whalen was my favorite priest. I got to work with him when I was an altar boy. He was really good at his job, and I will always remember him.

This paragraph is short on detail. In what sense was Father Whalen good at his job? If he really does live on in memory, what exactly is it about him that is being remembered?

Now consider a well-developed paragraph by an experienced writer.

> *Working with Whalen was a pleasure; he was a real artist, someone who could have made his mark in any field.* He had all the tools—good hands, nimble feet, a sense of drama, a healthy ego, the unnerving itch to be loved that all great performers have. He did not rush his movements, mumble, or edit his work. He was *efficient,* yes—he'd send the right hand out for the chalice as his left hand was carving a blessing in the air, that sort of thing—but every motion was cleanly executed and held the air for the proper instant, and he had astounding footwork for such a slab of meat. He was one or two inches over six feet tall, 250 pounds maybe, big belly sliding around in his shirt, but he was deft on the altar and could turn on a dime in the thick red carpet. He cut a memorable double pivot around the corners of the altar table on his way to his spot, and he cut that sucker as cleanly as a professional skater before a Russian judge. —BRIAN DOYLE, "Altar Boy"

Notice how the series of details in this paragraph support the main idea (italicized) or the topic sentence (see **3c(1)**). There is no need to "break it up"; readers can see how one sentence leads to another.

(2) Examples

Like details, examples contribute to development by making specific what otherwise might seem hard to grasp. Details describe a person, place, or thing; examples illustrate an idea. In college writing, you will be expected to provide examples to support your ideas. (See **5e**.)

The author of the following paragraph uses several closely related examples (as well as details) to support the main idea with which he begins.

The civility that lingers on in Japan is the most charming and delightful aspect of life here today. Taxi drivers wear white gloves, take pride in the cleanliness of their vehicles, and sometimes give a discount if they mistakenly take a long route. When they are sick, Japanese wear surgical masks so they will not infect others. The Japanese language has almost no curses, and high school baseball teams bow to each other at the beginning of each game.

—NICHOLAS KRISTOF, "In Japan, Nice Guys
(and Girls) Finish Together"

2e Experimenting with development strategies can help you generate additional paragraphs.

Development strategies can be used to frame entire essays by providing a way to organize ideas. For example, you could compose an essay devoted exclusively to defining a concept or explaining a process. More frequently, however, these strategies, or **modes** as they are sometimes called, are used to generate ideas and determine a focus (see **2a(2)**) or to facilitate effective communication between writer and audience by developing a point that might otherwise be unclear. When drafting an essay, you may discover that you need to add a paragraph defining a term or explaining a process before you can expect your audience to understand your essay as a whole.

Development strategies are often used in combination. For example, a formal definition can be developed through both comparison and contrast, and narration can be developed through description. The point is to choose a strategy—or combination of strategies—that will satisfy your purpose and your audience within a particular context. Considering the needs of your audience (see **1g(2)**) will help you determine which points to develop and which strategies can facilitate that development.

(1) Narration

A narrative discusses a sequence of events, normally in the order in which they occur, to develop a particular point. This mode often uses time markers such as *then, later, that evening,* or *the following week.*

(2) Description

By describing a person, place, object, or sensation, you can make your material come alive. Descriptions are often visual, but they can appeal to senses other than just sight. Description should suit your purpose and audience. In describing your car, for example, you would emphasize certain features to a potential buyer and others to a mechanic who is going to repair it.

(3) Process

Process paragraphs explain how something is done or made. Add an explanation of process to your draft if doing so can illustrate a concept that might otherwise be hard for your audience to grasp.

(4) Cause and effect

Writers who explore causes raise the question *Why?* and must answer it to the satisfaction of their audience. Be sure to avoid the fallacy of assuming that because one event precedes another it necessarily caused it. (See **5i**, false cause.) Writers can also demonstrate effects by discussing what results from a specific choice or action.

(5) Comparison and contrast

A comparison points out similarities, and a contrast points out differences. When drafting, consider whether a comparison would help your readers see a relationship that they might otherwise miss or whether a contrast would establish useful distinctions.

(6) Classification and division

To classify is to categorize things in large groups that share certain characteristics. **Classification** is a way to understand or explain a subject by establishing how it fits within a category or group. For example, a book reviewer might classify a new novel as a mystery—leading readers to expect a plot that inspires suspense. **Division,** however, breaks objects and ideas into smaller parts and examines the relationships among them. Divided into chapters, a novel can also be discussed according to components such as plot, setting, and theme (see chapter 9).

(7) Definition

By defining a concept, a term, or an object, writers increase clarity and focus discussion. Definition locates a concept, a term, or an object in a class and then differentiates it from other members of that class: "A concerto [the term] is a symphonic piece [the class] performed by one or more solo instruments and orchestra [the difference]." The difference distinguishes the term from all other members of the class.

Use these strategies to make your essay as a whole more understandable to your audience. Make sure, however, that you are using them to support your thesis and purpose. If a paragraph devoted to definition or another mode is contributing to the main idea of your draft, then it is contributing to development. If you added this paragraph simply because you ran out of other things to say, then you will probably need to drop it as you revise your essay (see chapter 3).

2f Your first draft allows you to further explore your topic and to clarify what you think.

Get your ideas down quickly. Spelling, punctuation, and usage are not as important in the first draft as they are in the final one. Your first draft gives you something you can improve on later. If you are not sure how to begin, you could start by simply stating your thesis and the main points you hope to cover. Similarly, you could conclude by restating your thesis or summarizing your main points. Later, when you revise this first draft, you can experiment with other ways of introducing and concluding an essay (see 3b).

If you find yourself losing track of where you want to go, consult your plan and reread what you have written. If you are stuck, you could move ahead in your plan and write paragraphs that will appear later; the intervening material may occur to you if you keep on writing. For example, if you have trouble writing the introduction, start with a supporting idea you feel sure of, and write about it as long as you can. When you are actually writing, you will probably generate new ideas. You can then move on to another part that will be easy to write. What is important is to begin writing, to write as quickly as you can, and to save your early work so that you can refer to it as you revise. (See chapter 3.)

Although some writers like to draft in longhand, using a computer when drafting offers distinct advantages: you can easily move from drafting one part to another, knowing that you can scroll up or down as you generate new ideas. And when you save a draft in an electronic file, you are well positioned for revising your work later.

Finally, bear in mind that writing is a form of thinking. As you draft, you are likely to discover that you had more to say than you realized. Although you may choose to suppress any idea not directly related to your initial plan, writers often benefit from developing an unexpected idea. When drafting leads you to a place you did not intend to visit, allow yourself to explore if you sense that you are making a useful discovery. You can consider how to integrate this material into your plan when you prepare to revise, or you may simply choose to delete it.

Chapter

3

Revising and Editing Essays

To **revise** means "to see again." This activity, which is at the heart of writing well, implies that you take a fresh look at your draft—rethinking what you have written and what you still need to write by distancing yourself from your work and evaluating it from a reader's point of view. To **edit** means to polish a piece of writing by making word choice more precise (chapter **24**), prose more concise (chapter **25**), and sentence structure more effective (chapters **18** through **22**), in addition to eliminating any errors in grammar, punctuation, and mechanics. Although revising and editing can overlap, they are essentially very different activities.

Revising usually comes before editing. This does not mean that you cannot correct errors as you move along; but the more time you invest in editing at an early stage, the harder it is to make major changes to your essay. When something looks perfect on the surface, it can be tempting not to touch it. As you revise, you should be willing to rearrange paragraphs and make significant cuts and additions.

This chapter will help you revise and edit your essays by discussing how to

- consider your work as a whole (**3a(1–2)**),
- evaluate your tone (**3a(3)**),
- write a good introduction (**3b(1)**),
- write a good conclusion (**3b(2)**),
- choose an appropriate title (**3b(3)**),
- improve the unity and coherence of paragraphs (**3c**),
- create transitions (**3d**),

- work effectively in a writing group (3e),
- edit to improve style (3f), and
- proofread to eliminate errors (3g).

3a Revision is essential to good writing.

In one way or another you revise throughout the writing process. For example, even in the earliest planning stages, as you consider a possible subject and then discard it in favor of another, you are revising. Similarly, after choosing a subject, you might decide to change your focus or emphasize some new part of it. That, too, is a kind of revision. And, of course, you are revising when you realize that a sentence or a paragraph you have just written does not belong where it is, so you delete or move it.

Nevertheless, experienced writers usually revise after they have completed a draft. They not only revise certain sentences and paragraphs, but also they review the draft *as a whole*. Whenever possible, plan your writing process so that you can put a draft aside and then see it later with fresh eyes.

(1) What is on the page

When you review your essay as a whole, ask yourself whether your main point comes through clearly and whether you ever digress from it. (See 2b.) Writers frequently get off track as they generate ideas through the act of writing. Now is the time to eliminate those side trips. It is also wise to make sure you are developing a point rather than simply repeating the same thing in different words—or, as sometimes happens, contradicting yourself by saying two very different things.

Revising also demands paying close attention to the expectations of your readers. (See 1g(2).) Have you provided enough examples or other details? Are your ideas expressed in language appropriate for that audience? Will your audience understand the purpose of your essay? In other words, revising successfully requires that you examine your work both as a writer and as a reader. As a writer, ask yourself whether you have succeeded in saying what you wanted to say. As a reader, ask yourself whether what is clear to you will also be clear to your audience.

Moreover, you should examine your paragraphs to make sure they are well developed (see 2d), unified, and coherent (see 3c). Assess how well each paragraph leads to the next and whether your transitions are effective (see 3d).

CAUTION When you move or delete paragraphs, check to see whether your new arrangement works and whether you need to write new transitions.

(2) What is not on the page

One of the most challenging tasks in revision is to look for what you have left out that your audience might expect or that would strengthen your essay as a whole. Your best ideas will not always surface in your first draft; you will sometimes have an important new idea only after you have finished your draft and taken a good look at it.

Inexperienced writers sometimes end an essay prematurely because they cannot think of anything else to say. One way to get past this block is to use such strategies as listing and questioning (pages 31–33). Another way is to share your work with other readers and ask them to let you know if there is anything they find confusing or want to know more about (see 3e).

(3) Tone

Tone reflects your attitude toward your subject and must be appropriate to your purpose, audience, and context (see 1g). When revising, experienced writers consider how they sound. They may find that they sound confident and fair minded; they may also discover that they sound sarcastic, angry, apologetic, or arrogant. Your challenge, when revising, is to make sure that your tone contributes to how you want your readers to respond.

3b Introductions, conclusions, and titles help shape how readers respond to your essay.

Because they are prominently located in an essay, introductory and concluding paragraphs are especially important. Readers often look closely at these paragraphs, expecting guidance and clarification from them.

(1) Introductions

Of all the paragraphs in your essay, your opening paragraph may be the most important. If the introduction seems boring or confusing, some readers will stop reading. And those who persevere may misunderstand your essay if they misunderstood your introduction. For long or complex essays especially, a good introduction helps readers know what to expect.

Introductions have no set length; they can be as brief as a couple of sentences or as long as several paragraphs. Experienced writers compose introductions at any time during the writing process. Because getting started can be difficult, writers sometimes draft openings that are inefficient, misleading, or dull. When they revise, they usually find ways to introduce their ideas more effectively and to clarify the thesis statement (see 2b). Writers must also decide how to locate the thesis statement within an introduction that leads to it or develops it.

You can arouse the interest of your audience by writing introductions in a number of ways.

- Start with an interesting fact or unusual detail.
- Use an intriguing statement.

- Open with an anecdote.
- Begin with a question your essay will answer.
- Start with an appropriate quotation.
- Open with an illustration.
- Begin with general information about the subject or show how you came to choose it.
- Simply state your thesis.

Whatever type of introduction you choose to write, use your opening paragraph to indicate your subject, engage readers' attention, and establish your credibility (see **1f**).

(2) Conclusions

Writers sometimes stop drafting before they have come to a conclusion that draws their ideas together. They may also go on too long—drafting additional paragraphs after what is, in effect, the end of the paper in terms of its focus (see **2a(2)**). An essay should not merely stop; it should finish. Some suggestions follow.

- Conclude by rephrasing the thesis.
- Direct attention to larger issues.
- Encourage your readers to change their attitudes or to alter their actions.
- Conclude with a summary of the main points covered.
- Clinch or stress the importance of the central idea by referring in some way to the introduction.

Whatever strategy you choose, provide readers with a sense of closure. Bear in mind that they may be wondering, "So what? Why have you told me all this?" Your conclusion gives you an opportunity to respond to that concern. If there is any chance readers may not understand your purpose, use your conclusion to clarify your reason for writing (see **5g(5)**).

(3) Titles

The title is the reader's first impression and, like the introduction, should fit the subject and tone of the paper. Writers who are confident that they have chosen a subject likely to interest their audience might choose a title that simply announces their topic as in "How to Pay for a Good College." Other writers might draw attention with a title that involves a play on words, as in "Cents and Sensibility." A good title could also take the form of a question designed to arouse the reader's curiosity, as in "Who Killed the Bog Men of Denmark? And Why?"

When you are ready to title your essay, a good way to begin is to try condensing your thesis statement. Or reread your introduction and conclusion, and examine key words and phrases for possible titles. And when revising your essay, consider whether you need to revise your title (as Peter Geske chose to do when revising his paper, pages 68–73).

3c When revising, experienced writers consider whether paragraphs are unified and coherent.

Although readers may have special expectations for your introductory and concluding paragraphs (see **3b(1)** and **3b(2)**), they will expect to be able to follow all your paragraphs without getting confused. When revising an essay, you are likely to find opportunities to improve the unity and coherence of your paragraphs, especially if they are well developed (see **2d**). In a **unified** paragraph, every sentence relates to a single main idea. In a **coherent** paragraph, ideas progress easily from sentence to sentence.

Because drafting often generates unexpected ideas, some of which may be unrelated to your main idea, you should study the unity and coherence of your paragraphs as you revise.

(1) Topic sentences

Stating the main idea in a single sentence, often called a **topic sentence,** will help you achieve unity. As a critical reader (see chapter 1) you will find that this sentence may appear at any point in a paragraph. Because experienced writers try to avoid using the same patterns repeatedly, they organize paragraphs in different ways.

But if you are new to writing, or making a special effort to improve your paragraphing, you should begin by placing your topic sentences at the beginning of your paragraphs. Placing the topic sentence at the beginning helps readers grasp your main point immediately and helps you stay focused. For example, the topic sentence of the following paragraph (in italics) announces that the author will discuss why people become interested in the lives of celebrities.

> *Celebrity is a modern myth, an attempt by studying the lives of others to find answers for ourselves.* The pantheon changes but always is full of incarnate human gods, sacred marriages, taboos, kings killed when their strength fails, human scapegoats, expulsion of embodied spirits. Supermodels, rock and TV stars, shaman-priests, and Elvis are examples of contagious magic, the myths created by many. Myths were explanations, and Elvis still explains how the lowly can rise, how the high can fall, how the magician can enchant, how the ritual can thrill and the man-god convince each he has come only for them.
>
> —**JULIE BAUMGOLD,** "Midnight in the Garden of Good and Elvis"

If you want to emphasize the main idea of a paragraph or give its organization some extra support, you can begin and conclude the paragraph with two versions of the same idea. This strategy is especially useful for long paragraphs because it gives readers a second chance to grasp the main idea in case their attention has wandered.

As you prepare to revise, try underlining the topic sentences you can identify in your draft. If you cannot find one where you expect to see it, add a sentence stating the main idea of that paragraph.

(2) Unified paragraphs

Unity is violated when a sentence unrelated to the main idea appears in a paragraph, and this can easily happen when drafting. Consider the following example.

> New York has a museum to suit almost any taste. The Metropolitan Museum and the Museum of Modern Art are famous for their art collections. Other important collections of art can be found at the Frick, Guggenheim, and Whitney Museums. Visitors interested in the natural sciences will enjoy the Museum of Natural History. Those interested in American history should visit the Museum of the City of New York. *Getting around the city is easy once you have mastered the subway system.* Part of Ellis Island has become a museum devoted to the history of immigration. Exhibits devoted to social and cultural history can also be found at the Jewish Museum and the Asia Society.

In this paragraph, the italicized sentence about the subway system violates the unity of a paragraph devoted to museums. If pertinent to the essay, public transportation in New York could be discussed in a separate paragraph.

As you check your paragraphs for unity, use the following strategies to solve problems.

Strategies for Improving Paragraph Unity

Eliminate	Any information that does not clearly relate to the main idea should be cut.
Add	If the relation between the main idea and some of the details is not clear, add a phrase or a sentence to make their relevance clear.

| **Separate** | If more than one major idea appears in a single paragraph, develop them in different paragraphs. |
| **Rewrite** | If you want to convey more than one idea in a single paragraph, revise your topic sentence so that it establishes a relation between both ideas. |

(3) Coherent paragraphs

In a coherent paragraph, each sentence leads to the next. In a unified paragraph, every sentence relates to the main idea of the paragraph. The following paragraph has unity but lacks coherence.

> The inside of the refrigerator was covered with black mold, and it smelled as if something had been rotting in there for years. I put new paper down on all the shelves, and my roommate took care of lining the drawers. The stove was as dirty as the refrigerator. When we moved into our new apartment, we found that the kitchen was in horrible shape. We had to scrub the walls with a wire brush and plenty of Lysol to get rid of the grease. The previous tenant had left behind lots of junk that we had to get rid of. All the drawers and cabinets had to be washed.

Although every sentence in this paragraph concerns cleaning the kitchen after moving into an apartment, the sentences are not arranged in any meaningful pattern.

A paragraph is **coherent** when the relationship among the ideas is clear and the progression from one sentence to the next is easy for the reader to follow. Study the following patterns and consider which ones to adopt in your own writing.

(a) In chronological order

In chronological order, you report events according to the order in which they occurred.

Standing in line at the unemployment office makes you feel very much the same as you did the first time you ever flunked a class or a test—as if you had a big red "F" for "Failure" printed across your forehead. I fantasize myself standing at the end of the line in a crisp and efficient blue suit, chin up, neat and straight as a corporate executive. As I move down the line I start to come unglued and a half hour later, when I finally reach the desk clerk, I am slouching and sallow in torn jeans, tennis shoes and a jacket from the Salvation Army, carrying my worldly belongings in a shopping bag and unable to speak.

—JAN HALVORSON, "How It Feels to Be out of Work"

(b) In order of importance

When you arrange ideas according to **order of importance,** you go from most to least important. (See **21c.**) The author of the following paragraph focuses on a hierarchy of intelligence, moving from lower to higher forms of life.

An ant cannot purposely try anything new, and any ant that accidentally did so would be murdered by his colleagues. It is the ant colony as a whole that slowly learns over the ages. In contrast, even an earthworm has enough flexibility of brain to enable it to be taught to turn towards the left or right for food. Though rats are not able to reason to any considerable degree, they can solve such problems as separating round objects from triangular ones when these have to do with health or appetite. Cats, with better brains, can be taught somewhat more, and young dogs a great deal. The higher apes can learn by insight as well as by trial and error.

—GEORGE RUSSELL HARRISON, *What Man May Be*

(c) From the specific to the general or from the general to the specific

Sometimes the movement within a paragraph is from **specific to general** or from **general to specific.** A paragraph may begin with a series of details and conclude with a summarizing statement, as in the paragraph by Robert Sullivan, or it may begin with a general statement or idea, which is then supported by particular details, as in the paragraph by Amy Tan.

> This winter, I took a vacation from our unfinished mess. Getting back to it was tough, and one morning, I found myself on my knees before the dishwasher, as if in prayer, though actually busting a water-pipe weld. To my right were the unfinished cabinets, to my left the knobless backdoor, behind me a hole I'd torn in the wall. There in the kitchen, a realization hit me like a 2-by-4: for two years I'd been working on this house, and there was still no end in sight. It had become my Vietnam.
>
> —ROBERT SULLIVAN, "Home Wrecked"

> It was not the only disappointment my mother felt in me. In the years that followed, I failed her so many times, each time asserting my own will, my right to fall short of expectations. I didn't get straight As. I didn't become class president. I didn't get into Stanford. I dropped out of college. —AMY TAN, "Two Kinds"

3d Transitions improve coherence within and between paragraphs.

Sentences can be arranged in a clear sequence (see 3c(2)) but still lack coherence if the movement between them is abrupt. When revising, you can improve the coherence of your writing by using transitional devices such as pronouns, repetition, conjunctions, transitional phrases, and parallel structure.

(1) Pronoun links

In the following paragraph, the writer links sentences by using the pronouns *their* and *they*. Although these same two pronouns are used repeatedly, their referent, "easy victims," is always clear.

Several movements characterize easy victims: **their** strides were either very long or very short; **they** moved awkwardly, raising **their** left legs with **their** left arms (instead of alternating them); on each step, **they** tended to lift **their** foot up and place it down (less muggable sorts took steps in which **their** feet rocked from heel to toe). Overall, the people rated most muggable walked as if **they** were in conflict with **themselves; they** seemed to make each move in the most difficult way possible.

—CARIN RUBENSTEIN, "Body Language That Speaks to Muggers"

(2) Repetition

In the following paragraph, the repetition of the key word *wave* links the sentences and also provides emphasis. (See **21e**.)

The weekend is over, and we drive down the country road from the cottage to the pier, passing out our last supply of **waves.** We **wave** at people walking and **wave** at people riding. We **wave** at people we know and **wave** at people who are strangers.

—ELLEN GOODMAN, "Waving Goodbye to the Country"

Repeating a key word is also a common way of establishing a transition between paragraphs, as in the next two paragraphs.

For those who pray or chant with great perseverance, there is the suggestion that their **waiting** has been converted into purposefulness.

Of course we do not only **wait** for love; we **wait** for money, we **wait** for the weather to get warmer, colder; we **wait** for the plumber to come and fix the washing machine [. . .].

—EDNA O'BRIEN, "Waiting"

(3) Conjunctions and other transitional phrases

Conjunctions and other transitional phrases demonstrate the logical relationship between ideas, helping writers to make their work coherent. Here is a checklist of frequently used transitional connections arranged according to the kinds of relationships they establish.

CHECKLIST of Transitional Connections	
Alternative and addition	or, nor, and, and then, moreover, besides, further, furthermore, likewise, also, too, again, in addition, even more important, next, first, second, third, in the first place, in the second place, finally, last
Comparison	similarly, likewise, in like manner
Contrast	but, yet, or, and yet, however, still, nevertheless, on the other hand, on the contrary, conversely, even so, notwithstanding, in contrast, at the same time, although this may be true, otherwise, nonetheless
Place	here, beyond, nearby, opposite to, adjacent to, on the opposite side
Purpose	to this end, for this purpose, with this object, in order to
Result or cause	so, for, therefore, accordingly, consequently, thus, thereupon, as a result, then, because, hence
Summary	to sum up, in brief, on the whole, in sum, in short, in any event
Repetition	as I have said, in other words, that is, to be sure, as has been noted
Exemplification	for example, for instance, to show, to see, to understand, in the case of
Intensification	in fact, indeed, to tell the truth
Time	meanwhile, at length, soon, after a few days, in the meantime, afterward, later, now, then, in the past, while

Coherence can also be achieved through parallel structures. (See chapter 20.)

CHECKLIST for Revising Paragraphs

- Does the paragraph have a topic sentence (3c(1))?

- Do all the ideas in the paragraph belong together? Do they link to previous sentences? Is the order of sentences logical (3c(2))?

- Are sentences connected to each other with transitions (3d)?

- Is the paragraph linked to the preceding and following ones (3d)?

- Is the paragraph adequately developed? Are any ideas left out? Will analyzing the strategy used to develop the paragraph help to improve it (2d and 2e)?

3e Writers benefit from sharing their work with others.

Writers benefit from checking to see whether they are communicating their ideas effectively. When they consult with readers, writers usually gain a clearer sense of how they can improve their drafts.

(1) Evaluation standards

Whether working in a writing group or with a single reader such as a tutor or instructor, it is important to have agreed-on evaluation standards. Without such standards, you may get advice that is inappropriate or unhelpful.

Instructors usually indicate their evaluation standards in class, on assignment sheets, or in separate handouts. Be mindful of these standards when reviewing a draft. For example, if your instructor has told you that he or she will be evaluating the paper primarily in terms of whether you have a clear thesis (**2b**) and adequate support for it (**5e**), you could be at risk if you ignore these criteria because you are focusing on sentence length and variety (chapter **22**).

In addition to working with the evaluation criteria, writing groups must often negotiate how to use their time productively so that every member of the group gets help within a limited time period. Groups often benefit from reviewing evaluation criteria at the beginning of a working session and using them to decide how to proceed. Writers who raise specific concerns about their drafts (see **3e(2)**) can also help focus the group's attention.

Whether you have been given criteria for evaluation or not, the following checklist can help you get started.

CHECKLIST for Revising Essays

- Is the purpose of the work clear (**1g(1)**)? Does the work stick to its purpose?

- Does the essay address the appropriate audience (**1g(2)**)?

- Is the tone (**3a(3)**) appropriate for the purpose, audience, and context?

- Is the subject focused (**2a(2)**)?

- Does the essay make a clear point (**2b**)? Is this point well supported?

- Are paragraphs arranged in a logical, effective order (**2c**)?

- Are the introduction and conclusion effective (**3b(1–2)**)?

---

(2) Identifying concerns

When submitting a draft for review, you can increase your chances of getting helpful advice by introducing your work and indicating what your concerns are. You can do so orally within a writing group that has gathered to review drafts. When this is not possible, you can attach a cover letter to your draft. In either case, adopting the following model can help your reviewers give you useful responses.

Topic and purpose	Tell your readers what your topic is, why you have chosen it, and what you hope to accomplish by writing about it. Indicate your thesis (see **2b**), and explain why you have taken this position.
Strengths	Identify those parts of the draft that you are confident about. Doing so directs attention away from any area that you do not want to discuss.
Concerns	Being clear about your concerns is essential to effective problem-solving. Let your readers know exactly what kind of help you want from them. For example, if you are worried about your conclusion, say so.

(3) Listening to criticism

When you write about your ideas, you are putting part of yourself on paper. So hearing honest criticism of those ideas can be difficult. Even experienced writers sometimes feel anxious when they submit their work for evaluation.

Before asking for responses to a draft, remind both your readers and yourself that the work in question is *only a draft.* Saying this aloud signals readers that it is safe for them to criticize, and it reassures you that they are responding to a piece that is not yet finished.

Some readers may retreat into silence because they do not know what to say or settle for identifying a minor error in order to look as if they are being helpful. Others may be unnecessarily assertive, giving you more advice than you had bargained for and insisting that you follow it. But if you allow yourself to hear what other people have to say about your work, you will often get helpful responses.

When reading or listening to responses to a draft, try not to become defensive. If you cut other people off, you may miss the advice that could have been the most useful. However, you are responsible for evaluating the responses you received—rejecting those that would take you in a direction you do not want to pursue and honoring those that would help you fulfill your purpose (see **1g(1)**).

(4) Providing thoughtful responses

When you are asked to read a draft written by someone else, ask what concerns the writer has about it. Read the draft carefully before you respond, and when you do, be specific. Be sure to address the concerns the writer has expressed. If you see other problems in the draft, ask whether the writer wants to know about them. Praise whatever the writer has done well, and identify what you think could be improved. In either case, draw attention to passages that illustrate what you mean.

Whenever possible, frame your comments as a personal response. For example, if you tell a writer, "Your second page is confusing," you are putting yourself in the position of speaking for all readers. If, on the other hand, you say, "I have trouble following your organization on page 2," you alert the writer to a potential problem while speaking only for yourself.

Remember, then, that it is possible to be honest without being unkind. You will not be helping a writer if you ignore problems in a draft you are reviewing. On the other hand, dwelling on every problem can also be unhelpful. Help others write the papers they want to write, not the paper you want to write.

3f Editing makes ideas clearer and more engaging.

After you are satisfied with the revised structure of your essay and the content of your paragraphs, edit individual sentences for clarity, effectiveness, and variety (see chapters **18** through **26**). Consider combining choppy or unconnected sentences and reworking long, overly complicated ones. If you overuse some structures, try to experiment with other patterns. Eliminate any needless shifts in tense, person, tone, style, or point of view.

Examine your diction, and make sure the words you have used are the best choices for this particular essay. Eliminate any unnecessary words (see chapter **25**). If you have experimented with words new to your vocabulary, make sure you have used them accurately.

Check whether your punctuation is correct and whether you have followed standard conventions for mechanics. Even if you have already used a spell checker (see **32a**), use it again because new errors may have been introduced in the revision process. Double-check that you are using words like *there* and *their* or *who's* and *whose* correctly—and remember that even correctly spelled words might be the wrong words in a specific sentence.

CHECKLIST for Editing
Sentences
• Are ideas related through subordination and coordination (**19**)?
• Are all sentences unified (**18**)?

- Do any sentences contain misplaced parts or dangling modifiers (**15**)?

- Is there any faulty parallelism (**20**)?

- Are ideas given appropriate emphasis within each sentence (**21**)?

- Are the sentences varied in length and in type (**22**)?

- Are there any fragments (**13**), comma splices, or fused sentences (**14**)?

- Are all verb forms appropriate (**17**)? Do all verbs agree with their subjects (**17e**)? Do all pronouns agree with their antecedents (**16d**)?

Diction

- Are any words overused or imprecise (**24c, 24a**)?

- Have all unnecessary words and phrases been eliminated (**25**)? Have any necessary words been left out by mistake (**26**)?

- Is the vocabulary appropriate for the audience, purpose, and context (**1g, 23**)?

- Have all technical words that might be unfamiliar to the audience been eliminated or defined (**23b(6)**)?

Punctuation and Mechanics

- Is all punctuation correct (**27–31**)? Are any marks missing?

- Are all words spelled correctly (**32**)?

- Is capitalization correct (**33**)?

- Are titles identified by either quotation marks (**30c**) or italics (**34a**)?

- Are abbreviations (**35**) appropriate and correct?

3g Proofreading can help you avoid irritating or confusing your readers with careless errors.

Once you have revised and edited your essay, format it carefully (see chapter 4) and proofread it. The product you submit should be error-free. Proofreading may alert you to problems that call for further editing.

With the computer, you can easily produce professional-looking documents. Remember, however, that presentation is only one aspect of a successful project. No matter how beautiful your paper looks when you print it out, proofread it carefully.

Watch for three common word processing errors: accidentally leaving a word out, leaving in a word you meant to delete, or inserting in the wrong place a passage that you moved. Errors of this sort are common with electronic composition. A spell checker can alert you to repeated or misspelled words, but you have to proofread to see whether deleting or moving material led to other errors.

Because the eye tends to see what it expects to see, many writers miss errors—especially minor errors, such as a missing comma or apostrophe—even when they think they have proofread carefully. Not only should you proofread more than once, but also you may find it beneficial to read your work aloud.

3h The final draft reflects the care the writer took.

After following the process of planning and drafting an essay described in chapter 2, Peter Geske submitted an early draft for peer review (see 3e). Guided by the responses he received and working to improve the unity and coherence of his paragraphs (see **3c**), he revised that draft extensively. Here is an early draft of his essay, followed by his final draft. Like Peter, you can benefit from drafting on a computer, printing out hard copy, making changes in pencil, and then going back to the computer for another round of revision.

Early draft

Peter Geske
English 101, sec. 2
                              Title?
              High School
    In today's society education is becoming more and more important. The children of today need education to get good jobs and keep up with this fast paced modern society. Nobody ever explained this to my teachers though. High school was the worst. The teachers at my school were losers and didn't know what they were doing. The building was falling apart also and their was alot of violence in it.
Picture a building that looks like a run-down warehouse or prison. That's what my high school looked like.
Standards were so low that I learned very little and became discouraged about school.

combine somehow

    Central was built about a hundred years ago and that's probably the last time it got a coat of paint. *Inside* The walls were cracked and we used to flick off loose paint chips all the time. On the outside it looked like a prison. It used to have big windows but they got bricked up to save energy. There was *there were* also graffiti all over the place. No trees anywhere but plenty of broken cement and crumbling asphalt.

First outside then inside

move up →The school had at least twice as many kids squeezed into it than it was designed for. Even with plenty of people cutting to party, (every classroom was crowded.) Sometimes at the beginning of the year there wasn't even a desk for everyone. Computers were a joke. We had one small lab for two thousand students and they were these old machines that you couldn't run good programs on. If you wanted to use the internet you had to go to the library and there was always somebody else using the terminal there which was the only one in the school with access to the Web.

Science equipment was also bad. I really hated my chemistry teacher but maybe she wouldn't of been so bad if we had a decent lab.

Once you got past your sophomore year you could do pretty much what you wanted to. You were supposed to take English every year and you had to take math and science too. You also had to take blow off courses you could sleep through like social problems where Mr. Thorp used to talk about the problems his kids were having and how students today aren't as good as they used to be. But juniors and seniors could take lots of electives and you could pass your English requirement by reading science fiction or taking a course where you did nothing but watch tapes on a VCR.

Discuss teacher by personality first then the teaching! together!

The teachers were the worst. They couldn't control their classes and everybody took advantage of that. Mr. Kleinberg was my geometry teacher. He wore these green socks everyday and I swear it was always the same pair. When you got close to him it was really gross he smelled so bad. Kids never paid attention to him and he would usually start screaming at one person while knives were being pulled in another corner and other kids were strung out on ~~drugs~~. *nodding off from* My chemistry teacher, was just as bad. Her name *never did anything* was Mrs. Fiorelli, ~~and she was real skinny.~~ *except* ~~All she would ever do was~~ read from the text- book. Her class was out of control also and when somebody would try to ask a question she would just keep on reading. She gave these killer tests though, and I ended up *because I learned so little in it* ~~flunking~~ her course ~~not that I need to know~~ *failing* ~~chemistry for anything.~~

It wasn't all bad though. Mr. Rodriguez ∧ *who* taught American history ~~and he was~~ ~~cool. He~~ *good* ~~tied the textbook to current events which~~ ~~made it more interesting and~~ also was good *Mrs. Sullivan who taught* ~~about giving extra help.~~ My English teacher *Creative Writing good* sophomore ~~year~~ was also ok. ~~I liked some of~~ ~~the books we read and getting the chance to~~ ~~be creative.~~ *But these were the exceptions to the rule.* *As I look back on my high school years, I am amazed that I learned* ~~This is just my opinion. There might be~~ *anything except how to party. Now that I am in college, I wish I had gone to a* ~~other kids who had a good experience at~~ *better high school.* ~~Central and maybe someday I'll laugh about~~ ~~it.~~

Final draft

Peter Geske
Professor Henrikson
English 101, Section 2
12 May 2000

School Daze

Picture a run-down building that looks
like a warehouse and feels like a prison.
You approach through a sea of broken cement
and crumbling asphalt. There are no trees
near the building, although a few tufts of
uncut grass struggle to grow in a yard of
baked-down dirt. Many of the windows have
been bricked in, and the ground floor is
covered with graffiti. Inside, inadequate
lights reveal old tiles, broken lockers, and
flaking paint. The school is empty because
it is only seven o'clock. Within an hour,
however, it will be overcrowded with students
who are running wild and teachers who do not
know how to respond. You have entered
Central High School, the institution where my
education suffered because of poor facilities
and low standards.

Built a hundred years ago, Central had
a good reputation when the neighborhoods
around it were prosperous. Now it is the
worst high school in the city, and the
school board seems to have given up on it.
The more run-down it gets, the worse the
morale gets, and as morale gets lower, the
school goes farther downhill.

After the condition of the building itself, the most obvious problem at Central is the overcrowding. Almost every classroom is filled to capacity, and sometimes there are more students than desks--especially at the beginning of the school year when most people are still showing up for school. The situation gets a little better by Columbus Day, because kids soon discover that one of the advantages of going to Central is that they can skip school without anybody caring.

Our textbooks were usually ten years out of date. And if more expensive supplies ever made it through the door, they did not last long. We had only one computer lab for two thousand students, and it was equipped with old machines that could not access the Internet. Science supplies were almost as bad. In the chemistry lab, for example, there was never enough equipment for individual experiments even when we were teamed with a lab partner. We were put in groups of four and had to wait half the class period before we got the chance to work. By then, most people had checked out. What usually happened is that one person would do the work, and the rest of the team would coast on those results.

My chemistry teacher, Mrs. Fiorelli, is a good example of another problem at Central: bad teachers. All she would ever do was read from the textbook. When somebody would try to ask a question, she would just keep reading. Then she would turn around every few weeks and give difficult tests. It was as if she hated us and wanted to punish us when she couldn't ignore us any longer.

I had many other teachers who were just as bad. Mr. Kleinberg, my geometry teacher, could not control the class. When we got out of control--which was every day--he would start screaming at one person (usually a girl who wasn't doing anything) while other students were flashing knives and plenty were nodding off from drugs. Would you be surprised to hear that I now have a problem with both science and math?

To be fair, I did have some good teachers at Central: Mr. Rodriguez, who taught American history, and Mrs. Sullivan, who taught creative writing. But they were the exceptions. For every good teacher, there were at least three who should consider a career change. And for every course in which you might actually learn something, there were two blow-off courses in which all you had to do was read science fiction, watch tapes on a VCR, or listen to some guy talk about the problems he was having with his own kids.

As I look back at the four years I spent at Central, I am amazed that I learned anything at all. By the time I reached senior year, all I wanted to do was party. I had lost interest in school--which explains why I have been working in a warehouse for the past five years instead of going straight to college. Now that I am here, I sure wish I were better prepared.

Chapter 4

Document Design

This chapter contains information on presenting your writing so that it is as readable as possible. As the volume of information grows, so does the importance of its delivery—the visual design that gives readers the cues that lead them to the information they require and that enable them to read it efficiently.

This chapter gives guidance on

- using the proper materials (**4a**),
- using layout, headings, and graphics (**4b**),
- using appropriate form for electronic documents (**4c**), and
- proofreading for matters of format (**4d**).

Visual design sends messages to readers. A dense, tightly packed page with narrow margins signals difficult material. Ample white space signals openness and availability. White space frames the material on the page, preventing it from seeming oppressive and burdensome and so contributes to ease in reading, regardless of the difficulty of the content. But too much white space can send a negative message: for instance, a triple-spaced research paper with huge margins announces that the writer has little to say.

4a Using the proper materials enhances readability.

(1) Paper and binding

Use good 20-pound white $8\frac{1}{2}$-by-11-inch paper (neither onion-skin nor erasable bond); this kind of paper is suitable for use with typewriters, word processors, and most printers linked to a computer. If you write your papers by hand, use regular $8\frac{1}{2}$-by-11-inch lined white notebook paper and follow your instructor's recommendations.

Use a paper clip or a staple to fasten pages. Do not use any other method of binding pages unless you are specifically asked to do so.

(2) Format

If you submit your work electronically (for instance, by e-mail, on a bulletin board, in a Web document, or on some kind of removable disk), follow your instructor's directions exactly. If you use a disk, make sure that you use the proper size, density, and format. Label disks clearly. If you submit your work via e-mail or a bulletin board, use the subject line correctly and ensure that your work is free of errors before you send it. Whatever the requirements, the computing facilities to meet them are likely to be available on campus at no cost.

(3) Type, fonts, and justification

Although laser and ink-jet printers can print different typesizes and styles (fonts) on a single page, most academic papers should be printed using a font that looks like typewriter type, such as `Courier`, or a simple proportional font such as Times Roman. It is usually best to avoid the sans serif fonts such as Arial because they are hard to read. Fancy display fonts such as PTBarnum or *Script* are seldom appropriate, and using a variety of fonts detracts from the content. Although word processing makes it easy to use italics or boldfacing for emphasis, resist the temptation. (See 34f.) Also, resist the impulse to justify your right margins (make them straight).

Pages from a good ink-jet or laser printer are always acceptable. Before you start, make sure that the printer cartridge has enough ink or toner to complete your document. If you use a typewriter or dot matrix printer, the ribbon must be fresh enough to type clear, dark characters. If your instructor accepts handwritten papers, write in blue or black ink on one side of the paper only.

4b Clear and orderly arrangement contributes to ease in reading.

The advice here follows the guidelines in the *MLA Handbook for Writers of Research Papers,* fifth edition (New York: Modern Language Association, 1999). If your instructor requires another style manual, check the most recent edition of that manual.

(1) Effective layout

Word processing software can number your pages, print a certain number of lines per page, and incorporate appropriate word divisions. Software also allows you to vary the spacing between lines, but unless your instructor agrees to different spacing, double-space all papers and leave margins of one inch (or no more than one and one-half inches) on all sides of the text to give your reader room for comments and to prevent a crowded appearance. The ruled vertical line on notebook paper marks the left margin for handwritten papers. You can adjust the margin control on a typewriter to provide the margins you need.

(2) Indentation

The first lines of paragraphs should be uniformly indented. You can set your word processing software to indent the first lines of all paragraphs one-half inch. (Indent five spaces on a typewriter, or one inch if writing by hand.) Indent block quotations one inch from the left margin (ten spaces on the typewriter). (See **30b**.)

(3) Page numbers

Place Arabic numerals—without parentheses or periods—at the right margin, one-half inch from the top of each page. Put your last name immediately before the page number so that your instructor can identify a page that gets misplaced.

(a) The first page

Unless your instructor requests a title page, place your name, your instructor's name, the course and section number, and the date in the top left-hand corner (one inch from the top and one inch from the left edge of the page), double-spacing after each line. Double-space between the lines of a long title and center all titles. The page number should appear in the upper right-hand corner.

Begin your first paragraph on the second line below the title (the first double-spaced line). (See the models in chapters 3 and 7.) Most research papers do not require a title page, but if you use one, follow your instructor's directions about the form.

MLA Style (First page)

Bohn 1

Dietrich Bohn
Dr. Miller
English 299, Section 4
30 June 1999
Rigoberta Menchú and Representative Authority
    The 1983 publication of Rigoberta
Menchú's _I, Rigoberta Menchú_, has done much
to help her work to improve human rights in
her native country, Guatemala. Recently,
however, there has been a great deal of
controversy--especially since the 1999
publication of David Stoll's _Rigoberta Menchú
and the Story of All Poor Guatemalans_--
surrounding the truth of Menchú's
autobiography. Stoll, an anthropologist at
Middlebury College in Vermont, proves that
Menchú did not tell the whole truth about
her life in the book that made her famous.
When Menchú told her story, her goal was to
call international attention to the plight
"of all poor Guatemalans." She achieved this
goal by changing her story to make it more
compelling to her audience. These changes
have undermined her authority as a
representative figure and threaten to damage
her cause as well. The example of
I, Rigoberta Menchú shows why it is wrong to
fictionalize an autobiographical account
that claims to speak for a whole people.

Title Page

Rigoberta Menchú and
Representative Authority

Dietrich Bohn

English 299, Section 4
Professor Miller
30 June 1999

(b) Subsequent pages

Place your name and the page number in the upper right-hand corner, one-half inch from the top. Begin your text at the left margin, one inch from the top and double-space throughout.

(4) Headings

Headings are particularly useful for helping the reader manage information in research papers, technical and business reports, and other kinds of complex documents. (See chapter 10.) Headings can also highlight the organization of a long block of information or make it easy to combine several brief statements to avoid choppiness.

If you use headings, make them consistent throughout your document, and if you have two levels of headings, treat all occurrences of each level alike.

(5) Graphics

Visual examples help most readers understand complex information more readily. **Tables** organize information into columns and rows so that relationships are more easily noted. They are also particularly good for presenting numeric information. When you design a table, be sure to label all the columns and rows accurately and give your table a title and a number.

Table 1

Mean Annual Temperature in Reno, Nevada

Month	Temp.	Month	Temp.
January	40	July	79
February	43	August	85
March	50	September	80
April	60	October	65
May	70	November	53
June	72	December	44

Charts and **graphs, drawings, maps,** and **photographs** demonstrate relationships among data and spatial concepts or call attention to particular points, people, objects, or events. They are referred to as **figures. Pie charts** are especially useful for showing the relationship of parts to a whole.

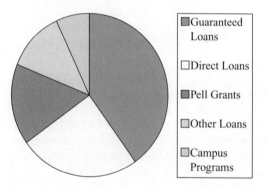

Fig. 1. Financial aid sources. Source: *Chronicle of Higher Education* 12 Feb. 1999: A31.

Graphs show relationships over time. For instance, a graph can show increases or decreases in enrollment or in student achievement or highlight differences in financial trends.

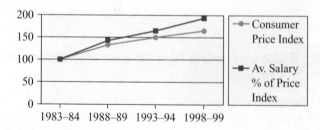

Fig. 2. Increase in buying power of faculty salaries, 1983–99. Source: *Chronicle of Higher Education* 26 Mar. 1999: A50.

Bar charts show other kinds of correlations. They might illustrate stock market performance over several decades or the relative speeds of various computer processors.

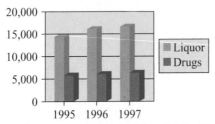

Fig. 3. Arrests on college campuses for liquor and drug violations. Source: *Chronicle of Higher Education* 28 May 1999: A1.

Other kinds of graphics such as **diagrams** and **drawings, maps,** and **photographs** help readers understand other kinds of concepts—dimensions and specific details, spatial relationships, emotional impact, and so on.

Remember that each visual element you use should be numbered (for example, Table 1, Fig. 4). Table numbers and labels appear before the table, and table sources as well as figure numbers and labels are placed after the material they illustrate. If there are many illustrations, consider placing all of them in an appendix. Occasionally, text will also flow around a table or a figure, especially if it is otherwise difficult to place the image near the text it illustrates.

4c The appropriate form for electronic documents can vary.

Electronic documents may be presented on the Internet, on your campus network, on a class or organization's electronic bulletin board, or even on a disk that you hand to your instructor or fellow student. Electronic documents, which are usually easy to modify, permit new kinds of collaboration and use of materials.

(1) E-mail

E-mail is much less formal than a letter or a memo but more enduring than conversation. It also fosters speedy and convenient communication. E-mail uses a format like that of an interoffice memo, with "TO" and "SUBJECT" lines for entering the address of the person you are writing to and the topic of your message. (See also **10a**.)

Using e-mail puts concern for the audience (see **1g(2)**) in the foreground and requires special care to communicate ideas clearly. Experienced users have developed guides (referred to as **netiquette**) to help new users avoid some common hazards. Some standard advice appears below.

- Keep messages concise and paragraphs short.
- Make the subject line short and descriptive.
- Include your e-mail address in a short signature.
- Don't use all capital letters. It's rude.
- Credit any quotations, references, or sources you use, even messages from friends.

(2) The World Wide Web

The World Wide Web contains **pages** that a reader can view using a **browser.** (A browser is a computer program that fetches the text and graphic images that make up a Web document—a page—and enables the user to view them.) Web pages can be dynamically linked to other Web pages to form a new sort of document set that is very different from a book and that permits users to determine the sequence in which they will view information.

Constructing a Web page is not technically difficult if you have the right equipment. Web pages are written in a fairly simple language called hypertext markup language (html). Although it is fairly easy to learn to write html code, you can make adequate Web pages using html-capable word processing software or a recent version of a Web browser. The planning that goes into making the page and the choices you make while you are building it are more important than knowing html.

When you plan a Web page, you decide what your rhetorical stance will be—identify your audience and your purpose, determine the context for the page, and decide on the tone you will take. And constructing a Web page, like writing an essay, means you must determine what information you will include and design a strategy for presenting it.

A Web document can be linear, like an essay, presenting each of its points in sequence; it can be hierarchical, branching out at each level; or it can be radial, allowing the reader to decide the final sequence of points.

Linear

Hierarchical   **Radial**

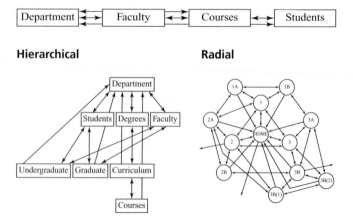

Web pages generally use about half as much text as paper pages. On a Web page, placement of the information, use of numbered lists, and visual elements substitute for directly stated transitional expressions and extensively described examples. A Web page should normally not exceed a couple of screens of carefully spaced information surrounded by meaningful white space—space that is not occupied by either text or images. Typically, the top part of the page—the upper part of the first screen—should identify the document: the title, a visual element, a few bulleted points. Browsers show the top of the page first, and it should be distinctive enough to make the reader want to explore more.

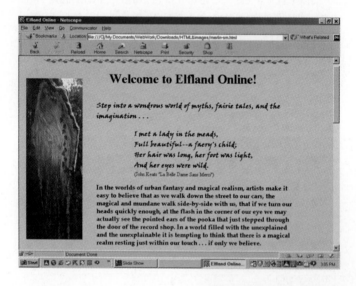

Kay Robinson's first design for this page displayed a large amount of text on this first screen, but she revised it by moving text down the page so it would appear when the user scrolled to the next screens (not shown).

At the bottom of every page are the links to other sites, the date created or modified, and any copyright information. If your personal safety is assured, it can be a good idea to include an e-mail address where readers can contact you about the document.

Keep visual elements under 30k (kilobytes) in size. Graphics larger than that make your Web page slow to load. Similarly, choose the background and text colors with care. A dark background with light text will print as a blank page. Many designers recommend no more than three colors (although you can use varying intensities of each). Backgrounds with designs can make text very difficult to read, so make sure you choose one that enhances your text rather than overwhelms it.

Select a clear, easy-to-read font in a size that will show about sixty characters per line. Much more makes text hard to read, so you need to select a font size accordingly.

The external links on your page are part of your text, so you should have a clear reason for using each one and keep them up to date.

Finally, you must get permission for any text or graphics you draw from another source.

For more detailed help with designing a Web site, you might look at some of the following.

Tim Berners-Lee, the creator of the World Wide Web, is the author of this Web-based design manual.

http://www.w3.org/Provider/Style/Introduction.html

Jeff Glover, the Web manager for XOOM.COM, has good advice to offer at his Web site.

http://jeffglover.com/ss.php

Check out library science professor Alastair Smith's list of nearly four dozen Web site evaluation guides.

http://www.vuw.ac.nz/~agsmith/evaln/evaln.htm

Be aware that Web addresses may change and that if there is no forwarding mechanism you may still be able to find the page by dropping the last element(s) of the address and trying again. You may also need to run a search (see **6d(2)**) or look at the links on other Web sites.

CHECKLIST for Designing Web Pages

1. Understand the difference between a paper page and a Web page.

2. Plan and organize your page before you construct it.

3. Make a template for all pages in a single Web document.

4. Limit each page to two or three screens of information.

5. Don't crowd your page with text.

6. Use graphics sparingly.

7. Make your document easy to navigate.

8. Include your name and the date you last worked on the page.

4d Proofreading provides quality control.

Proofreading pays particular attention to the conventions of grammar, mechanics, and punctuation and to spelling errors that may have slipped through the revising and editing process. (See chapter 3.)

Proofreading also checks for and corrects layout errors and serves as a final check to make sure all necessary revising and editing have been done. Proofreading can be done manually or with a word processing program; doing both is insurance against error.

Chapter

5   Writing Arguments

This chapter will help you write persuasively by discussing how to

- understand the purpose of your argument (**5a**),
- choose an appropriate subject (**5b**),
- distinguish fact from opinion (**5c**),
- take a position or make a claim (**5d**),
- provide evidence to support your claims (**5e**),
- establish that you are fair minded and well informed (**5f**),
- decide whether it would be appropriate to appeal to the feelings of your audience (**5f**),
- organize your ideas (**5g**),
- use logic (**5h**), and
- avoid logical fallacies (**5i**).

As you proceed, you should understand the importance of arguing ethically and treating your opponents with respect. Argument is a way to discover truth and negotiate differences. It should not be used to punish people with whom you disagree.

5a   Different arguments have different purposes.

When you write an argument, your purpose may be to pursue the truth until you have formed an opinion that seems reasonable. Or it may be to persuade an audience to agree with an opinion that you already hold.

When you are writing to pursue the truth, you are writing to **inquire.** An argument does not involve quarreling; it is shaped instead by the give-and-take of dialogue as different ideas are exchanged. Philosophers and rhetoricians call this kind of search for truth **dialectic.**

If you have already reached a conclusion to which you are committed, then your purpose is probably to **convince** other people to accept your position to some extent. This purpose can take at least four different forms.

- If there is little chance that you can convince an audience to change a strongly held opinion, then you have achieved much if you convince the audience your position deserves to be taken seriously.
- If the members of your audience are not firmly committed to a position, then you might write in the hope of convincing them to agree with you.
- If they agree with you in principle, then you might persuade them to undertake a specific action, such as supporting your candidate.
- If, however, there are fundamental differences within your audience, then you might write to reduce the extent of the conflict by establishing common ground and negotiating a compromise.

5b Argument assumes that views differ.

The first step toward finding a subject for argumentation is to consider issues that inspire different opinions. If your audience already agrees with you, then there is little point in writing an argument espousing that view.

Behind any effective argument is a question that can generate more than one reasonable answer. If you ask "Is there poverty in our country?" almost anyone will agree that there is. But if you ask "What can we do to eliminate poverty?" you will hear very different answers. Answers differ because people approach questions with different assumptions and have different information. They may look only for evidence that supports what they already believe. Be careful not to do so when preparing your own arguments. To be persuasive, you must give fair consideration to diverse views (see **5e(2)**).

When you write an argument, you are either looking for an answer to a question or showing that you have found the answer you want your audience to accept. If you choose a question, then focus (see **2a(2)**) on the part of this question you will address in your essay. Consider your own values and how they differ from those of your audience so that you can decide what to take for granted and what you will need to establish.

A good subject may occur to you if you note how you respond to the views of others. Your response to a class discussion or an article you have read could lead to a good essay. When you are free to choose your own subject, you should be able to think of many suitable ones if you stay abreast of current events.

CHECKLIST for Assessing a Subject

- Is there more than one possible answer? Would anyone be likely to disagree with you?

- Do you know enough about this subject? Can you find out what you need to know?

- Have you narrowed the subject so that you can do justice to it?

- Do you have a purpose in writing about this subject?

- Are the subject and purpose appropriate for your audience?

If you can answer "yes" to all these questions, you can feel confident about your subject and move further into the writing process. If you answer "no" to any of them, use them for further planning. For example, you can learn more about your subject by researching in your library or on the World Wide Web (see chapter **6**).

5c Preparing to write an argument requires the ability to distinguish between fact and opinion.

When you explore your subject, you must be able to distinguish between facts and opinions. **Facts** are reliable pieces of information that can be verified through independent sources or procedures. They are valued because they are believed to be true. **Opinions** are assertions or inferences that may or may not be based on facts. When opinions are widely accepted, they may seem to be factual when actually they are not.

Facts are not necessarily more valuable than opinions. In an effective argument, you need to show why the facts you use are significant, because the same set of facts can often lead to different conclusions. To assume that the facts speak for themselves is to assume that your audience already thinks the same way you do—and if that were true, you would not need to be arguing. To assume that you are using facts when you are really using opinions will look as if you are not thinking seriously about the issue. First, you must be able to distinguish facts from opinions.

If a statement can consistently be proven true, then it is a fact. If it can be disputed, then it is an opinion.

Fact	Spinach contains iron.
Opinion	Americans should eat more spinach.

To say that spinach contains iron is to state a fact; it can be verified by consulting published studies or by conducting laboratory tests. Whether or not this fact is significant depends on how a writer chooses to use it. To say that Americans need to eat more spinach is to express an opinion that may or may not be supported by facts.

Because the facts themselves can change, writers and readers need to remain flexible as they distinguish between fact and opinion. The erroneous belief that the sun revolves around the earth was once considered a fact. No matter how knowledge-able, a person who is unwilling to assimilate new information and question old ideas cannot expect to meet the challenges of a rapidly changing world. Both writers and readers of argument are thus prepared to ask themselves what kind of **verification** would be necessary to determine the reliability of information. Reliability depends not on the ease with which data can be verified, but on whether verification is possible. Whether you are considering a fact or an opinion, ask yourself, "What kind of evidence is necessary, how could that evidence be obtained, and what would happen if conflicting evidence is discovered?"

5d An argument takes a position or makes a claim.

When making an argument, writers take a position on the topic they have chosen. When writing to inquire, this position is likely to appear in the conclusion. When writing to convince, it can appear at almost any point (see **5a** and **5g**). The position you take is the main idea, or thesis (see **2b**) of your argument. This idea is called the **claim** or the **proposition.** Your claim states what you want your audience to accept or do.

(1) The extent of claims

Claims vary in extent; they can be absolute or moderate, large or limited. A writer who makes an absolute claim will need to provide more evidence than a writer who makes a moderate one. Absolute claims assert that something is always true or false, completely good or bad, whereas moderate claims make a less sweeping assertion.

> **Absolute claim**   Ronald Reagan was the best president we ever had.

Moderate claim   Reagan's foreign policy helped bring about the collapse of the Soviet Union.

The stronger the claim, the stronger the evidence needed to support it. Be sure to consider the quality and significance of the evidence you use (see 5e and 6c)—not just its quantity.

(2) The kinds of claims

Rhetoricians traditionally recognize three kinds of claims.

(a) *Substantiation* claims

Without making a value judgment, a substantiation claim asserts that something exists.

> Graduates of our law school often have difficulty finding a job.
>
> There is bumper-to-bumper traffic on Highway 94 during rush hour.

(b) *Evaluation* claims

According to an evaluation claim, something is good or bad, effective or ineffective, successful or unsuccessful.

> Our law school is failing to produce well-trained attorneys.
>
> Our current transportation system is inadequate.

(c) *Policy* claims

When making policy claims, writers call for something to be done.

> We must find the funds to hire better faculty for our law school.
>
> We need to build a light-rail system linking downtown with the airport and the western suburbs.

Policy claims typically draw on substantiation and evaluation claims: you cannot persuade an audience to do something without first demonstrating that there is a problem that needs to be fixed.

5e A persuasive argument is well developed.

You will sometimes need to do research on your subject. (See chapter 6.) At other times you will be able to write directly from your own experience and observations. (See pages 107–12.) In either case, you should explore your subject in enough depth to have the evidence to support your position. In addition, you should consider the reasons why other people might disagree with you and be prepared to respond.

(1) Reasons behind a claim

If you want to persuade readers to take your ideas seriously, then you must establish why you think as you do. That means communicating the reasons that have led to your position, as well as the values and assumptions that support your thinking. When you are exploring your subject, make a list of the reasons that have led to your belief. When you are ready to begin drafting (see 2d), think critically about the reasons on your list. Some may need to be eliminated because they overlap; others, because you would have trouble supporting them. You can then base your argument on the remaining reasons. If additional reasons occur to you as you write, you can incorporate them into your draft.

Be sure to support what you claim with sufficient evidence from credible sources:

- facts,
- statistics,
- examples, and
- testimony.

This evidence must be accurate, representative, and sufficient. (See 6c.) Accurate information should be verifiable (see 5c). Recognize, however, that a writer may provide you with information drawn from an exceptional case or a biased sample. If, for example, you are writing an argument about airline safety and draw all your evidence from material distributed by a major airline, this evidence is unlikely to represent all the available data on this topic. Your data in this case would be representative if you were seeking only to report the position taken by airline management. For data representative of the airline industry as a whole, you would need to consult other sources. (See chapter 6.) Similarly, think critically about the results of polls and other statistics you plan to use as evidence. How recent is the information, and how was it gathered?

Whatever form your evidence takes, be sure to show readers *why* it supports your claim. Do not assume that the relationship between claim and evidence will be clear to others simply because it is clear to you. Make the connection explicit so that your audience can understand your thinking.

(2) Opposing views

In addition to listing reasons for your claim, you should list reasons why people might disagree with you. Good arguments are never one sided. If you want to be persuasive, you must demonstrate that you are familiar with other views. The most common strategy for doing so is to introduce opposing views and then show why you do not find these reasons convincing. This strategy is called **refutation.** By showing not only the reasons for your position but also the weakness of the objections that can be made against it, you bolster your case.

As you consider opposing views, you are likely to discover some you cannot refute. Issues are often controversial precisely because good arguments can be made by all sides. When you find yourself agreeing with a point raised on another side of the issue, you can benefit from offering a **concession.** By openly conceding that you agree with opponents on a specific point, you show that you are fair minded (see 1f) and increase your credibility. It is hard to persuade people to agree with you if you insist that they are entirely wrong. If you admit that they are partially right, they are more likely to admit that you could be partially right as well.

Arguments that are exchanged electronically—by e-mail or in discussion groups—can easily become one sided when writers forget that they are using the computer to communicate with other human beings. Even if you can- not see your readers, you will be more persuasive if you imagine that they are in the same room with you.

When deciding what arguments to refute and what points to concede, consider how long your essay will be and what you know about your audience. In a short argument, you will need to limit yourself to a brief discussion of opposing views. In a longer one, you can afford to explore such views more fully. In either case, however, consider what your audience is likely to believe, and write with those assumptions in mind.

5f Persuasion usually requires appealing to an audience in more than one way.

If people were entirely rational, persuasion could be achieved through the logical use of facts (see 5c). But because people are often caught up in their own concerns, feel threatened by differences, or see argument as a kind of combat, they may not even hear what you say. Getting a fair hearing is essential if you want your views to be understood. Theories of argument offer advice on how to gain this hearing.

(1) Classical appeals

Aristotle and other important thinkers in the ancient world be-lieved that persuasion is achieved through a combination of three appeals: ethos, logos, and pathos. **Ethos** (an ethical appeal) means demonstrating that you have good character, good will toward the audience, and good knowledge of your subject. **Logos** (a logical appeal) is the effective use of critical thinking and the judicious use of information. It is what you employ when you support your claims, make reasonable conclusions, and avoid logical fallacies (see 5i). Both logos and ethos are essential to effective argumentation. **Pathos** (an emotional appeal) involves using language that will stir the feelings of your audience. Although pathos can be misused by people who wish to obscure thought, it can be effective when used to establish empathy. When you are trying to be persuasive, remember that human beings have feelings as well as thoughts. Appeal to these feelings if you can, but do not rest your entire case on them.

(2) Rogerian appeals

Rogerian argument derives from the work of Carl R. Rogers, a psychologist who believed that many problems are the result of misunderstanding, causing a breakdown in communication. In his book *On Becoming a Person* (1961), Rogers argues that people often fail to understand each other because of a natural tendency to judge and evaluate, agree or disagree. He emphasizes the importance of listening carefully to what others say and of suspending judgment until you are able to restate accurately what others believe. When each person in a conflict demonstrates this ability, the likelihood of misunderstanding is significantly reduced.

Skills such as paraphrasing and summarizing (see 7c) are essential to Rogerian argument. This model is especially useful when building consensus. A writer making a Rogerian argument says, in effect, "I have heard your concerns, and I am responding to them to the best of my ability. I am also offering some ideas of my own from which we can both benefit. I want to work with you and will not try to push you around." Emphasis on being fair minded and nonconfrontational gives

ethos (see **5f(1)**) an essential place in Rogerian argument. For information on how to organize a Rogerian argument, see page 97.

5g There are several ways to organize an argument.

The decisions you make about organization should be based on what would be most effective when writing about your subject in a specific context for the audience you have in mind. (See **1g**.) There are, however, a few basic principles that are useful to remember.

(1) Classical arrangement

The plan recommended by classical rhetoric assumes that an audience is prepared to follow a well-reasoned argument.

Introduction	Introduce your issue and capture the attention of your audience. Try using a short narrative or a strong example. (See **3b**.)
Background information	Provide your audience with a history of the situation and state how things currently stand. Define any key terms. Draw the attention of your audience to those points that are especially important and explain why they are meaningful.
Proposition	Introduce the position you are taking. Frame it as a thesis statement or claim. (See **2b** and **5d**.)
Proof	Discuss the reasons why you have taken your position. Provide facts, expert testimony, and any other evidence that supports your claim.
Refutation	Show why you are not persuaded by differing viewpoints. Concede any point that has merit but show why this concession does not damage your own case.

Conclusion   Summarize your most important points and appeal to your audience's feelings.

This plan can be effective if your audience has not yet taken a position on your issue.

(2) Rogerian arrangement

To write an argument informed by Rogerian appeals (pages 95–96), you can be guided by the following plan.

Introduction   Establish that you have paid attention to views different from your own. Build trust by stating these views clearly and fairly.

Concessions   Reassure the people you hope to persuade by showing that you agree with them to an extent and do not think they are completely wrong.

Thesis   Now that you have earned the confidence of your audience, state your claim or proposition.

Support   Explain why you have taken this position and provide support for it.

Conclusion   Conclude by showing how your audience could benefit from accepting your position. Indicate the extent to which this position will resolve the problem. If you are offering a partial solution to a complex problem, concede that further work may be necessary.

This plan can help you gain a fair hearing from an audience strongly opposed to you.

(3) Refutation

Unless you are required to follow a specific plan, you should respond to opposing views when your audience is most likely either to expect this discussion or to be willing to hear it. You must assess your readers carefully (see 1g(2)), determining what opinions they are likely to have about your subject and how open they are to new ideas. If your audience is receptive, you can place refutation and concessions after launching your own case, as in classical arrangement. If your audience adheres to a different position, you should respond to its views toward the beginning of your essay, as in Rogerian argument.

(4) Paragraph development

You can list several reasons in a single paragraph if its purpose is to summarize why you hold your position. Writers sometimes also include several reasons in a single paragraph near their conclusion if these reasons consist of additional advantages that do not call for detailed discussion. But if you try to develop two separate reasons in the same paragraph, it may lack unity and coherence. (See 3c.) Discussing separate reasons in separate paragraphs can help readers follow your argument.

You will need at least a full paragraph to develop any reason for your claim (see 5d), and some reasons could easily take several paragraphs. But no matter how many paragraphs you write, or how long any one of them may be, make sure that every paragraph is **unified** and **coherent** (see 3c).

When responding to an opposing argument, it is useful to state that view at the beginning of a paragraph. If you follow this strategy, the rest of the paragraph is available for your response, and readers make only one shift between differing views. If you begin a paragraph with your view, then introduce an opponent's view, and then return to yours, readers must shift direction twice and may miss the point.

(5) Conclusions

If you are writing to inquire, you might conclude with the truth you have reached. If you are writing to convince others, you might end by restating your position and summarizing your reasons for holding it. Ideally, however, a good conclusion does more than repeat points that have already been made. When considering how to conclude an argument, imagine readers who are interested in what you have to say but unsure about what you expect. "So what?" they might ask. "How does all this affect me, and what am I supposed to do about it?" When writing to persuade others, your conclusion could indicate how all opposing parties would gain from accepting your position. Your conclusion could also state a specific action that you want your audience to take (see 3b(2)). Or you could conclude with an ethical or emotional appeal (see 5f).

5h Understanding logic can improve your ability to argue effectively.

Logic is a means through which you can develop your ideas, reach new ones, and determine whether your thinking is clear enough to persuade readers. By arguing logically, you increase the likelihood that your arguments will be taken seriously.

(1) Inductive reasoning

Most people use inductive reasoning to make decisions in daily life. For example, if you get indigestion several times after eating sauerkraut, you might conclude that eating sauerkraut gives you indigestion. This use of evidence to form a generalization is called an **inductive leap,** and the leap should be in proportion to the amount of evidence gathered. It is reasonable to stop eating sauerkraut if it consistently makes you ill, especially if you have sampled sauerkraut from more than one source. But if you conclude that no one should ever eat sauerkraut, your claim would be too large for the amount of evidence in question.

Because induction involves leaping from discovering evidence to interpreting it, this kind of reasoning helps writers reach probable, believable conclusions, but not some absolute truth. Making a small leap from evidence to a probable conclusion is not the same as jumping to a sweeping conclusion that is easily challenged (see **5d(1)**). Generally, the greater the evidence, the more reliable the conclusion.

Science's use of inductive reasoning is known as the scientific method. For instance, early medical studies equated diets high in fat with coronary artery disease. The scientific community reserved judgment since the early studies were based on only a small sample, but later studies involving larger numbers of subjects confirmed the early reports. Although everyone with coronary artery disease cannot be studied, the sample is now large enough and representative enough to draw the conclusion with more confidence. Nevertheless, a critical thinker would still examine the available evidence carefully and ask a number of questions about it. If the research had been conducted primarily on men, would the conclusions be equally applicable to women? Are the conclusions equally applicable to people of all races? To what extent have the researchers controlled all variables? Because scientists have been trained to think critically, they are often motivated to do further research.

(2) Deductive reasoning

At the heart of a deductive argument is a **premise**, or a principle that is assumed to be true, which leads to the writer's conclusion or claim. For example, if you know that all soldiers must complete basic training and that Martha has enlisted in the army, then you could conclude that Martha must complete basic training. This argument can be expressed in a structure called a **syllogism.**

Major premise	All soldiers must complete basic training.
Minor premise	Martha has become a soldier.
Conclusion	Martha must complete basic training.

Sometimes premises are not stated.

> Martha has enlisted in the army, so she must complete basic training.

In this sentence, the unstated premise is that all soldiers must complete basic training. A syllogism with an unstated premise, called an **enthymeme,** can be very effective when used in an argument. For example, the argument "we need to build a new dormitory because those we have are seriously overcrowded" contains the unstated premise that dormitories should house only the number of people they were designed for. Writers with a good sense of audience understand that readers can lose interest in a discussion of what can be safely assumed.

Critical thinkers, however, should examine enthymemes with care because the omitted statement may be inaccurate. "Samuel is from Louisiana, so he must like Cajun food" contains the unstated major premise that "everyone from Louisiana likes Cajun food." This premise is unacceptable because there is no reason to assume that everyone from a particular region shares the same taste in food. When you use deductive reasoning in your arguments, be sure to work from a premise with which your audience can agree.

Because syllogisms are too absolute for questions that do not have absolute answers, they are often more effective as exercises in critical thinking than as outlines for written arguments. Nevertheless, familiarity with syllogistic reasoning can help you evaluate the arguments you read and write.

(3) The Toulmin model

Another way of using logic is through the method devised by Stephen Toulmin in *The Uses of Argument* (New York: Cambridge UP, 1964). To create a method suitable for the needs of writers, Toulmin drew on deductive reasoning but put less emphasis on the conventions of a syllogism. His approach sees argument as the progression from accepted facts (**data**) to a conclusion (**claim**) by way of a statement (**warrant**) that establishes a reasonable relationship between the two. For example, in the argument,

> Since soldiers are required to complete basic training, and since Martha has become a soldier, Martha must complete basic training,

the claim is that Martha must complete basic training, and the data consist of the fact that she has become a soldier. The warrant, that soldiers are required to complete basic training, ties the two statements together, making the conclusion follow from the data.

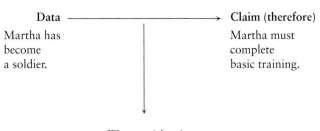

Data   **Claim (therefore)**

Martha has become a soldier.   Martha must complete basic training.

Warrant (since)
Soldiers must complete basic training.

Of course, few arguments are as simple as this example. For instance, Martha may have been exempted from basic training because she has a special skill for which there is an urgent need. Writers can use qualifiers such as *usually, probably,* and *possibly* to show the degree of certainty of their conclusion and use rebuttal terms such as *unless* to indicate exceptions.

> **Since** Martha is a soldier, she **probably** completed basic training **unless** an exception was made for her.

When using the Toulmin model to write arguments, you may be able to identify the claim, the data, and the qualifiers more easily than the warrant. Like the unstated premise in an enthymeme (see **5h(2)**), the warrant is often assumed. To discover the warrant, examine the assumptions with which you began your thinking. Recognize that warrants can take different forms. A warrant may be

- a matter of law or requirement (such as military regulations),
- an assumption that the data came from a reliable source (see **1f** and **6c**),
- an assumption that what is true of a sample is true of a larger group (**5h(1)**), or
- a value that is widely accepted in the writer's culture.

In addition, the Toulmin model requires that warrants have **backing,** or support. The backing may or may not appear within a written argument, but a writer should be able to produce it to support a warrant that has been questioned. Writers who assume that they are drawing their evidence from reliable authorities, for example, should be able to cite the credentials of those authorities. And those who base their argument on a legal principle should be able to cite the exact statute, precedent, or regulation.

5i Logical fallacies can weaken an argument.

Fallacies are lapses in logic that can result from relying on faulty premises, from misusing or misrepresenting evidence, or from distorting the issues. They can be the result of poor thinking, but they can also be a deliberate attempt to manipulate. Many fallacies are what logicians call *non sequiturs,* which is Latin for "it does not follow." Any conclusion that is based on a faulty premise—or does not follow from its premises—can be described as a *non sequitur*. For example, the statement "Billy Joe is honest; therefore, he will get a good job" is a *non sequitur* because it rests on a faulty premise: many honest people do not get good jobs (see **5h(2)**).

Both logicians and rhetoricians find it useful, however, to distinguish different kinds of fallacy. Here are some of the major ones. Be alert for them in your reading (see **1f** and **6c**) and when you revise the arguments you draft (see chapter **3**).

Ad hominem is a personal attack on an opponent in order to draw attention away from the issues.

> **Faulty** He is unfit to be governor because he drank too much when he was a college student. [Although this candidate's drinking when he was young may reveal something about his character, voters might decide that he now has political skills and principles that could benefit the state.]

Appeal to tradition is an argument that says something should be done a certain way simply because it has been done that way in the past.

> **Faulty** We should not allow women to join this club because we have never let women join before. [Times change; what was acceptable in the past is not necessarily acceptable in the present.]

Bandwagon is an argument saying, in effect, "Everyone's doing or saying this, so you should too."

> **Faulty** Everyone cheats on exams, so why shouldn't you? [The majority is not always right.]

Begging the question is a statement that assumes what needs to be proved.

> **Faulty** We need to fire the thieves in the police department. [If there are thieves working in the police department, this point needs to be established.]

Equivocation is an assertion that falsely relies on the use of a term in two different senses.

> Faulty   We know this is a natural law because it feels natural. [When first used, *natural* means principles derived from nature or reason; when used again, it means easy or simple because of being in accord with one's own nature.]

False analogy is the assumption that because two things are alike in some ways, they must be alike in others.

> Faulty   Bill Collins will be a good senator because he used to be a good quarterback. [The differences between playing football and serving in the Senate are greater than the similarities.]

False authority is the assumption that an expert in one field can be a credible expert in another.

> Faulty   The defense budget must be cut, as the Surgeon General has shown. [Medicine is unrelated to economics or political science.]

False cause is the assumption that because one event follows another, the first is the cause of the second.

> Faulty   Our new school superintendent took office last January, and crime has increased 14 percent. [The assumption is that the school superintendent is responsible for the increase in crime, an assumption unlikely to be true.]

False dilemma means stating that only two alternatives exist when in fact there are more than two (sometimes called the *either/or* fallacy).

> Faulty   We have only two choices: to build more nuclear power plants or to be completely dependent on foreign oil. [Other possibilities exist.]

Guilt by association is an unfair attempt to make someone responsible for the beliefs or actions of others.

> **Faulty**   Judge Barlow must be dishonest because she belongs to the same club as that lawyer who was recently disbarred. [People can belong to the same club without engaging in the same behavior.]

Hasty generalization is based on too little evidence or on exceptional or biased evidence.

> **Faulty**   Ellen is a poor student because she failed her first quiz. [Her performance may improve in the weeks ahead or be good in all her other subjects.]

Oversimplification is a statement or argument that leaves out relevant considerations about an issue to imply that there is a single cause or solution for a complex problem.

> **Faulty**   We can eliminate hunger by growing more food. [Increasing the amount of food produced does not guarantee that the hungry will have access to it.]

Red herring means dodging the real issue by drawing attention to an irrelevant one (sometimes called *ignoring the question*).

> **Faulty**   Why worry about overcrowded schools when we ought to be trying to attract a professional hockey franchise? [Professional sports have nothing to do with overcrowded schoolrooms.]

Slippery slope is the assumption that if one thing is allowed, it will be the first step in a downward spiral.

> **Faulty**   Handgun control will lead to a police state. [Handgun control has not led to a police state in England.]

What looks like a logical fallacy may be acceptable under some circumstances, however. Although personal attacks on an opponent (*ad hominem* arguments) should normally be avoided, a writer may have good reason to question someone's character. For example, if a candidate for public office has been cheating on his income tax, a writer may decide that voters should be advised of this information because it raises issues of public trust. Similarly, people should normally make their own decisions and not simply go along with the crowd (*bandwagon* arguments). But if you are part of a team that is working on a project and achieving consensus is essential to getting the job done, your teammates could legitimately point out that everyone else has agreed to the plan you have rejected.

Be alert for logical fallacies in your own writing. When you find one, fix it by moderating your claim, clarifying your thinking, or, if necessary, eliminating the fallacious point. Even if your argument as a whole is persuasive, logical fallacies can damage your credibility (see **1f** and **5f**).

5j   You can improve your ability to write persuasively by studying the arguments of other writers.

As you read the following paper, consider whether the author has argued her case effectively.

Janet Kowolsky
Professor Hayes
English 112, Section 1
25 April 2000

Making the Grade

Imagine how it feels to go to class every day, take careful notes, study hard for an exam, and end up with a grade that is even lower than you

Writer engages attention.

Writer engages the attention of audience she hopes to persuade.

feared. Then imagine that this has happened in your favorite subject and you limp back to your room wondering whether you should change your major or maybe even drop out of school. College professors, especially those who have not been tested recently, might benefit

Writer identifies her audience.

from imagining this scene and considering how it would feel to take one of the tests they have devised under the same conditions their students experience.

Last semester I had four midterm exams and three finals. This semester I have already had another three exams, and more will be coming up in a few weeks. The results have been all over the place, even though I studied hard for each of these tests. Surprisingly, some of my worst results have been in my best subjects. I have come to understand that performance on an exam is determined not only by how much you study for it and what the questions are like. It is also determined by the

Introduction of topic

circumstances under which the exam is given.

Of the ten exams I have had so far, eight were taken in class and two were taken outside of class. The eight in-class exams differed in terms of how

Background

they were set up. Three involved studying like crazy without having any clear sense of what I would be asked to do. My teachers simply said to review everything we had covered so far because this exam was cumulative. The others were less stressful. When I was preparing for finals in December, my psychology professor and my biology professor distributed copies of previous exams so that my classmates and I could have a rough idea of what our exam was going to be like. That was helpful. This semester, my history teacher gave us a list of six questions a week before our midterm and told us she would choose three of them for our test. This was also helpful. I still had to study hard, because I wanted to be able to do a good job with any of these questions, but I had less anxiety preparing for the test.

Unfortunately, each of these exams had to be taken in a room crowded with other students and filled with tension. Whenever I wanted to pause to think, I would look around and see other people scribbling away and worry that I was falling behind. When people would start to leave early, I would become anxious -- thinking something must be wrong with me because I needed all the time that still remained. Then there were the many irritations and distractions: losing my concentration when someone arrived late and squeezed into the seat next to me, listening to people rummage in their backpacks for supplies, being asked if I had an extra pen, catching sight of other students passing material between

Background

Writer concedes that some professors are helpful.

Additional background and an appeal to feeling

Appeal to feeling

them, and feeling like I was some kind of laboratory rat under the eye of the teacher monitoring the room.

Two of my other tests were entirely different because they were take-home exams. One of these was in my introduction to literature class; the other was in calculus. Although these two exams were set up somewhat differently, they were both excellent. I

Proposition or claim

think more professors should assign take-home exams.

First reason in support of proposition

Their big advantage is that you can work on them in a quiet place where you feel safe and comfortable. The questions on my two take-homes were challenging, but I did well on both of them because I was working in space that I selected. Because the circumstances are more comfortable does not mean that the exam itself has to be easy. If professors eliminated some of the stress of exam

Writer raises a concern of her audience.

taking, they would be able to tell more accurately how much their students really know. Is that not the purpose of exams?

Writer anticipates an opposing argument and makes a concession.

Some professors may be concerned that students will cheat if they take their exams at home. I have to admit that cheating could be a problem. However, students who really want to cheat can usually find a way of doing so on regular exams and other assignments. So avoiding take-home exams does not mean that cheating goes away. And take-

Refutation

home exams can be designed to minimize cheating. My literature exam, for example, was an open-book essay exam. It was very useful to be able to look up quotes to back up what I wanted to say, but there is no way I could have passed the exam if I had not read the material and thought about it in advance. Theoretically, somebody could probably get a friend to take an exam like this for him or her. But the same thing could happen when we have to write papers. When somebody cheats this way, the professor should be able to tell even if she was not there watching the person do it.

Another common argument against take-home exams is that they could become big productions. I have heard some students say that they would rather get an exam over with in two hours than have a take-home that takes as much work as writing another big paper. I understand these concerns. My literature teacher told us that we could take as long as we wanted on the exam just as long as we handed it in on time, and I ended up spending a whole morning on it. But my calculus professor insisted that we limit ourselves to the two hours we would get during the standard final exam period. We got to choose which two hours we would devote to the exam--and where we would take it--but the exam itself took no longer than any other exam.

Margin annotations:
- Refutation
- Concession
- Refutation
- Writer raises a second opposing argument.
- Writer identifies with opposition.
- Refutation

Refutation

In other words, take-homes can be designed in different ways to make them appropriate for different classes.

There are a number of other advantages to take-home exams. Finals are not scheduled during the same hours the class met, and this can be a problem for students who have jobs or children to care for. The take-home provides flexibility for such students by being sensitive to their needs. And just as

Summary of additional support

they are more student-friendly, they are also more professor-friendly. Teachers do not have to hang around monitoring a classroom when they have lots of other things they could be doing. And more important, they get to read better exams. Would professors not be happier to see their students doing well than to see them doing poorly?

A final concession

Take-home exams can be well designed or badly designed--just like any other assignment. But the flexibility they offer makes them preferable to traditional exams.

Writer calls for a specific action.

Professors who have never offered a take-home exam should experiment with them. They will get a chance to do so soon, and I hope they will take advantage of it.

Chapter 6

Research: Finding and Evaluating Sources

The distinctive feature of a research assignment is that it requires you to obtain information in order to clarify your thinking and support your claims (see 5d–e). Good research skills are essential when you are required to write papers incorporating outside sources. (See chapter 7.) But these skills may help with other writing assignments as well, because you may need to obtain information even when you are not specifically required to do research. These skills include knowing how to

- develop a research routine (6a),
- frame a research question (6b),
- evaluate the reliability of sources (6c),
- use a college or university library (6d(1)),
- use the World Wide Web (6d(2)),
- conduct surveys and interviews (6e), and
- compose a working bibliography (6f).

6a Writers need information.

Because downloading material from the World Wide Web is so easy (see 6d(2)), many students now go to it exclusively—overlooking other avenues that might give them better results. You can assume that there is information on the Web about most subjects. Sorting through hundreds of sites can be time-consuming, however. Before turning to the Web, consider whether material housed in your college library, and guidance from a reference librarian, would be useful (see 6d).

As you proceed, be aware of which sources are primary and which are secondary. **Primary sources** for topics in literature and the humanities are generally historical documents and literary works. In the social sciences, primary sources can be field observations, case histories, and survey data. In the sciences, primary sources are generally empirical—measurements, experiments, and the like. **Secondary sources** are commentaries on primary sources. So a review of a new novel would be a secondary source and so would a critical study of young adults based on survey data. Experienced researchers usually consult both primary and secondary sources, read them critically, and draw on them carefully. (See chapters 5 and 7.)

In addition to examining information that has already been published, consider whether you would benefit from discussing your project with others. An authority on your topic may be teaching at your college. Interview subjects could be nearby or available through e-mail. Thoughtful conversation about your topic could be generated through an electronic discussion list (see **6e**). And the instructor who assigned your project can help clarify what you need to do to complete it successfully.

(1) Resources

Research that people do in their daily lives involves looking in different places to find answers to questions. If you plan to buy a new car, you may read reviews published in magazines or on the Web, talk to people familiar with the cars that interest you, and take a test drive. A similar strategy may be appropriate for research assignments in school or at work: read, interview, and observe.

The following chart can help you see at a glance the advantages and disadvantages of different resources. (For additional information on developing a search strategy, see **6d**.)

Resource Assessment Table

Library Catalog (see page 121)

Advantages

It indexes books available on your campus. It may also link to catalogs at other schools. It identifies material that has been professionally edited, reviewed, and selected for purchase.

Disadvantages

It will not cover all books. A book you need may be checked out. Interlibrary loan may be necessary.

Electronic Indexes to Periodicals (see pages 121–27)

Advantages

They enable you to find material focused specifically on your topic. The most recent citations are identified first and direct you to current work in your field. They have a high percentage of credible sources.

Disadvantages

They provide citations to articles but usually not the full text of them. Articles must usually be located in library holdings or through interlibrary loan. Scholarly articles can be difficult reading for researchers unfamiliar with the field.

Web Sites (see pages 127–30)

Advantages

The Web contains a high volume of recent material. Many sites have links to other relevant sites. The full text can be downloaded and printed out on a personal computer.

Disadvantages

Researchers can be overwhelmed by the number of available sites and waste time investigating sites that prove unhelpful. A high percentage of sites lack credibility.

Conversation (see pages 131–32)

Advantages

Interviews can be conducted in person, by phone, or by e-mail and focus on a point you need to clarify. Dialogue can generate new ideas when you feel stuck.

Disadvantages

Ideas can be lost if not recorded. Misreporting is common. Sources may lack credibility.

(2) Time management

Make sure to allow enough time for the long process of choosing a subject (**2a**), reading extensively, taking notes (**7b**), preparing a working bibliography (**6f**), developing a thesis (**2b**), outlining (**2c(2)**), drafting (**2f**), revising (**3a–d**), and editing (**3f**). Do not procrastinate.

6b Researchers focus their subject and frame it as a question that needs to be answered.

You find the **topic** for a research paper the same way you find a topic for other papers: you are assigned a topic or you choose a question that you would like to answer. (See **2a** and **5b**.)

As you focus your subject, think in terms of a **research problem:** a question that can be resolved at least partly through research. While you may argue a position (see chapter 5), your paper should invite exploration rather than make a judgment. For example, the thesis "animal experimentation is wrong" is not a research problem because it is a conclusion rather than a question. Someone interested in animal research might begin with a question like "Are animals being treated responsibly in research labs?" Beginning with a question encourages researchers to look at diverse materials, not just material that reinforces their beliefs.

6c Researchers look for reliable sources.

When you are doing research, one important consideration is the reliability of your sources. (See **1f** and **5e(1)**.) As you discover sources, ask the questions in the following checklist.

CHECKLIST for Evaluating Sources

- What are the author's credentials?

- Do others speak of the writer as an authority?

- Does the work contain evidence indicating that the author is well informed?

- Does the work contain evidence that the author is prejudiced in any way?

- Is the work recent enough to provide up-to-date information?

- Does the work provide documentation to support important points?

- Does the work include a bibliography that can help you identify other sources?

- What can you discover about the company or organization that has published this work?

You can usually assume that university presses demand a high standard of scholarship. Additional information about books and publishers can be found by searching the Web. A directory of publishers with sites on the Web can be obtained through Vanderbilt University (http://www.library.vanderbilt.edu/law/acqs/pubr.html).

An article published in an **academic journal** (as opposed to a popular magazine) has usually been reviewed by experts before publication. Academic journals are usually published quarterly, which allows time between issues for the careful selection and editing of articles. Pieces that appear in **general-circulation magazines** (the kind that appear weekly or monthly and are available in a supermarket or drugstore) may also be reliable, but they are usually written more quickly and chosen for publication by someone on the staff—not by an expert in the field.

Some magazines are straightforward in identifying their affiliations. For instance, *Mother Jones* reveals its liberal credentials on its masthead, which identifies its namesake as "Mary Harris 'Mother' Jones (1830–1930), orator, union organizer, and hellraiser." Subscription forms for *Conservative Chronicle, The Capitalist's Companion,* and the Conservative Book Club published in *The American Spectator* also reveal their political stance. At other times, however, an apparently well-reasoned article can reflect the values built into a periodical that does not seem political. For example, an article on malpractice suits in the *Journal of the American Medical Association* is likely to be sympathetic to physicians.

Recognizing that periodicals may reflect the political values of their owners and editors does not mean, however, that you must necessarily distrust what you learn from them. Journals and newspapers can be committed to certain values and still have high standards for what they publish.

Distinguish between sources that are **committed** and those that are **biased.** A committed source represents a point of view fairly, whereas a biased source represents it unfairly. The difference is a matter of **ethos** (see **5f(1)**). It is possible to argue ethically for ideas you believe in; it is also possible to twist facts and misrepresent events to make your point. The same is true in publishing. If you read the *Wall Street Journal*, you will recognize that it has a conservative editorial policy sympathetic to business interests. This paper is also committed to honest reporting, however, so the articles it prints may reflect conservative political positions and still be reliable. Bias appears when politics interferes with honest reporting so that facts are distorted or suppressed. Be alert for such signs of bias as

- personal attacks on people,
- sarcastic language,
- sweeping generalizations unsupported by verifiable data,
- oversimplification of complex issues, and
- ignoring or belittling opposing views.

For additional signs of bias, see 5i.

Understanding the distinction between "committed" and "biased" is especially useful when you navigate the Web. Many sites are created by organizations or individuals strongly committed to specific values and goals. If you visit the Web site for Planned Parenthood or the National Rifle Association, you can expect to find information that advances the purposes of these organizations. You can learn much from committed sites such as these. You need to read critically (see 1e–f and 5c) and remember that you are likely to encounter other opinions at other sites, but you should not assume that a site is biased just because it is committed. Look for the signs of bias listed above.

Ask the following questions when determining the reliability of a Web site.

- How often is the site updated?
- Is the author acknowledged?
- Is the source sponsored by an organization about which information is available at other sites? Addresses such as **.edu** (edu-

cation), **.gov** (government), and **.org** (organization) signal sources of this kind.
- Does the work include citations to other sources or, in the case of hypertext, links to other reliable documents?

Additional information on evaluating sites can be found at http:// milton.mse.jhu.edu:8001/research/education/net.html (a site created and maintained by a librarian at Johns Hopkins University). Realize that addresses for Web sites can change. When this happens, you may be linked to the new address, or you may have to search for it.

As you read your sources, learn how to identify useful passages. Seldom will an entire Web site, book, or article be useful for your research. You will usually need to consult many sources, rejecting some and using only parts of others. Use the table of contents and the index of a book, and learn to skim until you find the passages you need. When you find them, read critically. (See **1d–f** and **5c**.)

6d Researchers need to know how to locate information efficiently.

Although different projects require different strategies, you can usually benefit from beginning your search in your college library. If you turn to the library only toward the end of your search, you may have the frustrating experience of discovering exactly the right material and being unable to obtain it on short notice because it is checked out by someone else or must be obtained through interlibrary loan (an arrangement among local or regional libraries for exchanging books and photocopied articles).

(1) Libraries

Libraries have diverse materials that have been carefully selected and organized. Moreover, libraries are staffed by information specialists who can help you find what you need. When you visit a library, be sure to look for both books and periodicals. Each requires a different system for retrieving information.

(a) Books

You locate a book by consulting the library's **main catalog,** which gives you the call number you need to find where the book is shelved. Reference books, encyclopedias, and indexes—materials that cannot usually be checked out of the library—are located in the **reference collection,** which may also include indexing information for electronic databases, either online or on CD-ROM.

Most libraries have computerized their main catalogs, which help users research efficiently. Catalog programs usually allow researchers to locate sources by searching for author, title, or subject—as well as by supplying the computer with other information, such as a keyword that may appear in the title or even a book's call number.

The catalog tells you where each book is located. When you go to the shelf where the book you are looking for is kept, you may find other relevant sources in the same place.

(b) Periodicals

Periodicals (magazines, journals, and newspapers in print or on microform) are usually stored in a special section of the library. To access information in periodicals, researchers use **electronic indexes.** Many periodicals are now also available online, and some allow for **full-text retrieval:** the option of downloading and printing out an article.

A variety of periodical indexes (usually accessed at work-stations within a library and increasingly via the Web) do for articles what the main catalog does for books: locate material by **subject, author,** or **keyword.** This information is stored electronically on CD-ROM and in online information storage and retrieval systems.

In addition to providing electronic access to periodical indexes, many college libraries provide bound volumes of printed indexes, each of which covers a single year. In either electronic or print form, each index includes many publications not listed in the others, so you may need to consult a number of indexes to find the information you need.

Virtually every specialized field has its own periodicals, which usually provide much more detailed information than can be found in magazines or newspapers aimed at the general public. Familiarize yourself with indexes that direct you to the kind of material being written and studied by professionals in your field.

Access to electronic information storage is provided by systems such as *FirstSearch,* which allow you to search in a large number of databases. If your school does not subscribe to *First-Search,* check to see whether you have access to *SilverPlatter* or *Infotrac.* (See pages 124 and 126–27.) Other databases that may be available include full-text search and retrieval databases such as *EBSCO Academic Search Elite* for periodicals and *LEXIS-NEXIS* for legal documents and newspapers. Most permit users to restrict searches to a specific time period, language, and type of record.

Choosing an index   *FirstSearch* enables you to search through a number of databases. It arranges its indexes in thirteen subject areas, such as Education, Life Sciences, and Social Sciences. After you choose from among these, you are presented with additional choices. Covering more than forty indexes, *FirstSearch*, as its name suggests, is a good place to begin your search for periodical literature.

The databases available through *FirstSearch* vary from one library to another. But the introductory screen will prompt you to choose a database, and each subsequent choice brings up a new screen. To research a topic like social injustice in Guatemala, as Dieter Bohn did for his paper (see **7f**), you could click on the database for News and Current Events or Public Affairs and Law. To research what happens when young adults return home to live with their parents, as Adrienne Harton did for her paper (see **7i**), you could click on Social Sciences. Then, once you are in a database, you need to decide what kinds of records to search. By clicking **Article1st,** you could access "nearly 12,500 journals." By clicking **NewsAbs,** you could limit your search to a little "over 25 newspapers."

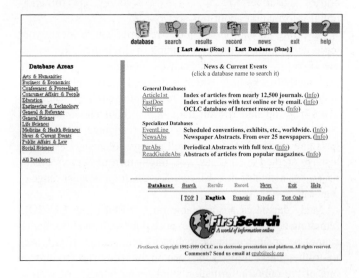

Most college libraries provide students with access to other indexing services. Many disciplines have their own indexes.

Literature	The *MLA Bibliography* is essential for research in American, English, French, German, and Spanish literature.
Education	*ERIC* indexes articles and conference papers in all areas of education.
Psychology	*PsychLit* provides short summaries, or abstracts, of articles in psychology as well as the citations that will help you find the full article.
Life Sciences	*Medline* provides abstracts of articles in medicine and biology from more than seven thousand journals.

These indexes and many others can be accessed through online service provided by *SilverPlatter,* to which many college libraries subscribe. See http://www.silverplatter.com/ for additional information about this service.

Selecting an appropriate index requires you to locate your topic within a discipline or grouping of disciplines. For example, if you are researching the causes of memory loss, you could go directly to *PsychLit,* which is devoted exclusively to scholarship in psychology. If you are researching cases in which students have opened fire on their high school classmates, you could also go to *PsychLit.* But if you recognize that sociologists and criminologists—as well as psychologists—are likely to have studied such cases, you might turn to *Social Science Abstracts,* available through *FirstSearch,* for a broader range of material.

Many databases are available on CD-ROM, but CD-ROM searching has one disadvantage: once published, the information cannot be updated without issuing a continuation. If you need up-to-the-minute information, you might need to search through one of the online information storage and retrieval systems to supplement what you find on CD-ROM. Because electronic databases of scholarly materials are much easier to search and update than print versions, most libraries have switched to them.

Searching an electronic index Whether your library provides indexing services online, via the Web, or on CD-ROM, you can use the following search strategy to locate periodical literature.

Basic Search Strategy

1. Identify the keywords used to discuss the topic.
2. Determine the databases to be searched.
3. Apply a basic search logic.
4. Log on and perform the search.
5. Identify the citations you want to keep.
6. Refine the search strategy if the first search returned too many or too few citations or (worse) irrelevant ones.
7. Obtain the articles for which you have citations.

Identifying **keywords** for your topic, the first step in this strategy, echoes the beginning steps for locating information in your research process as a whole (see **6b**). Many databases permit keyword searches of the entire database, identifying **records** that use the keyword in titles or other parts of the record. If your search yields **no records,** try substituting a synonym or another closely related term for your keyword.

Basic search logic enables you to guard against retrieving too many or too few records. A search result that says, "Found: 2,493,508 records containing the descriptor 'film,' " is as useless as one that reports, "Sorry, no records found." You can use certain words to broaden or narrow your search:

or   broadens a search—**young adults or single adults** finds all records that contain information about either category;

and   narrows a search—**young adults and single adults** returns only those records that contain both categories;

not excludes specific items—**young adults and single adults not homeless** will exclude any records that mention homeless young single adults;

near instructs the computer to find a link based on proximity of terms and prevents inclusion of widely separated terms—**young adults near single adults** lists only those references to both young adults and single adults that occur within a preset number of words (this option is often not available, however).

After you have performed your search, evaluate the records you have retrieved and discard any that are irrelevant.

Searching indexes in bound volumes Although searching electronic indexes is more efficient than searching through bound and printed indexes, many college libraries continue to purchase bound volumes in addition to subscribing to comparable databases. Bound volumes provide essential backup when computers are out of service. Searching through them takes more time than searching a database, but it is preferable to having your research disrupted.

(c) Abstracting services

An **abstract** is a short summary of a longer work. Articles in the social and natural sciences often begin with an abstract so that readers can quickly determine whether they wish to read the whole article. Abstracts can also be accessed electronically.

Whereas bound printed indexes provide only a list of citations for articles, some of their electronic counterparts also provide abstracts. The bound volumes of the *Social Science Index,* for example, provide only the bibliographical information necessary for locating each article. *Social Science Abstracts* (available through *FirstSearch*) is now providing these citations, as well as short summaries of most articles.

Infotrac, a widely used electronic index to articles in periodicals, now provides an abstracting service through its *Expanded Academic ASAP* database. Other **abstracting services** support specific academic disciplines. Your library may have CD-ROMs for *Academic Abstracts, Biological Abstracts,* and *Chemical Abstracts*. When using one of these services, you can quickly scan the short summaries and decide which seem likely to be the most useful. You can print out a list of citations, a list of citations with abstracts, and the full text of some of the articles. Be aware, however, that abstracting services sometimes include material published in languages other than English. An abstract may be in English even if the article is not.

(d) Reference works

When doing research, you may need to consult a variety of reference works. A general encyclopedia, such as *Encyclopaedia Britannica* (now available by subscription on the Web at http://www.eb.com/), can provide useful information, especially at an early stage in your research. You may be able to access an electronic encyclopedia through the software you are using before turning to the Web, where many other reference works, such as dictionaries, can be located.

You may also need to consult a specialized encyclopedia or dictionary in your college library to identify names and understand concepts in the books or articles you have discovered. Sources written for a specialized audience (see **1g(2)**) will assume that readers do not need help with basic terms. Reference books can help you fill in the gaps that keep you from understanding the other sources you have found. For a detailed list of reference books and a short description of each, consult *Guide to Reference Books* by Robert Balay and *American Reference Books Annual* (*ARBA*).

(2) The World Wide Web

The **World Wide Web** is a huge and rapidly expanding collection of information, much of which is useful for research papers and some of which is not. The easiest way to find information on the Web is to use one of the many search systems (often called search engines), such as *AltaVista, InfoSeek, Lycos,* or *Yahoo!*

After you type keywords into a text entry box, these engines will return a list of Web sites that meet the searching criteria.

There are important differences among search engines. Some, like *Yahoo!,* match keyword searches against Web sites submitted by owners and entered by human indexers (who also classify them into basic categories). Others, like *AltaVista,* are best known for their **spiders,** automatic programs that visit millions of Web sites to index the actual content of the pages, word by word.

Because of differences such as these, different search systems will return different results. One system may search only for the titles of documents, another may look at document links, and a few search the full text of every document they index. Furthermore, some search only the Web, whereas others search parts of the Internet (such as Usenet Newsgroups) that are not part of the Web. For these reasons, one engine may be better for academic information, another for general information, and yet another for business information. Experiment with several of them and consult the help screens when necessary. The following screen from *AltaVista* shows that this search engine located 3,764 Web sites on Rigoberta Menchú, the subject of the research paper in **7f.**

The result of the successful search will be a list of addresses or Uniform Resource Locators (URLs) you can use to access the page(s) you need. Keep a log in which you record what sites you visited on which days. Because sites change or even disappear, scholarly organizations such as the Modern Language Association (MLA) (see **7e**) and the American Psychological Association (APA) (see **7h**) require that bibliographies include the date of access as well as the date the site was posted. The posting date (or date when the site was last modified) usually appears on the site itself. When you print material from the Web, you will usually find an access date on the top or bottom of the printout. When you take notes directly from the screen, however, you will have no record of the dates unless you write them down.

CAUTION Because anyone with access to a server can post information on the Web, a search can call up harebrained or tasteless information. However, you can avoid unsuitable or unreliable material by thinking critically (see **1f**, **5c**, and **6c**). As you do so, distinguish between **Web access** and **Web content.** Access signifies how the content was delivered. For example, you can access *Encyclopaedia Britannica* on the Web, but it was not composed exclusively for the Web. Whether you access it online or in bound volumes, you are using a source that has a well-deserved reputation for credibility. But when you turn to someone's home page, you are looking at a document that does not exist outside the Web. Although many Web sources have excellent content, they seldom go through the kind of careful reviewing and editing that a good publisher requires.

Web pages are best viewed with a graphically capable browser. The example on page 130 shows a Web page retrieved with *Netscape,* a widely used program. This page begins with an image accompanied by **links** to other pages. Identified by a different color from the text or by underlining, links can appear anywhere in a Web site. But they are especially likely to appear at the top or bottom of a given Web page.

The site on Rigoberta Menchú illustrated here provides access to an interview by her. Looking at this page, an experienced researcher would note a number of signs indicating a positive treatment of Menchú: a decorative border suggests sympathetic attention to her native culture. She is referred to by her first name and presented with a smiling face. And the text states, "Her life has been dedicated to bringing peace and justice to her country [. . .]" and also claims that she is "an inspiration." The site is committed to Menchú, and this stance must be taken into account when evaluating it for credibility (see **1f** and **6c**).

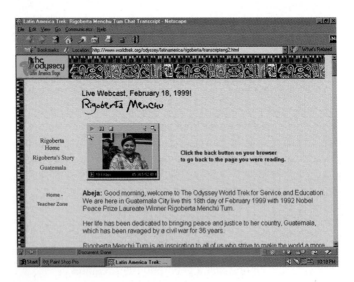

CAUTION Remember that the power that computers make available to you is also available to others. Protect yourself by being security conscious. Do not tell anyone your password, and change it if you have any reason to suspect that the security of your system has been breached. Moreover, protect your equipment by using a good virus checker.

6e Field research involves interviewing, experimenting, and conducting surveys.

For some topics, you may want to do field research, the most common of which is an **interview.** The faculty at your college, business and professional people, and even relatives and friends can be appropriate interview subjects if they have relevant first-hand experience with the subject you are researching.

Because well-informed interviewers usually ask the best questions, you should consider an interview only after you have done some reading on your subject. Schedule interviews well ahead, and if you plan to use a tape recorder, ask permission. Take a professional approach to the interview: have pens and paper ready for taking notes and fresh batteries and blank tapes for your tape recorder. Record the date of the interview on tape or in your notes.

Begin with questions that are broad enough to give people room to reveal their own special interests; then follow up with more specific questions. Be prepared to depart from your list of questions whenever your subject says something of particular interest that would be useful to pursue.

Less formal than an interview, a dialogue with other people interested in your topic can also be useful. You may be able to enjoy such a dialogue with people on your campus or in your community. Researchers often benefit, however, from using the Internet to discuss ideas with people in other parts of the world.

Discussion lists allow you to read messages posted to all the members of a group interested in a specific topic and to post messages yourself that those like-minded people will read. For instance, your instructor may belong to a specialized discussion list for composition teachers operated by the Alliance for Computers and Writing. Participants discuss issues related to using computers to teach writing. Your instructor can send e-mail messages to the **Listserv address,** which will redistribute them to hundreds of other writing teachers around the world. Similarly, your instructor can receive replies from anyone who subscribes to the list.

Anyone who wants to discuss a topic can join a discussion list. To find out if there are any lists that might discuss the topic you are researching, visit http://www.liszt.com, a Web site that provides a directory for thousands of lists and instructions that can guide your search.

Discussion lists can also give you a means of conducting an informal **survey,** in which you ask a number of people the same set of questions and then analyze the results. But a survey limited to people who are already familiar with and discussing a topic will not be representative of other groups, such as the citizens of your state. (See **5e.**) For some research questions (see **6b**), you may get better results by designing a survey specifically for the people whose views you wish to consider.

You can administer a survey orally like an interview, or you can distribute a written questionnaire by mail or in person. You may find the following checklist helpful.

CHECKLIST for Creating Survey Questions

- Does each question relate to the purpose of the survey?

- Are the questions easy to understand?

- Are they designed to elicit short, specific responses?

- Are they designed to collect concrete data that you can analyze easily?

- Are written questions designed to give respondents enough space for their answers?

- Are you able to present these questions to the population you want to survey?

6f A working bibliography lists sources.

A working bibliography contains information (titles, authors, dates, and so on) about the materials you think you might use. Write down the most promising sources you find. Often, the sources you consult will have helpful bibliographies. Draw on them, but do not ignore other ways of discovering sources.

Some people find it convenient to put each entry on a separate index card, which makes it easy to add or drop a card and to arrange the list alphabetically without recopying it. Others prefer to use a computer, which can sort and alphabetize automatically, making it easier to move material directly to the final paper.

From the beginning, you should follow consistently the bibliographical form you are instructed to use. The MLA bibliographic style can be found in 7e and the APA style in 7h. Using the specified style from the start will save you time later, when you must compile a formal list of the sources you used in your paper. Be sure to note the URL for Internet sites. Both MLA and APA styles require that you include this information in bibliographies.

Citations
MLA/APA

Chapter 7   **Research Using and
Citing Sources**

Citations MLA/APA

Chapter

7

Research: Using and Citing Sources

To write well from sources, you need to think critically (**1d–f** and **5c–i**) and discover relevant information (chapter **6**). That effort can be undermined if you do not document your sources accurately. But no matter how many sources you use or how carefully you document them, remember that you are a *writer,* not simply a compiler of data. *You* are the most important presence in a paper that has your name on it.

This chapter will help you understand how to

- determine the purpose of a research paper (**7a**),
- take notes accurately (**7b**),
- use direct quotations (**7c(2)**),
- paraphrase (**7c(3)**),
- summarize (**7c(4)**),
- avoid plagiarism (**7d**),
- use MLA-style documentation (**7e–f**),
- use footnotes or endnotes (**7g**), and
- use APA-style documentation (**7h–i**).

Different disciplines usually employ different documentation styles, so there is no single way to document or to prepare a bibliography that can be used in every department of a college or university. Use the style your instructor specifies. If your instructor does not require a specific documentation style, follow the one set forth by the discipline appropriate for your paper. When you do not know what type of documentation is appropriate, model your documentation on the style you find used in one of the journals in your field.

This chapter discusses the two documentation styles most widely used in college writing: MLA (Modern Language Association) style, used for papers in English and other modern languages (see chapter **9**), and APA (American Psychological Association) style, most often used for papers in psychology and other courses in the social sciences.

7a Research papers have a purpose.

Inexperienced writers sometimes assume that they are fulfilling the purpose of a research project by demonstrating that they have done some research. But research could be indicated simply by submitting a working bibliography (see **6f**) and a collection of notes. A research paper uses the results of research to make or prove a point. In other words, research papers are either **expository** or **persuasive.** (See **1g(1)**.)

If you have begun with a **research problem** (see **6b**), your paper will be expository if it explains

- the nature of the problem,
- its causes,
- its effects, or
- the way others are responding to it.

Your paper will be persuasive if it

- asks readers to recognize that a problem exists,
- offers a solution to the problem,
- calls on readers to undertake a specific action, or
- reconciles conflicting parties.

As you work toward fulfilling your purpose, you must establish that you are a credible source (see **1f** and **5f(1)**). To be

credible in a research paper, you must show your audience that
you have

- done serious research,
- understood what you have discovered,
- integrated research data into a paper that is clearly your own,
- drawn accurately on the work of others, and
- honored academic conventions for citing such work.

The rest of this chapter focuses on how to use sources to fulfill your purpose in writing a research paper. For information
on how to conduct research, see chapter 6.

7b Taking notes demands accuracy.

There are four widely used methods for taking notes. Match
your choice to your own work style.

Using a notebook

A ring binder into which you can insert pages of notes as well
as photocopies is an excellent organizational tool, particularly
if you have a system for sorting notes into the main subject categories your work covers. Identify the source on every page of
notes, and use a fresh page for each new source.

Using photocopies

On a photocopy you can mark quotable lines and jot down your
own ideas. Make sure you document the source on the photocopy.

Photocopied source with notes

The testimonials of Rigoberta Menchú and others, and the large number of indigenous combatants in the guerrilla organizations, suggest that many <u>Maya found them a hospitable site of struggle.</u> In turn, the revolutionary organizations were pushed by the incorporation of so many indigenous people (C. Smith 1990b, 271) to theorize the relations among class, ethnicity, and nationalism and to create more equal relations among Maya and ladino, supporting Mayan customs as much as possible given their mobility and attacking racism in self-criticism sessions (Simon 1988; Díaz-Polanco 1987; Harbury 1994; author interviews). <u>However many other indigenous people left the organizations,</u> some as part of larger splits, some fed up with what they perceived as <u>ongoing racist discrimination.</u> <u>What is undeniable is that despite the large numbers of Mayan combatants, there were no indigenous commanders representing the guerrillas in the peace talks, and there are few ranking officials who are Maya.</u>[29]

Complex political situation-Link with Stoll

Check these sources?

problem

evidence

Diane Nelson, A Finger in the Wound (Berkeley: U of California P, 1999) 59.

Using notecards

Researchers sometimes take notes on index cards, which they can arrange as their research proceeds. If you are using this system, show the author's name (and a short title for the work) on each card, and include the exact page number(s) from which the information is drawn. Put no more than a single note, however brief, on each card and a heading of two or three keywords at the top, so that you can arrange your cards in the order you will use them.

Using computer files

You may use your computer for taking notes. Doing so gives you the advantage of recording notes quickly and keeping them stored safely. Using a computer also makes it easy to copy and paste information into subject files and ultimately into the finished paper.

Whatever system you use to create your notes, consider the questions in the following checklist.

CHECKLIST for Taking Notes

- Does every note clearly identify its source? Have you put the full bibliographic citation on the first page of every photocopy?

- Is the bibliographic information for the source of every note accurate? Double-check to be sure.

- Have you accurately recorded any useful passage that you think you may later quote? Have you been especially careful to put quotation marks around any words you copy directly?

- When a source has sparked your own thoughts, have you distinguished between the source and your own ideas?

- Have you incorporated every source you are using into your working bibliography? (See **6f**.)

7c Integrating sources fosters mastery of information.

Writers of research papers borrow information in three ways: quoting the exact words of a source, paraphrasing them, or summarizing them. With any of these methods, make sure that you use sources responsibly.

A research paper that consists primarily of material taken from other writers is unlikely to be successful even if the sources are well chosen and meticulously cited (6 and 7d). You must understand how to integrate your research into a paper that is clearly your own. In a good paper, sources support a thesis (2b) that has grown out of the writer's research, but they do not obscure the writer's own ideas. Integrate your source material with your own statements. Make sure to use your own words and your own style throughout.

(1) Introducing and discussing sources

Introduce sources to readers by establishing where material came from; for example, in a research paper about the value of vitamin C, readers might find it useful to know that the author of a quotation praising the vitamin was a Nobel laureate in chemistry. Moreover, introduce research with a phrase that indicates the author's attitude or the importance of the information. The following list of verbs that introduce quoted, paraphrased, or summarized information can be helpful in deciding how to integrate that information with your own ideas.

Sixty-Four Lead-In Verbs

acknowledge	assert	confirm	emphasize
add	believe	consider	endorse
admit	charge	contend	explain
advise	claim	criticize	express
agree	comment	declare	find
allow	compare	deny	grant
analyze	complain	describe	illustrate
answer	concede	disagree	imply
argue	conclude	discuss	insist
ask	concur	dispute	interpret

list	oppose	reply	speculate
maintain	point out	report	state
note	reason	respond	suggest
object	refute	reveal	suppose
observe	reject	see	think
offer	remark	show	write

Adding an adverb to one of these verbs can emphasize your attitude toward the material you are introducing: *persuasively* argue, *briefly* discuss, *strongly* oppose.

The following examples of quotation, paraphrase, and summary show MLA documentation style. For additional information on MLA-style documentation, see 7e–f.

(2) Using direct quotations

A direct quotation should contribute an idea to your paper. As a rule, anything worth quoting is worth discussing, and the longer the quotation, the greater your responsibility to discuss it. Select quotations only if

- you want to retain the beauty or clarity of someone's words, or
- you need to reveal how the reasoning in a specific passage is flawed, and
- you plan to discuss the implications of what you quote.

Keep quotations as short as possible and make them an integral part of your text. (See 7f.)

Quote **accurately.** Enclose every quoted passage in quotation marks. Any quotation of another person's words should be placed in quotation marks or, if longer than four lines, set off as an indented block. (See 30b.)

Cite the exact source for your quotation. If you think your audience might be unfamiliar with a source, establish its authority by identifying its author the first time you refer to it. (Note that this citation is in MLA style.)

```
Mike Rose, a nationally recognized authority
on education, claims that learning is
facilitated not by fear but by "hope,
everyday heroics, the power and play of the
human mind" (242).
```

This reference clearly establishes that the quotation can be found on page 242 of a work by Mike Rose, additional information about which would be found in a list of works cited at the end of the paper. (See 7e(2).)

CHECKLIST for Direct Quotations

• Have you copied all the words and punctuation accurately? (See 30f.)

• Do you need to observe a special form or special spacing? (See 30a and 30b.)

• Have you used ellipsis points correctly to indicate anything that is left out? (See 31i.)

• Have you used square brackets around everything you added to the direct quotation? (See 31g.)

• Have you used too many quotations? (Doing so suggests inability to think independently or to synthesize material.)

---

(3) Paraphrasing

A **paraphrase** is a restatement of someone else's ideas in close to the same number of words. Paraphrasing enables you to demonstrate that you have understood what you have read. Paraphrase when you want to

- clarify difficult material by using simpler language,
- restate a crudely made point in more professional terms,
- use another writer's idea but not his or her words to demonstrate that you understood what you read, or
- create a consistent tone (see 3a(3)) for your paper as a whole.

Your restatement of someone else's words should honor two important principles: Your version should be in your own words, and your words should accurately convey the content of the original passage.

Using your own words

Unless you enclose an author's words in quotation marks, do not mix them with your own. Equally important, do not make the mistake of thinking that you can substitute synonyms for an author's words while you preserve his or her sentence structure. Moreover, you must indicate where the paraphrase begins and ends.

As you compare the source below with the paraphrases that follow, note the similarities and differences in sentence structure as well as word choice. The parenthetical citations at the end of the paraphrases are in MLA-style documentation (see 7e(1)).

Source (from "The Trouble with Wilderness," by William Cronon, in *Uncommon Ground: Toward Reinventing Nature* [New York: Norton, 1995], pp. 80–81)

> This, then, is the central paradox: wilderness embodies a dualistic vision in which the human is entirely outside the natural. If we allow ourselves to believe that nature, to be true, must also be wild, then our very presence in nature represents its fall. The place where we are is the place where nature is not.

Inadequate paraphrasing

```
Here is the main problem: wilderness is a
two-sided ideal in which people have no
place. When we convince ourselves that real
nature means the wilderness, then nature has
no people in it. This means that we could
never visit nature because as soon as we got
to a natural place it would no longer be
natural (Cronon 80-81).
```

Adequate paraphrasing

```
William Cronon has shown why it is
problematic to associate "nature" with
"wilderness." Wilderness means a place that
is unspoiled by human presence. When we
define nature as wilderness, we are
ultimately saying that people have no place
in nature (80-81).
```

CAUTION You may be charged with plagiarism if the wording of your version follows the original too closely, even if you provide a page reference for the source. A page reference after an inadequate paraphrase would acknowledge the source of the idea but not your debt to another writer's language.

Maintaining accuracy

A paraphrase must accurately convey the sense of the original. If you accidentally misrepresent the original because you did not understand it, you are being **inaccurate.** If you deliberately change the gist of what a source says, you are being **unethical.** Compare the original statement below with the paraphrases.

Source (from *Heaven's Coast*, by Mark Doty [New York: Harper, 1996], p. 159)

We trivialize pain if we regard it as a preventable condition the spirit need not suffer. If we attempt to edit it out, will it away, regard it as our own creation, then don't we erase some essential part of the spirit's education? Pain is one of our teachers, albeit our darkest and most demanding one.

Inaccurate

```
Pain can never be prevented. It is
completely outside our control, but it makes
us grow stronger (Doty 159).
```

Unethical

```
Mark Doty argues that you are doing people a
favor when you hurt them (159).
```

Accurate

```
According to Mark Doty, pain cannot always
be alleviated. In a spiritual sense, however,
people can grow through suffering if they
are willing to learn from what is happening
to them (159).
```

(4) Summarizing

A summary omits much of the detail that a writer used but accurately reflects the essence of that writer's work. In most cases, then, a summary reports a writer's **main idea** (see 2b) and the most important support given for it. Because summarizing enables writers to report the work of others without unnecessary detail, it is a highly useful skill in writing research papers.

A paraphrase (see 7c(3)) is usually close to the same length as the original material. A summary must be shorter. When you paraphrase, you are helping readers understand another writer's work. When you summarize, you are saving space. The two skills are closely related, however. Although summaries consist primarily of paraphrasing, they can also include short quotations, in quotation marks, of key phrases or ideas.

Source   (from "What's Wrong with Animal Rights," by Vicki Hearne, *Harper's,* Sept. 1991, p. 61)

> A human being living in the "wild"—somewhere, say, without having the benefits of medicine and advanced social organization—would probably have a life expectancy of from thirty to thirty-five years. A human being living in "captivity"—in, say, a middle-class neighborhood of what the Centers for Disease Control call a Metropolitan Statistical Area—has a life expectancy of seventy or more years. For orangutans in the wild in Borneo and Malaysia, the life expectancy is thirty-five years; in captivity, fifty years. The wild is not a suffering-free zone or all that frolicsome a location.

Summary

```
Because of the risks posed by living in the
wild, both humans and animals lead
significantly shorter lives under such
conditions than they do when cared for
within an "advanced social organization"
(Hearne 61).
```

CAUTION If you retain some of another writer's phrasing when you are summarizing, be sure to put quotation marks around those words.

7d Plagiarism is a serious offense.

Taking someone else's words or ideas and presenting them as your own leaves you open to criminal charges. In the film, video, music, and software businesses, this sort of theft is called **piracy.** In publishing and education, it is called **plagiarism** or **cheating.**

You would be putting yourself at a great disadvantage, however, if you felt it was unsafe to draw on the work of others. One purpose of this chapter is to help you use such work responsibly so that you can enter into a thoughtful conversation with other writers.

You must give credit for all information you use except for common knowledge and your own ideas. Common knowledge includes dates and other facts: the stock market crashed in 1929; water freezes at thirty-two degrees Fahrenheit. It also includes information such as "The *Titanic* sank on its maiden voyage." This event has been the subject of many books and movies, and some information about it has become common knowledge: the *Titanic* hit an iceberg, and many people died because the ship did not carry enough lifeboats. But if you are writing a research paper about the *Titanic* and wish to include details about the ship's construction, then you are providing *un*common knowledge that must be documented.

After you have read a good deal about a given subject, you will be able to distinguish between common knowledge and the contributions of specific writers. When you use the ideas or information these writers provide, be sure to cite your source. If you have been scrupulous in recording your own thoughts as you took notes, you should have little difficulty distinguishing between what you knew to begin with and what you learned through your research and must therefore cite.

Source (from "Returning Young Adults," by John Burnett and Denise Smart, *Psychology and Marketing* 11 [1994], p. 254)

Both generations want their rights. The RYAs want the autonomy they have grown accustomed to and expect their parents to treat them like adults. The parents, meanwhile, have come to recognize their own rights. They may resent that the time, money, and emotional energy they planned to invest in themselves after the child's departure are instead allocated to the RYA.

Undocumented paraphrase

```
Parents may get upset when resources they
had planned to use on themselves must be
used to support an adult child who has
returned home.
```

Documented paraphrase

```
Marketing professors John Burnett and Denise
Smart note that young adults who return to
live at home can make their parents resent
supporting them with resources they had
planned to devote to themselves (254).
```

This idea is introduced with a reference establishing where the paraphrase begins. The sentence structure and phrasing have changed. A parenthetical citation marks the end of the paraphrase and provides the page number on which the source can be found.

Documented quotation

```
Marketing professors John Burnett and Denise
Smart note that parents "may resent that the
time, money, and emotional energy they
planned to invest in themselves after the
child's departure are instead allocated to
the RYA" (254).
```

Quotation marks show where the copied words begin and end, and the number in parentheses tells the reader the exact page on which the words appear. In this case, the sentence identifies the authors. An alternative is to provide the authors' names within the parenthetical reference: (Burnett and Smart 254). If you cannot decide whether you need to cite a source, the safest policy is to cite it.

CHECKLIST of Information That Should Be Cited

- Writings, both published and unpublished:
    direct quotation, paraphrase, and summary

- Opinions and judgments not your own

- Statistics and other facts that are not widely known

- Images and graphics:
    works of art, drawings, tables and charts, graphs, maps, advertisements, and photographs

- Personal communication:
    interviews, letters, and e-mail

- Public electronic communication:
    television and radio broadcasts, films and videos, recordings, Web sites, and discussion lists

---

CAUTION There is another form of plagiarism that is never excusable: Do not ever submit as your own a paper you did not write.

7e MLA-style documentation is required for research papers in literary studies and useful for other courses in the humanities.

Directory of MLA-Style Parenthetical Citations

(1) Parenthetical citations

Parenthetical citations identify the source of specific material and refer the reader to a list of works cited at the end of the paper. The MLA suggests reserving numbered notes for supplementary or explanatory comments. Superscript numbers are inserted in the appropriate places in the text, and the notes are gathered at the end of the paper. (See pages 198–99.)

The basic elements of the parenthetical citation are the author's last name and the page number of the material used in the source. However, it is not necessary to repeat any information that is already provided. Omit the author's name from the parenthetical citation if you have identified it in the text shortly before the material being cited. Study the following examples, as well as the discussion of punctuation and mechanics that follows these examples (pages 157–59).

Work by one author

```
Olivier creates Richard III's "central device
of coherence" by using a cyclical theme of
the crown (Brown 133).
```

In this citation, the author's name is included within the parentheses because it is not mentioned in the text. A page number is included because the reference is to a specific passage. Note how the citation changes if the text includes more information about the source.

```
Constance Brown argues that in Richard III,
Laurence Olivier uses a cyclical theme of
the crown to create a "central device of
coherence" (133).
```

Work by two or three authors

```
High software prices mean that "education
must do without this resource, prices must
come down, or new strategies for development
must be devised" (Holdstein and Selfe 27).
```

Provide the last name of each author. Commas are necessary in a citation involving three authors, for example: (Bellamy, O'Brien, and Nichols 59).

Work by more than three authors

For a work by more than three authors, use the same form as the bibliographic entry (see pages 163–64), giving either the first author's last name followed by the abbreviation *et al.* (from the Latin *et alii,* meaning "and others") or all the last names. (Do not italicize or underline the abbreviated Latin phrase.)

```
In one important study, women graduates
complained more frequently about "excessive
control than about lack of structure"
(Belenky et al. 205).
```

OR

```
In one important study, women graduates
complained more frequently about "excessive
control than about lack of structure"
(Belenky, Clinchy, Goldberger, and Tarule
205).
```

Multivolume work

Include the volume number (followed by a colon and a space) before the page number.

```
As Katherine Raine has argued, "true poetry
begins where human personality ends" (2:
247).
```

You do not need to include the volume number if your list of works cited includes only one volume of a multivolume work.

More than one work by the same author

When your list of works cited includes more than one work by the same author, your parenthetical citations should include a shortened title that reveals which of the author's works is being cited. Use a comma to separate the author's name from the shortened title when both are in parentheses.

```
According to Gilbert and Gubar, Elizabeth
Barrett Browning considered poetry by women
to be forbidden and problematic
(Shakespeare's Sisters 107). That attitude
was based on the conception that male
sexuality is the "essence of literary power"
(Gilbert and Gubar, Madwoman 4).
```

This passage cites two different books by the same authors, Sandra M. Gilbert and Susan Gubar. The authors' names are not necessary in the first citation because they are mentioned in the text; they are included in the second because their names are not mentioned in connection with *Madwoman.*

Works by different authors with the same last name

Occasionally your list of works cited will contain sources by two authors with the same last name—for example, rhetoricians Theresa Enos and Richard Enos. In such cases, you must use the first name as well as the last.

> Richard Enos includes a thirteen-page bibliography in <u>Greek Rhetoric before Aristotle</u> (141-54). In her collection of articles by prominent figures in modern rhetoric and philosophy, <u>Professing the New Rhetorics</u>, Theresa Enos discusses contemporary reliance on pre-Aristotelian rhetoric (25, 331-43).

In these references, the citation of more than one page, "(141–54)," identifies continuous pages, whereas "(25, 331–43)" indicates that the reference is to two separate sets of pages.

Indirect source

If you need to include material that one of your sources quoted from another work and cannot obtain the original source, use the following form.

> The critic Susan Hardy Aikens has argued on behalf of what she calls "canonical multiplicity" (qtd. in Mayers 677).

A reader turning to the list of works cited should find an entry for Mayers (which was the source consulted) but not for Aikens (because the quotation was obtained secondhand).

Poetry, drama, and the Bible

When you refer to poetry, drama, and the Bible, you must give numbers of lines, acts, and scenes, or of chapters and verses, rather than page numbers. This practice enables a reader to consult an edition other than the one you are using.

Act, scene, and line numbers (all Arabic) are separated by periods with no space before or after them. The MLA suggests that biblical chapters and verses be treated similarly. In all cases, the progression is from larger to smaller units.

The following example illustrates a typical citation of lines of poetry.

```
Emily Dickinson concludes "I'm Nobody! Who
Are You?" with a characteristically
bittersweet stanza:
            How dreary to be somebody!
            How public, like a frog
            To tell your name the livelong June
            To an admiring bog! (5-8)
```

Quotations of three lines or less are not indented (see **9f**).

The following citation shows that the "To be, or not to be" soliloquy appears in act 3, scene 1, lines 56–89 of *Hamlet.*

```
In Hamlet, Shakespeare presents the most
famous soliloquy in the history of the
English theater: "To be, or not to be
[. . .]" (3.1.56-89).
```

Biblical references identify the book of the Bible, the chapter, and the pertinent verses. In the following example, the writer refers to the creation story in Genesis, which begins with chapter 1, verse 1, and ends with chapter 2, verse 22.

```
The Old Testament creation story (Gen. 1.1-
2.22), told with remarkable economy,
culminates in the arrival of Eve.
```

Names of books of the Bible are neither italicized—underlined—(see chapter **34**) nor enclosed in quotation marks (see chapter **30**), and abbreviation is preferred (see chapter **35**).

Sources produced for access by computer

Although electronic sources are treated differently from print sources in your bibliography (see **7e(2)**), many can be treated identically for parenthetical documentation in the text. An on-line book, for example, could easily have both an author and page numbers just like a printed book.

If an electronic source does not have page numbers but does provide another numbering scheme, use those numbers. If paragraphs are numbered, cite the number in question, beginning with the abbreviation *par.* or plural *pars.* If screen numbers are provided, cite the screen, beginning with *screen*.

If the source includes no numbers distinguishing one part from another, then you must cite the entire source.

```
Raymond Lucero's Shopping Online offers
useful advice for consumers who are concerned
about transmitting credit card information
over the Internet.
```

The Uniform Resource Locator (**URL**) for this site and additional information about it would be included in the list of works cited.

Punctuation and mechanics

Punctuation and numbers Commas separate the authors' names from the titles (Brown, "Olivier's *Richard III:* A Reevaluation") and indicate interruptions in a sequence of pages or lines (44, 47). Hyphens indicate continuous sequences of pages (44–47) and lines (1–4). Colons separate volume and page numbers (Raine 2: 247); one space follows the colon. Periods separate acts, scenes, and lines in drama (3.1.56–89). Periods (or colons) distinguish chapters from verses in biblical citations (Gen. 1.1 or Gen. 1:1). (See **31d.**)

Ellipsis points (see **31i**) indicate omissions within a quotation and should be enclosed in brackets: "They lived in an age of increasing complexity and great hope; we in an age of [. . .] growing despair" (Krutch 2). Brackets (see **31g**) also indicate interpolations within quotations: "The publication of this novel

[*Beloved*] establishes Morrison as one of the most important writers of our time" (Boyle 17).

When a question mark ends a quotation (see **31b**), place it before the closing quotation mark; then add a period after the parenthetical citation.

```
Paulo Freire asks, "How can the oppressed,
as divided, unauthentic beings, participate
in developing the pedagogy of their
liberation?" (33).
```

The MLA favors Arabic numbers throughout, except when citing pages identified by Roman numerals in the source itself (such as the front matter of a book: Garner ix).

Placement of citations   Wherever possible, citations should appear just before a mark of punctuation in the text of the paper.

```
Richard Enos provides a bibliography of
sources for the study of Greek rhetoric
before Aristotle (141-54), and Theresa Enos's
edited collection, Professing the New
Rhetorics, includes Michael Halloran's essay
"On the End of Rhetoric, Classical and
Modern" (331-43).
```

Richard Enos's citation falls just before a comma; Theresa Enos's just before a period. However, in a sentence such as the following, the citations should follow the authors' names to keep the references separate.

```
Richard Enos (141-54) and Theresa Enos (25)
address classical rhetoric from very
different perspectives.
```

Lengthy quotations   When a quotation is more than four lines long, set it off from the text by indenting one inch (or ten spaces) from the left margin (see **30b**). Although the final punctuation mark comes *after* the citation in quotations fewer than four lines long, it comes *before* the final punctuation mark in longer quotations set off by indentation.

```
Susan Sontag asks how European governments
should respond when another government
commits genocide within its borders:
                Imagine that Nazi Germany had had
                no expansionist ambitions but had
                simply made it a policy in the
                late 1930's and early 1940's to
                slaughter all the German Jews. Do
                we think a government has the right
                to do whatever it wants in its own
                territory? Maybe the governments of
                Europe would have said that 60
                years ago. But would we approve now
                of their decision? (55)
```

No indentation is necessary if you quote only one paragraph or if you quote the beginning of a paragraph. When quoting more than one paragraph, indent the first line of each paragraph by three additional spaces.

(2) Works-cited list

For MLA-style papers, the list of sources from which you have cited information is called the **Works Cited.** This list appears at the end of the paper.

When you are ready to produce the final draft of your paper, eliminate from your working bibliography (see **6f**) any sources that you did not use and include every source that you did use.

- Arrange the list of works alphabetically by author.
- If a source has more than one author, alphabetize by the last name of the first author.

- Type the first line of each entry flush with the left margin and indent subsequent lines five spaces or one-half inch (a hanging indent).
- Double-space throughout.

As you study the following MLA-style entries, observe both the arrangement of information and the punctuation. (See also pages 459–61 for a list of abbreviations that are used in works cited, notes, and tables.)

Directory of MLA-Style Works-Cited Entries

Books

Articles

Sources Viewed or Heard

Sources Produced for Access by Computer

Books

Most book entries consist of three units separated by periods.

Author	Title	Publication data

Lastname, Firstname. <u>Title Underlined</u>. City: Publisher, date.

1. *Author.* Give the last name first, followed by a comma and the first name.
2. *Title.* Underline the title of the book, and capitalize all major words. (See **33c**.) Always include the book's subtitle. Make underlining continuous, not separate under each word.
3. *Publication data.* Provide the city of publication, an abbreviated form of the publisher's name, and the latest copyright date shown on the copyright page. Type a colon after the city and a comma after the publisher. (To shorten the name of the publisher, use the principal name: Alfred A. Knopf becomes Knopf; Random House becomes Random; Harvard University Press becomes Harvard UP; University of Michigan Press becomes U of Michigan P.)

Book by one author

Smith, Jeanne Rosier. <u>Writing Tricksters: Narrative Strategy and Cultural Identity in Maxine Hong Kingston, Louise Erdrich, and Toni Morrison</u>. Berkeley: U of California P, 1997.

Use a colon to separate a main title from a subtitle. Capitalize all words in both the title and subtitle, except for articles, prepositions, and coordinating conjunctions (see **33c**). To cite books published by universities, abbreviate "University" and "Press" without periods. Indent all lines after the first by five spaces.

More than one work by the same author

Angelou, Maya. <u>A Brave and Startling Truth</u>. New York: Random, 1995.

---. <u>Kofi and His Magic</u>. New York: Potter,
      1996.

Alphabetize the works by the first major word in each title.
Give the author's name with the first title, but substitute three
hyphens followed by a period for the name in subsequent
entries.

Book by two or three authors

West, Nigel, and Oleg Tsarev. <u>The Crown
      Jewels: The British Secrets at the Heart
      of the KGB Archives</u>. New Haven: Yale
      UP, 1999.
Spinosa, Charles, Ferdinand Flores, and
      Hubert L. Dreyfus. <u>Disclosing New
      Worlds: Entrepreneurship, Democratic
      Action, and the Cultivation of
      Solidarity</u>. Cambridge: MIT P, 1997.

Invert the name of the first author (or editor), but do not invert
the second or third name.

Book by more than three authors

When a book has more than three authors, give all names in
full as they appear on the title page or add the abbreviation *et
al.* after the first author.

Bell-Scott, Patricia, Beverly Guy-Sheftall,
      Jaqueline Jones Royster, Janet Sims-
      Wood, Miriam DeCosta-Willis, and Lucille
      P. Fultz, eds. <u>Double Stitch: Black
      Women Write about Mothers and Daughters</u>.
      New York: Harper, 1993.

OR

Bell-Scott, Patricia, et al., eds. <u>Double Stitch: Black Women Write about Mothers and Daughters</u>. New York: Harper, 1993.

Book by a corporate author

Institute of Medicine. <u>Blood Banking and Regulation: Procedures, Problems, and Alternatives</u>. Washington: Natl. Acad. P, 1996.

Alphabetize by the first major word in the corporate name.

Book by an anonymous author

<u>Primary Colors: A Novel of Politics</u>. New York: Warner, 1996.

Begin the entry with the title. Do not use "Anonymous."

Book for which the editor appears as author

Warhol, Robyn R., and Diane Price Herndl, eds. <u>Feminisms: An Anthology of Literary Theory and Criticisms</u>. New Brunswick: Rutgers UP, 1993.

Edition after the first

Fromkin, Victoria, and Robert Rodman. <u>An Introduction to Language</u>. 6th ed. Fort Worth: Harcourt, 1998.

Work from an anthology (a collection of works by different authors)

Bishop, Wendy. "Students' Stories and the Variable Gaze of Composition Research."

Writing Ourselves into the Story:
Unheard Voices from Composition Studies.
Ed. Sheryl I. Fontane and Susan Hunter.
Carbondale: Southern Illinois UP, 1993.
197-214.

Use this form for an article or essay that was first published in an anthology; use it also for a story, poem, or play reprinted in an anthology.

For an article or essay that was published elsewhere before being included in an anthology, use the following form.

Chaika, Elaine. "Grammars and Teaching."
College English 39 (1978): 770-83. Rpt.
in Linguistics for Teachers. Ed. Linda
Miller Cleary and Michael D. Linn. New
York: McGraw, 1993. 490-504.

Note where the essay first appeared and then show where you read it. Use the abbreviation *Rpt.* for "reprinted." Both forms require you to cite the complete range of pages where the material can be found, not just the pages the researcher borrowed material from. In the second example, you must cite both the pages of the original publication (770–83 in this case) and the pages of the anthologized version (490–504).

Translated book

Duras, Marguerite. The North China Lover.
Trans. Leigh Hafrey. New York: New P,
1992.

Republished book

Alcott, Louisa May. Work: A Story of
Experience. 1873. Harmondsworth:
Penguin, 1995.

The original work was published over a century before this paperback version. (For reprinted articles, see "Work from an anthology," pages 164–65.)

Multivolume work

Odell, George C. D. <u>Annals of the New York
      Stage</u>. 15 vols. New York: Columbia UP,
      1927-49.

This multivolume work was published over a period of years. Cite the total number of volumes in a work when you have used more than one volume.

   If you use only one volume, include the number (preceded by the abbreviation *Vol.*).

Browning, Robert. <u>The Complete Works of
      Robert Browning: With Variant Readings
      and Annotations</u>. Ed. John C. Berkey and
      Allan C. Dooley. Vol. 6. Athens: Ohio
      UP, 1996.

Encyclopedia or almanac

Hile, Kenneth S. "Rudolfo Anaya."
      <u>Contemporary Authors</u>. New Rev. Ser.,
      1991.
Petersen, William J. "Riverboats and
      Rivermen." <u>Encyclopedia Americana</u>. 1999
      ed.

Full publication information is not necessary for a well-known reference work organized alphabetically. Use abbreviations to specify edition or series (such as New Rev. Ser. for New Revised Series). For sources that are more unusual, you should reveal more about the source.

Dreyer, Edward L. "Inner Mongolia."
    Encyclopedia of Asian History. Ed.
    Ainslee T. Embree. 4 vols. New York:
    Scribner's, 1988.

When an author's name is indicated only by initials, check the table of contents for a list of contributors. When an article is anonymous, begin your entry with the article title and alphabetize according to the first important word in the title.

Book in a series

Kelly, Richard Michael, and Barbara Kelly.
    The Carolina Watermen: Bug Hunters and
    Boat Builders. Twayne English Author
    Ser. 577. Winston-Salem: Blair, 1993.

Provide the name of the series and the number designating the work's place in it (if any).

Introduction, foreword, or afterword to a book

Elbow, Peter. Foreword. The Peaceable
    Classroom. By Mary Rose O'Reilley.
    Portsmouth: Heinemann, 1993. ix-xiv.

Begin with the author of the introduction, foreword, or afterword. Include the name of the book's author after the title. Note the pages at the end, using Roman numerals if they appear as such in the work.

Pamphlet or bulletin

Safety Data Sheet: Kitchen Machines. Chicago:
    Natl. Restaurant Assn., 1970.

If the pamphlet has an author, begin with the author's name (last name first) as you would for a book.

Government publication

```
United States. Office of Management and
     Budget. A Citizen's Guide to the Federal
     Budget. Washington: GPO, 1999.
```

When citing a government publication, identify the government (e.g., "United States," "Minnesota," "Great Britain," "United Nations") followed by the agency that issued the work. Indicate the city of publication. Federal publications are usually printed by the Government Printing Office (GPO) in Washington, DC, but be alert for exceptions.

Articles

The documentation format for articles differs slightly from that for books. The three units are the same, and they are still separated by periods, but note the differences in treatment for titles and publication information.

Author	Title	Publication data

Lastname, Firstname. "Title of Article." <u>Journal</u> volume (year): pages.

Lastname, Firstname. "Title of Article." <u>Periodical</u> day/month/year: pages.

1. *Author.* Give the last name first, followed by a comma and the first name.
2. *Article title.* Type the article title in regular (Roman) face, and put it in quotation marks with the period inside the final quotation marks. Capitalize all major words in the title. (See 33c.)
3. *Publication data.* The exact kind of information differs according to the type of periodical, but all references provide the periodical title, the date of publication, and the page numbers on which the article appeared. Continuously underline the periodical title, and capitalize all major words. (See 33c.) Note that no punctuation follows the periodical title and that a colon introduces the inclusive page numbers. If a periodical entry requires both a volume number and a date, put the date in parentheses.

Article in a journal with continuous pagination

A *journal* is a scholarly publication written for a specific profession, whereas a *magazine* is written for the general public.

Diaz, Gwendolyn. "Desire and Discourse in
    Maria Luisa Bombal's <u>New Islands</u>."
    <u>Hispanofila</u> 112 (1994): 51-63.

Citing a specific issue is not necessary when a journal's pages are numbered continuously throughout the year.

Article in a journal with each issue paginated separately

Ray, Robert B. "How to Teach Cultural
    Studies." <u>Studies in the Literary
    Imagination</u> 31.1 (1998): 25-36.

When each issue begins with page 1, put a period after the volume number and add the issue number.

Article in a monthly magazine

Shenk, Joshua Wolf. "America's Altered
    States: When Does Legal Relief of Pain
    Become Illegal Pursuit of Pleasure?"
    <u>Harper's</u> May 1999: 38-49.

MLA style abbreviates the names of months (except for May, June, and July). A period goes between the last word in the title and the closing quotation marks unless the title ends with a question mark or exclamation point. A space (without punctuation) separates the magazine title from the date of issue.

Magazine articles are often interrupted by other articles. If the first part appears on pages 45–47 and the last on pages 213–21, give only the first page number followed by a plus sign: 45+.

Article in a weekly newspaper or magazine

Karps, Richard. "Risk's Rewards." <u>Barrons</u> 19
    Apr. 1999: 22-24.
Stille, Alexander. "The Man Who Remembers."
    <u>New Yorker</u> 15 Feb. 1999: 50-63.

Article in a daily newspaper

Leroux, Charles. "Reading Frenzy." <u>Chicago
    Tribune</u> 20 Apr. 1999, final ed., sec.
    2: 1+.

When it is not part of the newspaper's name, the name of the
city should be given in brackets after the title: *Star Tribune*
[Minneapolis]. If a specific edition is not named on the masthead, put a colon after the date and then provide the page reference. Specify the section by inserting the section number or
letter immediately before the page number just as it appears in
the newspaper: A7 or 7A. When an article is continued elsewhere in the section (but not on the next page), add + to indicate this continuation.

Editorial in a newspaper or magazine

Lewis, Anthony. "Deeper Than Politics."
    Editorial. <u>New York Times</u> 24 Apr. 1999,
    natl. ed.: A29.

If the editorial is not signed, begin the citation with the title.

Sources viewed or heard

Motion picture

<u>Shakespeare in Love</u>. Dir. John Madden.
    Miramax, 1998.

When you cite the contribution of a specific person, put the person's name first. Additional information can be included immediately after the title.

Fiennes, Joseph, perf. <u>Shakespeare in Love</u>.
    Screenplay by Marc Norman and Tom
    Stoppard. Dir. John Madden. Miramax,
    1998.

Radio or television program

"'Barbarian' Forces." <u>Ancient Warriors</u>. Narr.
    Colgate Salsbury. Dir. Phil Grabsky. The
    Learning Channel. 1 Jan. 1996.
Leavitt, David. <u>The Lost Language of Cranes</u>.
    Prod. Ruth Caleb. Dir. Nigel Finch.
    Great Performances. PBS. WNET, New York.
    24 June 1992.

Play performance

<u>Death of a Salesman</u>. By Arthur Miller. Dir.
    Robert Falls. Eugene O'Neill Theater,
    New York. 7 May 1999.

Cite the date of the performance you attended.

Compact disc sound recording

Franklin, Aretha. <u>Amazing Grace: The Complete
    Recordings</u>. Atlantic, 1999.

Provide the full title, including the subtitle. Adapt this form for other kinds of sound recording by including what kind it is (such as Audiocassette or LP), followed by a period, immediately before the name of the manufacturer.

    If citing the recording of a specific song, begin with the name of the performer, and place the song title in quotation marks. Identify the author(s) after the song title. If the performance is a reissue from an earlier recording, provide the original date of recording (preceded by Rec.) immediately before the title of the compact disc.

```
Horne, Lena. "The Man I Love." By George and
     Ira Gershwin. Rec. 15 Dec. 1941. Stormy
     Weather. BMG, 1990.
```

Lecture

```
Mikolajczak, Michael. "T. S. Eliot's The
     Waste Land." Class lecture. English 212.
     University of St. Thomas, St. Paul. 30
     Apr. 1999.
```

Use the title if available or provide a descriptive label for an untitled lecture and give the location and date.

Interview

```
Jones, Faustine. Personal interview. 16 Jan.
     2000.
```

Use this form for an interview you have conducted, giving the name of the person you interviewed. If the interview was conducted by someone else, begin with the name of the interviewer, then state the title of the interview followed by the title of the source in which you found it.

Sources produced for access by computer

The information required to cite sources such as software programs or databases that can be distributed on diskettes or CD-ROM disks and the information required to cite online sources differ in two important ways. Citations to CD-ROM disks and diskettes generally should identify the publisher, the place, and the date of publication. Citations for information obtained online should state the date of publication and the date of access because Web sites change frequently. You must also provide the correct **URL** for any Web site you use. By providing your readers with a complete address, including the access identifier (**http, ftp, telnet, news**), all punctuation marks, and both path and file names, you are telling them how to locate the source.

<http://stanfordmag.org.marapril99/>
<ftp://beowulf.engl.uky.edu/pub/beowulf>

The complete address is essential. It substitutes for the publication data that help readers find print sources. Place the address within angle brackets < > so that it is clearly separated from any other punctuation in your citation. Divide the address after a slash when it cannot fit on a single line.

The information cited varies according to the kind of electronic source. Arrange that information in the following sequence.

1. *Author*. Give the last name first, followed by a comma and the first name.
2. *Work title*. Capitalize all major words in the title, and either underline it or place it within quotation marks (see **30c** and **34a**). Begin with the title when there is no author.
3. *Publication data*. For online services, this includes the date of publication, the name of the sponsoring organization, the date of access, and the network address. For a CD-ROM or diskette, include the city where the program was published, the name of the manufacturer, and the date of issue.

CAUTION The World Wide Web contains material that is uneven in quality. *The MLA Style Manual and Guide to Scholarly Publishing*, 2nd edition, cautions scholars to evaluate carefully the quality of any sources that they intend to use, print or electronic. For information about evaluating Web sites, see **6c**.

Online book

Be sure to use a reliable source. Note that the following example was published at a well-respected university.

```
Shakespeare, William. Richard III. The
     Complete Works of William
     Shakespeare. 2 Aug. 1995. The Tech. MIT.
     20 Apr. 1998 <http://thetech.mit.edu/
     Shakespeare/History/kingrichardiii/
     kingrichardiii.html>.
```

In this case, the work was published on August 2, 1995, and accessed on April 20, 1998. Providing the date of publication tells readers how long the source has been available. Providing the date of access indicates how recently the site was still available, as well as the precise version used (because online sources can be updated after publication). Break URLs only at slashes.

Article in an online journal

```
Harnack, Andrew, and Gene Kleppinger. "Beyond
     the MLA Handbook: Documenting Sources on
     the Internet." Kairos 1.2 (1996).
     14 Aug. 1997 <http://www.english.ttu/
     acw/kairos/index.html>.
```

The date of access follows the volume and date of publication.

Article in an online magazine

```
Plotz, David. "The Cure for Sinophobia."
     Slate 3 June 1999. 8 June 1999
```

```
<http://www.slate.com/StrangeBedfellow/
99-06-03/StrangeBedfellow.asp>.
```

Give the date of access after the date of publication even if you consult the source the same day it is posted.

Article in an online newspaper

```
"Tornadoes Touch Down in S. Illinois." New
    York Times on the Web 16 Apr. 1998.
    20 May 1998 <http://www.nytimes.com/
    aponline/a/AP-Illinois-Storms.html>.
```

Begin with the article title when an author is not identified.

Review in an online magazine or newspaper

```
Koeppel, Fredric. "A Look at John Keats."
    Rev. of Keats, by Andrew Motion. Nando
    Times News 16 Apr. 1998. 27 Aug. 1998
    <http://www.nando.net/newsroom/ntn/enter/
    041698/enter30_20804.html>.
```


Online government publication

```
United States. Dept. of State. Bur. of
    Democracy, Human Rights, and Labor.
    Guatemala Country Report on Human Rights
    Practices for 1998. Feb. 1999. 1 May
    1999 <http://www.state.gov/www/
    global/human_rights/1998_hrp_report/
    guatemal.html>.
```

Begin with the government responsible for this publication, followed by the division or agency that issued it. If a subdivision of a larger organization is responsible, name the larger division first, followed by the subdivision. If an author is identified, provide the name(s) between the title and the date of issue.

Online work of art

```
Vermeer, Johannes. Young Woman with a Water
    Jug. c. 1660. Metropolitan Museum of
    Art, New York. 27 Apr. 1999 <http://
    www.metmuseum.org/htmlfile/gallery/second/
    euro5.html>.
```

Place the date of the painting, sculpture, or photograph immediately after its title. If the precise date is not known, use the abbreviation *c.* (for *circa*) to indicate the approximate date attributed to it. Include the date of access after the name of the institution or organization making the work available for viewing.

Online map

```
"Virginia 1624." Map. Map Collections 1544-
    1996. Library of Congress. 26 Apr. 1999
    <http://memory.loc.gov/cgi-bin/map_...mp/
    ~ammmem_8kk3::&title=Virginia++>.
```

Include the word *Map* followed by a period immediately after the map's title.

E-mail

E-mail is treated much the same as personal letters and memos. Give the name of the writer, a description of the message (usually the subject line), the receiver of the message, and the date.

```
Peters, Barbara. "Scholarships for Women."
    E-mail to Rita Martinez. 10 Mar. 2000.
```

Academic discussion list

Whenever possible, cite an archived version of a posting to a discussion list to make it easier for your readers to find your source.

```
Schipper, William. "Re: Quirk and Wrenn
     Grammar." Online posting. 5 Jan. 1995.
     Ansaxnet. 12 Sep. 1996 <http://
     www.mun.ca/Ansaxdat/>.
```

Identify the name of the forum (in this case, Ansaxnet, a group of scholars interested in England before 1100 C.E.) between the date of posting and the date of access.

Newsgroup

```
May, Michaela. "Questions about RYAs." Online
     posting. 19 June 1996. 29 June 1996
     <news:alt.soc.generation-x>.
```

Newsgroups are open forums, unconfined by a subscription list. Most have no moderator to ensure the quality of the postings, and messages are not usually retrievable after a few weeks. Make a hard copy of the posting so that you can refer back to it.

CD-ROM

For a source on CD-ROM, provide the author (if available) and the title, the publication medium, the place of publication, the publisher, and the publication date.

```
"About Richard III." Cinemania 96. CD-ROM.
     Redmond: Microsoft, 1996.
```

Publication on diskette

Provide the title, a descriptive label, the version number, the publisher or distributor, and the copyright date. Add other information at the end of the entry, including, if pertinent, the operating system and units of memory necessary to run the program. When a program is attributed to an author, insert the name (last name first) immediately before the title.

```
Hieatt, Constance, Brian Shaw, and Duncan
     Macrae-Gibson. Beginning Old English:
     Exercise Disk. Diskette. Vers. 6.4.
     Binghamton: OEN Subsidia, 1994.
```

Publication in more than one medium

```
English Poetry Plus. CD-ROM, diskette. New
     York: Films for the Humanities and
     Sciences, 1995.
```

7f Producing the final draft of a research paper requires time and attention.

After investing much time and effort into researching and drafting, writers sometimes fail to review their final draft carefully. Planning your time (see 6a(2)) reduces the risk of being forced to submit a final draft that was prepared too quickly.

(1) Revising and editing

After writing and carefully documenting the first draft of your paper, make needed revisions. An outline can help you determine whether your organization is logical (see 2c). Revise each paragraph to make its purpose clear (see 3c), and edit each sentence to support its paragraph. Refer to chapters 3 and 4 as needed, particularly the revising, editing, and proofreading checklists. As you revise, make sure you continue to use your sources carefully and responsibly (see 7b–d). If you have questions about final manuscript form, refer to chapter 4 and to the sample research paper in 7f(2).

(2) Sample MLA-style research paper

After researching a case in which a Nobel Prize winner was found to have misrepresented the truth in the book that made her famous, Dieter Bohn focused his paper on what this case reveals about credibility. As you study his paper, note how he develops his thesis, considers more than one point of view (see 5e(2)), and observes correct form for an MLA-style paper.

Comments

A. All pages (including the first one) are numbered with Arabic numerals in the upper right-hand corner, one-half inch from the top. The page number is preceded by the author's last name. Notice that no period follows the page numbers.

B. The name of the author, the name of the professor, the course number, and the date of submission—appearing in that order—begin one inch from the top of the page and flush with the left margin. A margin of one inch is provided at the left, right, and bottom.

C. Double-space between the heading and the centered title of the paper. Double-space also between the title and the first line of the text. (A title consisting of two or more lines is double-spaced, and each line is centered.)

D. The thesis statement for this paper is placed where readers can easily locate it. The thesis emerged through the process of writing the paper. Note the uncertainty Bohn reveals when exploring ideas before writing his first draft.

Excerpt from the research log of Dieter Bohn

```
The central issue is not whether or not
she told the truth (she clearly didn't)
but the implications of that. [. . .]
     I'm having a hard time [. . .] because
all the options seem to put me in one camp
or the other. I'm not entirely happy with
either. I don't want to say that it was
propaganda intended to further the left's
cause because I think there is something
to their cause. On the other hand, condoning
the lies in her book seems tantamount to
saying that it is okay to distort the
facts for a political agenda, and even if
```

(*continued on page 182*)

B

Dieter Bohn
Professor Miller
English 299, Section 4
30 June 1999

Rigoberta Menchú and Representative Authority C

1   The 1983 publication of Rigoberta
Menchú's <u>I, Rigoberta Menchú</u> has done much
to help her work to improve human rights in
her native country, Guatemala. Recently,
however, there has been a great deal of
controversy--especially since the 1999
publication of David Stoll's <u>Rigoberta Menchú
and the Story of All Poor Guatemalans</u>--
surrounding the truth of Menchú's
autobiography. Stoll, an anthropologist at
Middlebury College in Vermont, proves that
Menchú did not tell the whole truth about
her life in the book that made her famous.
When Menchú told her story, her goal was to
call international attention to the plight
"of all poor Guatemalans" (<u>I, Rigoberta</u> 1).
She achieved this goal by changing her story
to make it more compelling to her audience.
These changes have undermined her authority
as a representative figure and threaten to
damage her cause as well. The example of
<u>I, Rigoberta Menchú</u> shows why it is wrong to D
fictionalize an autobiographical account that
claims to speak for a whole people.

2   In Guatemala, ladinos, or those of
European or mixed descent, make up
approximately fifty-six percent of the

Comments

E. Bohn provides background information so that his audience can understand the political situation that inspired the book he has chosen to discuss. A parenthetical citation appears without a page reference because it is to a Web site without pagination or paragraphing. (See page 184.)

F. A parenthetical citation does not include the author's name when the author is clearly identified in the text, as is the case here.

Excerpt from the research log of Dieter Bohn
(*continued from page 180*)

the guerrillas for which Menchú spoke were blameless (when I don't think they are), I wouldn't want to accept that.

    The one thing I feel obligated to put in this paper is that Menchú's book is <u>not</u> an autobiography, but a consciously formed story including her own life mixed with what her allies would like construed as the typical peasant experience in a dictatorship. What I am hesitant about is what to say about it. Condone it on the basis of her great victimization mixed with relativistic autobiographical theory? Say it was wrong? Try to make no judgments whatsoever? I don't know.

    Anyway, that's where I'm at right now.

population; the rest is composed mainly of different types of Amerindian, or Mayan, peoples ("Guatemala"). There has been tension E between these two ethnic groups; for many years, Mayans had suffered under a series of oppressive ladino dictatorships. At the same time, there were several guerilla groups fighting the Guatemalan army, also composed mainly of ladinos but claiming to speak for Mayans. Caught in the middle were Mayan peasants, trying to survive in this difficult environment by cultivating mountainside fields and working on coastal plantations called _fincas_, most of which are owned by wealthy ladinos. It was out of this war-torn country that Rigoberta Menchú, a Mayan, traveled to Europe in January 1982 so that she could tell her story to anthropologist Elizabeth Burgos-Debray. After recording a week's worth of conversation with Menchú, Burgos-Debray converted those tapes into the book-length memoir known as <u>I, Rigoberta Menchú</u> (xv-xxi). F

3   In this book, Menchú recounts her upbringing, the murder of four members of her family, oppression by the Guatemalan army, and the guerilla resistance. Telling how she and her village organized to fight the oppression of ladino landowners, she describes events and feelings she claims were typical of what most Mayan peasants experienced. Filled with powerful language and stories about her fight against

Comments

G. Although the period normally *follows* the parenthetical citation, MLA style makes an exception for block quotations. For quotations indented one inch from the left margin, place the period *before* the parenthetical citation as shown here.

H. When two sources are cited within the same parentheses, they are separated by a semicolon.

I. Bohn establishes the credibility of a source by identifying a name that would be unfamiliar to this audience.

J. A shortened version of the title appears within the parentheses because the works-cited list includes two works by Stoll.

K. When a Web site or other source accessed by computer includes neither page nor paragraph numbers, the MLA advises writers to refer readers to the complete source, which can be found in the list of works cited. The MLA has never asked writers to create numbers for unnumbered texts. In the case of sources accessed by computer, specific passages can usually be located by performing a *find* on the Web site or in the electronic document by entering a few words from the quotation in question. For additional information on citing electronic texts, see pages 156–57 and 172–78.

L. Recognizing the controversy provoked by David Stoll's book on Menchú, Bohn establishes that another source has verified Stoll's findings.

Bohn 3

injustice, Menchú's book has received
considerable attention because she tells
such a compelling story. For example, she
describes a confrontation between the
people of her village and the Guatemalan
army:

> The people raised their weapons and
> rushed at the army, but they drew
> back at once, because there was the
> risk of a massacre. The army had
> all kinds of arms, even planes
> flying overhead. [. . .] But nobody
> thought about death. I didn't think
> that I might die, I just wanted to
> do something, even kill a soldier.
> (179)   G

4   Menchú's book became an international
bestseller (Grandin and Goldman 25; Wilson   H
A14). One of the many results of this
success has been the widespread use of
<u>I, Rigoberta Menchú</u> in university classrooms.
According to Charles Lane, an editor for <u>The</u>   I
<u>New Republic</u>, the book

> has become required reading in
> anthropology, women's studies, and
> Latin American history and politics
> courses at universities across the
> United States. [. . .] According to
> Menchú herself, it has inspired
> some 15,000 scholarly papers. It
> has been translated into twelve
> languages. (36)

Another result of the book's success is
that Menchú has become an international
activist for human rights (Stoll, <u>Rigoberta</u>   J
5). All of this attention and acclaim
eventually helped Menchú win the 1992 Nobel
Prize. In a press release, the Norwegian
Nobel Foundation said that Menchú "stands out
as a vivid symbol of peace and
reconciliation across ethnic, cultural, and
social dividing lines [. . .]." Menchú's   K
status as a symbol of oppressed indigenous
people was an especially effective tool
against the problems in Guatemala. In 1995,
the Guatemalan government signed an agreement
to stop violating human rights (Stoll,
<u>Rigoberta</u> 268). It did this mainly because
of international pressure--the most
significant result of Menchú's work. Were it
not for Menchú, many believe, the human
rights violations in Guatemala would have
passed largely unnoticed by the international
community (Grandin and Goldman 25). Now,
although there are still problems, the
Guatemalan government cannot indiscriminately
kill peasants or destroy their villages.

5   But the book that inspired so much of
this progress is misleading, as David Stoll
has shown. Larry Rohter, a reporter for the
<u>New York Times</u>, corroborated Stoll's account: L
           Relatives, neighbors, friends and
           former classmates of Rigoberta
           Menchú [. . .] indicated that
           many of the main episodes

related by Ms. Menchú have either
been fabricated or seriously
exaggerated.

6   One of the major exaggerations that
Menchú made about her life as she told it in
her book concerns her childhood. She tells
us that most peasants try to eke out a
living from small farms in the mountains but
often cannot, and so travel down to the
fincas to work. The conditions in the fincas
are terrible; Menchú writes about working as
an eight-year-old:

> I went on working and [. . .] for
> two years they paid me only 20
> centavos [equivalent to 20 U.S.
> cents a day]. I picked more and
> more coffee. It increased by one
> pound, two pounds, three pounds.
> I worked like an adult. Then,
> finally, they started paying me
> more. By the time I was picking
> 70 pounds of coffee [a day],
> they paid me 35 centavos. (I,
> Rigoberta 35)

The workers were also exposed to toxins:
"They'd sprayed the coffee with pesticide by
plane while we were working, as they usually
did, and my brother couldn't stand the fumes
and died of intoxication" (Menchú, I,
Rigoberta 38). The conditions these workers
faced were terrible, and they were common to
most Guatemalan peasants. However, Stoll
discovered that Menchú never actually

Comments

M. A superscript numeral in addition to a parenthetical citation indicates that an explanatory note will follow on a separate page at the end of the paper. (See page 199.)

In an earlier draft, Bohn had extended his discussion of what happened to Menchú's siblings by including the following passage describing the fate of a brother who was part of a group of prisoners burned alive by the military:

> They all had marks of different
> tortures. The captain devoted
> himself to explaining each of the
> tortures. [. . .] You could only
> think that these were human
> beings and what pain those bodies
> had felt to arrive at that
> unrecognizable state. [. . .]
> Anyway, they lined up the
> tortured and poured petrol on
> them; and then the soldiers set
> fire to each one of them. (I,
> Rigoberta 177-79)

Bohn described this scene as "powerful enough to make even the hardest hearts sympathetic to Menchú's plight," but then went on to cite evidence showing that Menchú could not have witnessed this scene as she claims. When revising, he decided that he was dwelling too long on establishing how Menchú had misrepresented her story when he really wanted to focus on the political and ethical implications of these discrepancies. So he condensed this part of his paper and inserted an explanatory note. (See page 198.)

experienced these conditions. Menchú's
surviving family members and neighbors say
that she spent most of her childhood in
Catholic boarding schools (Stoll, <u>Rigoberta</u>
160). Nevertheless, Menchú did know from her
interactions with other Guatemalan peasants
what the conditions in the <u>fincas</u> were like,
even if she did not experience them first-
hand. Stoll himself points out that this is
not an especially problematic change: "Even
if the young Rigoberta did not watch her
siblings die on a plantation, other Mayan
children have" (<u>Rigoberta</u> 190).[1]   M

7   Unfortunately, there are other major
fabrications that misrepresent the common
experience of indigenous people. One change
Menchú makes is the source of the land
problems that many Mayans face. Menchú claims
that her village was primarily fighting
ladino landowners:

>   We started thinking about the roots
>   of the problem and came to the
>   conclusion that everything stemmed
>   from the ownership of the land. The
>   best land was not in our hands. It
>   belonged to the big landowners.
>   Every time they see that we have
>   new land, they try to throw us off
>   it or steal it in other ways.
>   (<u>I, Rigoberta</u> 116)

Although it is true that the rich plantation
owners, the <u>finca</u> owners, owned much of the

best land, in Menchú's particular case, her father's fight was not against ladino landowners, as Menchú asserts, but against other Mayans. She claims that "my father fought for twenty-two years, waging a heroic struggle against the landowners who wanted to take our land and our neighbors' land" (I, Rigoberta 103). However, Stoll's research has shown that people in Menchú's village agree that her father's "most serious land dispute was not with ladino plantation owners. Instead, it was with K'iche [Mayan] smallholders like himself: his in-laws" (Rigoberta 30). This type of situation is much more common than Menchú would like to admit. Thus, her claim that the main problem was between ladinos and Mayans is misleading; the major land problems were actually between Mayans and other Mayans.

8   Another disturbing fabrication is that Menchú claims her village was united with the guerillas against the army; instead, most villages were actually stuck between both forces. Menchú describes how her entire village organized as guerilla fighters: "Everyone came with ideas of how to defend themselves. [. . .] We began to get a much better idea of how to organise [sic] our community" (I, Rigoberta 126). However, most peasants were not on one side or the other, but trapped between a guerilla movement they did not wish to join

and an army that was killing everybody they thought was in collusion with the guerillas (Stoll, <u>Rigoberta</u> 110). Mayans were pressured into joining one side or the other simply to keep from getting killed.

9   By claiming that the guerillas formed spontaneously in the Mayan villages in response to oppression (<u>I, Rigoberta</u> 123), Menchú implies that guerilla warfare was inevitable. According to Stoll, "that view of the violence is incorrect" ("Literary"). The decision to fight was actually made by guerilla leaders who were ladino, not Mayan. Moreover, Diane Nelson, another anthropologist who has done research in Guatemala, argues that many Mayans felt the ladino leadership was racist. In <u>A Finger in the Wound</u>, Nelson writes that many "indigenous people left the [guerilla] organizations, [. . .] some fed up with what they perceived as ongoing racist discrimination" (59). Marc Becker, of the University of Kansas, also found evidence that the guerilla leadership "considered Indians to be politically and economically marginal to Guatemalan society with little promise of leading or contributing to a revolutionary uprising."

10   Menchú's version of events is
significantly different from what actually
happened. She changed what was a ladino-led
attempt at an uprising to a version that
sounded suspiciously like the perfect
Marxist revolt: the lowest class becoming
aware of its oppression and rising up.
David Horowitz, a conservative columnist,
noted this change and came to the
conclusion that "the fictional story of
Rigoberta Menchú is a piece of Communist
propaganda designed to incite hatred of
Europeans and Westerners [. . .]" (2).
Others agree with Horowitz; in fact, there
is now a group calling itself "Operation
Remove Rigoberta" that is angry about the
influence Menchú has gained as a result of
her less-than-truthful book. This group
has used advertisements in college
newspapers as well as a Web site in a
campaign to remove the book from college
campuses ("Operation").

11   Against opinions such as this, John
Beverly, of the University of Pittsburgh,
defends Menchú because he believes that she
was simply trying to gain support for her
cause, so her changes do not matter if they
are taken in that sense:

          [H]er primary purpose in making the
          text is not to humanize college
          students, or to give literary
          theorists something to argue over,

but to act tactically through the
text as a way of advancing the
interests of the group or class
represented in the <u>testimonio</u>
[autobiography]. (138)

Stoll argues along the same lines. He claims
that she changed her story to make it more
compelling to a mass audience: "One of the
simplifying functions of solidarity imagery
is that it offers a single platform to
support" (<u>Rigoberta</u> 236). The Rigoberta
Menchú Tum Foundation, which Menchú founded,
has defended the book on the grounds that it
gained that support: "The path for which
Rigoberta Menchú opted [. . .] was that of
involving the conscience of the international
community." The Foundation asserts that
Menchú's account is not weakened by
Stoll's findings and that her goal of
gaining international attention is what was
important for that text. Thus, her foundation
claims that a precise use of the truth was
not her goal. In other words, all three
defenders essentially argue that, in this
case, the ends (international attention for
Mayans) justified the means (Menchú's
fabrications).

12   Menchú is now attempting to sidestep the
political aspects of the controversy
surrounding her. In a recent interview she
spoke mainly about the problems of indigenous
peoples in a way that was clearly (and

probably purposefully) not Marxist in tone or
content: "Well I think it's not exactly a
conflict between the government and myself.
I'm not subject to any political party [sic]
I respect all the parties [. . .]"
("Webcast"). Menchú has asserted her
independence from the guerilla movement in
other ways. In a new autobiography, <u>Crossing
Borders</u>, she writes, "I am no philosopher. I
am simply a granddaughter of the Mayans
[. . .]" (87). This definition of herself is
significant. She claims to hold no
philosophical views, so that she is not tied
down by a political agenda. Yet she
identifies herself solely with the Mayan
people, which is, at many levels, a
political association--only it is a
slightly different arena of politics from the
guerilla associations. In the midst of the
controversy surrounding her,[2] Menchú has
tried to maintain her representative
authority as a Mayan by talking solely about
indigenous issues.

13   Ironically, while the book has been
attacked as being a piece of fiction, its
literary aspects have also been used to
defend it. The main argument has been that
Menchú is telling a deeper, more poetic
kind of truth. According to one critic,
"Menchú's reader must resist the temptation
of reading her <u>literally</u>, which would deny her
the capacity to represent herself <u>literarily</u>

[poetically] and symbolically [. . .]"
(Handley 68). He argues that Menchú should
not be read as strictly nonfiction, but
as a subjective account of how she perceived
what happened to her. Others have gone
even further. Allen Carey Webb, of
Western Michigan University, has argued
that, given Menchú's terrible situation,
her changes are actually true in a deeper
sense in that they reflect what it was
really like to be oppressed (qtd. in Wilson
A16).

14   This kind of defense, however, works
only so long as the "deeper truth"
actually corresponds to the changes
Menchú made. Unfortunately, it does not.
Menchú's autobiography does not represent
a deeper truth because it fails to meet
the claim that Menchú herself makes
for it: "My story is the story of all
poor Guatemalans. My experience is the
reality of a whole people" (I, Rigoberta 1).
Her story is not "the reality of a whole
people." Menchú claims that there was
solidarity among Mayans against landowners,
among Mayans with the guerillas, and within
the guerilla groups themselves. The reality
of the situation was much more complicated,
involving land disputes, coercion, and
racism.

15   When war and genocide are involved,
it is tempting to lie if doing so could

save lives. Along these lines, Menchú
oversimplified the situation as a means of
gaining support for her cause. That support
led to a peace agreement in Guatemala, so
she may have succeeded in saving lives. In
one sense, then, her success seems to
justify her means. However, other ends that
Menchú perhaps did not expect--international
attention of a different sort than she
wanted--resulted. Because her means involved
changing her story to fit what appears to be
a Marxist paradigm, her credibility as a
representative of the Mayans has been
damaged. The danger is that she has been so
successful in identifying herself with Mayans
that this damage could extend beyond Menchú's
person to the cause itself, equal rights for
indigenous people in Guatemala.

16   Although Menchú's misrepresentation of
the Mayan experience was understandable given
her situation, it was not right. Even if her
changes were not discovered, they would have
indirectly harmed her people. By
fictionalizing what most Mayans went through,
she caused the international community to act
on false information. Too often this led to
support for the guerilla movement rather than
the Mayans. It is clear that Menchú was able
to use her fame to accomplish some good
results in Guatemala; unfortunately, the
guerillas her book supported were not as
noble as she made them out to be. In fact,

in some cases the guerillas were exploiting
the Mayans. Nelson concludes that in some
cases, "the guerillas used the Maya[ns] as
cannon-fodder [. . .]" (59). The good that
Menchú eventually achieved came from building
support for indigenous rights, not from her
support of the guerilla movement.

17   Reflecting on this case raises the
question of whether it is ever right to
fictionalize an autobiographical account.
There is no easy answer, but what Menchú's
story reveals is this: when the
fictionalization deals not just with an
individual, but--as Menchú puts it--with the
"reality of a whole people," it is important
to strive to tell the most accurate version
of events possible. The reason is that the
"whole people" may be affected by the story.
Menchú did the exact opposite--she
intentionally changed a story that she knew
would be seen as representative. Her homeland
and her people deserved a more truthful
account.

Comments

N. Notes are coordinated with their location in the text by a super-script number that comes before the indented first line of the note and also at the appropriate location in the text.

According to the *MLA Handbook for Writers of Research Papers,* 5th edition,

> In research papers, make all notes endnotes, unless you are instructed otherwise. As their name implies, endnotes appear after the text, starting on a new page numbered in sequence with the preceding page. Center the title *Notes* one inch from the top, double-space, indent one-half inch (or five spaces, if you are using a typewriter) from the left margin, and add the note number, without punctuation, slightly above the line. Type a space and then the reference. If the note extends to two or more lines, begin subsequent lines at the left margin. Type the notes consecutively, double-spaced, and number all pages. (Gibaldi 269)

See page 188 for part of an earlier draft that was summarized and became part of note 1.

Notes such as these provide writers with a way to incorporate material that they decide is too important to discard even if they cannot incorporate it within the paper itself because they need to focus their ideas (see **2a(2)**) and work within the length appropriate for a specific assignment. Responsible writers do not use explanatory notes as a means for preserving everything they decide to cut from their texts, because doing so could make excessive demands upon the good will of their audience (see **1g(2)**). When you decide to add explanatory notes, remember that you are asking readers to turn away from your main text in order to make a side trip. Evaluate each of these detours by asking yourself if they help you fulfill your purpose (see **1g(1)**).

Notes

[1] Many other changes that Menchú made to her story do not damage its credibility. An example is Menchú's claim to have witnessed the army burning her brother alive (I, Rigoberta 179). Stoll has shown that nobody was ever actually burned alive in the village where Menchú claims to have seen the torturing (Rigoberta 69). Still, Menchú's brother was murdered by the army, as were many other Mayans. Changes of this nature do not detract from its representative authority, as they are in line with common Mayan experience.

[2] There is not enough space in this paper to fully develop the controversy surrounding Menchú's politics. Many people have oversimplified Stoll's book by depicting it as little more than an accusation of lying. Some people have jumped to Menchú's defense, claiming that Stoll is a racist who is trying to silence Menchú. The important issue is that the very fact that the controversy exists raises serious questions about Menchú's credibility.

Comments

O. Center the title *Works Cited,* one inch down from the top of the page, and double-space between this title and the first entry.

P. Include only those works you cited in the paper. If you consulted other sources but did not use them, do not include them in your list. Alphabetize entries according to the author's last name. Each entry should begin flush with the left margin. Lines after the first are indented five spaces (or one-half inch).

   When citing two or more works by the same author, arrange them in alphabetical order determined by the first important word in the title. After providing the author's name in the first entry, additional entries for this same author are indicated by typing three hyphens, then a period followed by a space.

Q. When citing Web sources, be scrupulously careful with the address and place it in angle brackets so that it will be clearly distinct from the rest of the entry. When the full address cannot fit on a single line, divide it after a slash.

Works Cited   O

Becker, Marc. "Ethnicity, Legitimacy, and the   P
    State: Understanding Ethnic Movements in
    Mexico, Guatemala, and Peru." 1997
    Update on Latin America Conference. 15
    Mar. 1997. 30 Apr. 1999 <http://
    falcon.cc.ukans.edu/~marc/update.html>.

Beverly, John. "The Real Thing (Our
    Rigoberta)." Modern Language Quarterly
    57.2 (1996): 129-39.

Burgos-Debray, Elizabeth. Preface.
    I, Riboberta Menchú. By Rigoberta Menchú.
    1983. New York: Verso, 1996. xi-xxi.

Grandin, Greg, and Francisco Goldman. "Bitter
    Fruit for Rigoberta." The Nation 8 Feb.
    1999: 25-28.

"Guatemala." The CIA World Factbook 1998. 20
    June 1999 <http://www.odci.gov/cia/
    publications/factbook/gt.html>.

Handley, George. "It's an Unbelievable Story:
    Testimony and Truth in the Work of
    Rosario Ferre and Rigoberta Menchú."
    Violence, Silence, and Anger: Women's
    Writing as Transgression. Ed. Diedre
    Lashgari. Charlottesville: UP of
    Virginia, 1995. 62-79.

Horowitz, David. "I, Rigoberta Menchú, Liar."
    Salon 11 Jan. 1999. 20 June 1999
    <http://www.salonmagazine.com/col/horo/   Q
    1999/01/11horo.html>.

Lane, Charles. "Deceiving is Believing." The
    New Republic 8 Mar. 1999: 36-40.

"Live Webcast, 18 Feb. 1999! Rigoberta
    Menchú." <u>Latin America Trek</u> 18 Feb. 1999.
    25 Apr. 1999 <http://www.worldtrek.org/
    odyssey/latinamerica/rigoberta/
    transcripteng2.html>.

Menchú, Rigoberta. <u>Crossing Borders</u>. Trans.
    and ed. Anne Wright. New York: Verso,
    1998.

---. <u>I, Rigoberta Menchú</u>. Ed. Elizabeth
    Burgos-Debray. Trans. Anne Wright. 1983.
    New York: Verso, 1996.

Nelson, Diane. <u>A Finger in the Wound</u>.
    Berkeley: U of California P, 1999.

The Norwegian Nobel Foundation. "The Nobel
    Peace Prize for 1992." 18 June 1998. 27
    Apr. 1999 <http://www.nobel.se/
    laureates/peace-1992-press.html>.

"Operation Remove Rigoberta." <u>Front Page
    Magazine</u> 11 May 1999. 17 May 1999
    <http://www.frontpagemag.com/campaign/
    rigobertacampaign.htm>.

The Rigoberta Menchú Tum Foundation.
    "Rigoberta Menchú Tum: The Truth
    That Challenges the Future." Jan. 1999.
    20 June 1999 <http://
    ourworld.compuserve.com/homepages/rmtpaz/
    mensajes/m990120i.htm>.

Rohter, Larry. "Nobel Winner Accused of
    Stretching the Truth." <u>The New York
    Times on the Web</u> 15 Dec. 1998. 20 June
    1999 <http://www.nytimes.com/library/
    books/121598cambodian-memoir.html>.

Stoll, David. "Literary Truth." <u>National</u>
<u>Public Radio Talk of the Nation</u>. 10
June 1999. 14 June 1999 <http://
search.npr.org/cf/cmn/
cmnpsosfm.cfm?SegID:513367>.

---. <u>Rigoberta Menchú and the Story of All</u>
<u>Poor Guatemalans</u>. Boulder: Westview,
1999.

Wilson, Robin. "A Challenge to the Veracity
of a Multicultural Icon." <u>The Chronicle</u>
<u>of Higher Education</u> 15 Jan. 1999: A14-
A16.

7g Some disciplines use the note style of documentation.

Some disciplines in the humanities still use either footnotes or endnotes for documentation. Both footnotes and endnotes require that a superscript numeral be placed wherever documentation is necessary. The number should be as close as possible to whatever it refers to, following the punctuation (such as quotation marks, a comma, or a period) that appears at the end of the direct quotation or paraphrase.

Footnotes should be single-spaced four lines below the last line of text on the same page where the documentation is necessary. Double-space between footnotes if more than one appears on any one page. **Endnotes** should be double-spaced on a separate page headed *Notes*. (For an example, see page 199.)

The following notes use the same sources as the ones in 7e(2). By comparing the model footnote with its corresponding works-cited entry, you will see differences between the two forms. (These numbered notes are arranged in a pattern for your convenience and are numbered sequentially, as your notes would be for documentation. But your notes, of course, would not begin with "book by one author" followed by "book by more than one author," and so on.)

Book by one author

[1] Jeanne Rosier Smith, <u>Writing Tricksters: Narrative Strategy and Cultural Identity in Maxine Hong Kingston, Louise Erdrich, and Toni Morrison</u> (Berkeley: U of California P, 1997) 143.

Indent one-half inch (or five spaces), then type the note number (without punctuation) followed by a space. Make additional lines flush with the left margin.

Book by more than one author or editor

[2] Nigel West and Oleg Tsarev, <u>The Crown Jewels: The British Secrets at the Heart of the KGB Archives</u> (New Haven: Yale UP, 1999) 158.

If the book has more than two authors, use commas to separate the authors' names.

[3] Charles Spinosa, Fernando Flores, and Hubert L. Dreyfus, <u>Disclosing New Worlds: Entrepreneurship, Democratic Action, and the Cultivation of Solidarity</u> (Cambridge: MIT P, 1997) 179.

Multivolume work

[4] George C. D. Odell, <u>Annals of the New York Stage</u>, 15 vols. (New York: Columbia UP, 1949).

[5] Robert Browning, <u>The Complete Works of Robert Browning: With Variant Readings and Annotations</u>, ed. John C. Berkey and Allan C. Dooley, vol. 6 (Athens: Ohio UP, 1996) 114.

Editor as author

[6] Robyn R. Warhol and Diane Price Herndl, eds., <u>Feminisms: An Anthology of Literary Theory and Criticisms</u> (New Brunswick: Rutgers UP, 1993) 165.

Work in an anthology

[7] Wendy Bishop, "Students' Stories and the Variable Gaze of Composition Research," <u>Writing Ourselves into the Story: Unheard Voices from Composition Studies</u>, ed. Sheryl I. Fontane and Susan Hunter (Carbondale: Southern Illinois UP, 1993) 211.

Introduction, preface, foreword, or afterword to a book

[8] Peter Elbow, foreword, <u>The Peaceable Classroom</u>, by Mary Rose O'Reilley (Portsmouth: Heinemann, 1993) xii.

Article from a journal with continuous pagination

[9] Gwendolyn Diaz, "Desire and Discourse in Maria Luisa Bombal's <u>New Islands</u>," <u>Hispanofila</u> 112 (1994): 61.

Article from a magazine

    ¹⁰ Alexander Stille, "The Man Who
Remembers," <u>New Yorker</u> 15 Feb. 1999: 56.

Article from a newspaper

    ¹¹ Charles Leroux, "Reading Frenzy,"
<u>Chicago Tribune</u> 20 Apr. 1999, final ed.,
sec. 2: 1.

7h **APA-style documentation is appropriate for research papers in psychology and most social sciences.**

Directory of APA-Style Parenthetical Citations

(1) APA-style parenthetical citations

In APA style, the basic elements of a parenthetical citation in the text are the author's last name, the year of publication, and the page number if the reference is to a specific passage in the source. If the author's name is mentioned in the text of the paper, give the date alone or the date and the page number in parentheses. In the following examples, note the details of punctuation and the treatment of the page number.

Work by one author

A prominent neurologist has concluded, "Pushing back the age at which the widespread form of Alzheimer's strikes--from, say, age seventy to age ninety--would be nearly tantamount to a cure" (Kosik, 1999, p. 17).

OR

Dr. Kenneth Kosik, a prominent neurologist, has concluded, "Pushing back the age at which the wide-spread form of Alzheimer's strikes--from, say, age seventy to age ninety--would be nearly tantamount to a cure" (1999, p. 17).

OR

Kosik (1999) has concluded, "Pushing back the age at which the wide-spread form of Alzheimer's strikes--from, say, age seventy to age ninety--would be nearly tantamount to a cure" (p. 17).

APA style requires the abbreviation *p.* (or *pp.* for "pages") before the page reference. Use commas to separate the author's name from the date and the date from the page reference.

Work by two authors

There is evidence that students in second and third grade respond favorably to guidance from elementary school students in higher grades (Bowman & Myrick, 1987).

Use an ampersand (&) to separate the authors' names. A page number is not necessary when the reference is to an entire work—a common practice in writing within the social sciences.

Work by more than two authors

```
One study has shown that people who fear
failure are not susceptible to hypnosis
(Manganello, Carlson, Zarillo, & Teeven,
1985).
```

For works with *three to five authors,* cite all the authors in the first reference, but subsequently give only the last name of the first author followed by *et al.* ("Manganello et al." in this case). For works with *six or more authors,* provide only the last name of the first author followed by *et al.,* even in the first citation.

Anonymous work

Use a shortened version of the title to identify an anonymous work.

```
Chronic insomnia usually requires medical
intervention ("Sleep," 2000).
```

This author has cited a short article identified in the bibliography as "Sleep disorders: Standard methods of treatment."

Two or more works in the same parentheses

```
Opponents of animal experimentation have
traditionally argued that it is both
unnecessary and cruel (Mayo, 1983; Singer,
1975).
```

Use a semicolon to separate different studies, and arrange them in alphabetical order.

(2) An APA-style reference list

Format the "References" (alphabetical list of works cited) in the APA style your instructor specifies. (See the commentary on final manuscript style, page 217.) As the fourth edition of the *Publication Manual* asserts, **final manuscript style** allows considerable freedom to format documents to enhance readability. Some instructors prefer that the first line of each entry in the reference list be typed flush left and that subsequent lines be indented five spaces—called a **hanging indent.** Other instructors prefer that you indent the first line of each entry five spaces and type subsequent lines flush with the left margin. The *Publication Manual* urges instructors to specify the style they prefer for the final manuscript.

The reference entries below have a hanging indent, but as the *Publication Manual* asserts, they could have been formatted just as correctly with an indented first line—the recommended approach for **copy manuscript** (see pages 217 and 230). Whichever format you use, be consistent and observe all details of indentation, spacing, and mechanics.

For additional information on APA-style documentation, visit the APA's Web site (http://www.apa.org).

Directory of APA-Style Entries for the Reference List

. . . .

Books

Books

Most book entries consist of four units separated by periods:

1. *Author.* Give the author's last name and use initials for the first and middle names. For entries with more than one author, invert all names and put an ampersand (&) before the last one. (If two authors have the same last name and initials, spell out their first names and list the references in alphabetical order by their first names.)
2. *Date.* Put the date in parentheses after the author's name.
3. *Title.* Capitalize only the first word in titles and subtitles. Do not capitalize other words (except for proper names that would be capitalized in other contexts). Separate titles and subtitles with a colon, and underline the title and any period immediately following it.

4. *Publication data*. Identify the city of publication. Add the two-letter U.S. Postal Service abbreviations for states unless the city is one of the following: Baltimore, Boston, Chicago, New York, Philadelphia, and San Francisco. When a work is published outside the United States, add the country's name unless it is published in Amsterdam, Jerusalem, London, Milan, Moscow, Paris, Rome, Stockholm, Tokyo, or Vienna—in which case the city alone is sufficient. Give only enough of the publisher's name so that it can be identified clearly.

Book by one author

Riordan, C. H. (1997). <u>Equality and achievement: An introduction to the sociology of education.</u> New York: Longman.

More than one work by the same author

If you use more than one work by the same author, list the works in order of the publication date, with the earliest first. Repeat the author's name for each work.

Gates, H. L. (1992). <u>Loose canons: Notes on the culture wars.</u> New York: Oxford.
Gates, H. L. (1995). <u>Colored people: A memoir.</u> New York: Vintage.

Book by two or more authors

Fish, B. C., & Fish, G. W. (1996). <u>The Kalenjiin heritage: Traditional religious and sociological practices.</u> Pasadena, CA: William Carney Library.

Note that APA style calls for identifying the state unless a work is published in a major city associated with publishing.

Edition after the first

Kelly, D. H. (1989). <u>Deviant behavior: A</u>
<u>text-reader in the sociology of deviance</u>
(3rd ed.). New York: St. Martin's.

Translation

Freud, S. (1960). <u>Jokes and their</u>
<u>relationship to the unconscious</u>
(J. Strachey, Trans.). New York: Norton.
(Original work published 1905)

Cite the date of the translation. Include the date of the original publication in parentheses at the end of the entry. A period does not follow the original publication date. In text, use the following form: (Freud, 1905/1960).

Government document

Department of Transportation. (1996).
<u>Liability cost and risk analysis</u>
<u>studies: Bus liability review for six</u>
<u>transit systems</u> (DOT-T-96-13). Washington,
DC: Technological Sharing Program.

Treat the issuing agency as the author when no author is specified. Include a document or contract number (but not a library call number) if either number is printed on or in the document.

Work with no author

Use the first significant words of the title to cite anonymous materials in the text, underlining the title of a book. Unless "Anonymous" is specifically designated as the author of a work, do not use it for in-text citations or the list of references.

Directory of mental health providers in
      Texas. (1996). Austin, TX: State
      Employees' Insurance Agency.

Articles

Capitalize only the first word and any proper nouns in article
titles, and do not put quotation marks around titles. (If the article has a subtitle, use a colon to separate the title and the subtitle and capitalize the first word of each.) For an article in an
edited book, provide both the title of the article and the title of
the book in which it appears. Give the name of the editor and
the complete page numbers for the article. For an anonymous
article, place the article title where the author's name would
normally appear, and alphabetize by the first important word
in the title.

Boomerang age. (1990). American Demographics,
      12, 25-30.

The title of a journal is capitalized differently from article or
book titles. Underline the journal title and continue the underlining so that it extends (without a break) to include the volume number and the commas preceding and following it. Include the issue number, when necessary, within parentheses but
do not underline it. The point is to make volume and issue numbers visually distinct from the page reference.

Article in a journal with continuous pagination

Lenfant, C. (1996). High blood pressure: Some
      answers, new questions, continuing
      challenges. JAMA, 275, 1605-1606.

Article in a journal with each issue paginated separately

Kolakowski, L. (1992). Amidst moving ruins.
     <u>Daedalus, 121</u>(2), 43-56.

The issue number appears in parentheses and is not underlined.

Article in a monthly or weekly magazine

Levy, D. H. (1992, June). A sky watcher
     discovers comets and immortality.
     <u>Smithsonian, 23,</u> 75-82.

For a monthly magazine, give the year first, followed by a comma and the full spelling of the month. For a weekly magazine, provide the exact date: (2000, February 18).

Article in a newspaper

Dershowitz, A. M. (1999, December 18). Why
     justice had to get out of town. <u>The New
     York Times,</u> p. A31.

Article in a collection of articles by different authors

Chlad, F. L. (1991). Chemical storage for
     industrial laboratories. In D. A.
     Pipitone (Ed.), <u>Safe storage of
     laboratory chemicals</u> (pp. 175-191). New
     York: Wiley.

Sources viewed or heard

Motion picture

Doran, L. (Producer), & Lee, A. (Director).
     (1995). <u>Sense and sensibility</u> [Film].
     London: Mirage.

Sound recording

```
Fellows, G. (Speaker). (1999). Nutritional
    needs for women with AIDS (Cassette
    Recording No. 8341). Cincinnati:
    Nutritionworks.
```

Sources produced for access by computer

APA recommends following the same sequence of information as provided for print sources. Any information, such as volume or page numbers, that is not available cannot be included. Information about how and when the source was retrieved appears at the end. Note also that the final period is omitted after URLs because trailing periods can cause difficulty in retrieving files.

> Lastname, I. (date). Title of article. *Name of Periodical, volume number*. Retrieved [access date] from retrieval path
> Lastname, I. (date). Title of article or chapter. In *Title of full work*. Place: Publisher. Retrieved [access date] from retrieval path
> Lastname, I., Lastname, I., & Lastname, I. (date). *Title of full work*. Place: Publisher. Retrieved [access date] from retrieval path

To supplement this discussion of APA-style documentation for sources produced for access by computer, visit the American Psychological Association (http://www.apa.org).

Article in an online journal

```
Fairbairn, G. L. (1998). Suicide, language,
    and clinical practice. Philosophy,
    Psychiatry, 5. Retrieved December 3,
    1999, from the World Wide Web:
    http://muse.jhu.edu/journals/
```

```
philosophy_p...y_and_psychology/v005/
5.2fairbairn01.html
```

The date of publication appears immediately after the author's name. Include the access date after the volume number (or after the journal title when a volume number is unavailable). Do not put a period at the end of the citation because it might be mistaken for part of the electronic address.

Article in an online magazine

```
Py-Lieberman, B. (1999, November). The colors
     of childhood. Smithsonian. Retrieved
     December 19, 1999, from the World Wide
     Web: http://www.smithsonianmag.si.edu/
     smithsonian/issues99/nov99/
     object_nov99.html
```

Place the year before the month for the date of publication.

Article in an online newspaper

```
Azar, B. (2000, January). What's in a face?
     APA Monitor. Retrieved January 6, 2000,
     from the World Wide Web:
     http://www.apa.org/monitor/scl.html
```

Indicate the database through which the newspaper is accessed. If the newspaper can be downloaded from the World Wide Web, provide the address of the site.

World Wide Web page

```
Dorman, B., & Lefever, J. (1999, December 28).
     The Autism Society of America home page.
     Bethesda, MD: Autism Society of America.
     Retrieved January 6, 2000, from the World
     Wide Web: http://www.autism-society.org/
```

When the name of the author (or creator) is not known, begin with the document title. Underline the document title, and provide additional information about this publication, if available, after the title (or after the date if the entry begins with the title). Conclude with the retrieval date and the retrieval path.

Cite e-mail, newsgroup, or bulletin board messages in the text but do not list them in the references. Not usually archived in any systematic way, these kinds of sources cannot be systematically retrieved and are regarded as ephemeral.

7i Studying a sample APA-style research paper can help you understand how to write in the social sciences.

The fourth edition of the APA *Publication Manual,* 1994, specifies two different styles of manuscripts, the **copy manuscript** and the **final manuscript.** The *Manual* explains,

> The author of a thesis, dissertation, or student paper produces a "final" manuscript; the author of a journal article produces a "copy" manuscript (which will become a typeset article). The differences between these two kinds of manuscripts help explain why the requirements for theses, dissertations, and student papers are not necessarily identical to the manuscripts submitted for publication in a journal. (p. 331)

The copy manuscript style is used for a document that will be sent to a publisher and set in type. The final manuscript style should be used for such documents as student papers, lab reports, master's theses, and doctoral dissertations because they are final—that is, they will not be sent elsewhere for typesetting. Final manuscript style permits a "number of variations from the requirements described in the *Publication Manual*" (p. 332) and should conform to the requirements of a specific university or instructor. For an example of final manuscript style, see the following paper.

Comments

A. A **title page** includes three double-spaced elements: running head, title, and author's full name and affiliation. Center the title and author horizontally (but not necessarily vertically).

B. The **running head** is a shortened version of the title. It appears in the upper right-hand corner of every page and the upper left of the title page, which is counted as page 1.

C. If an instructor asks that the course number be included, it generally appears instead of the affiliation. Unless specifically required, the instructor's name and the date the paper is due are not included.

Running head: GENERATION X   B

A

Generation X: Moving Back Home

Adrienne Harton

Texas Woman's University   C

Comments

D. An abstract is a short summary of a paper. The APA *Publication Manual* requires that an abstract be supplied on the second page of any essay that is to be submitted for publication (copy manuscript style). Check with your instructor to see whether an abstract is required for your paper.

E. An APA-style abstract should be between 75 and 120 words. According to the APA *Publication Manual,* a good abstract is

- accurate,
- self-contained,
- nonevaluative,
- coherent, and
- readable.

Readers should be able to understand what a paper is about simply by reading the abstract. Devoted to summarizing the paper's content, the abstract does not include an evaluation of the paper's quality.

Abstract   D
                                            E
During the last 20 years, young adults
returned to their parents' homes in record
numbers. Research indicates that education,
occupation, and personal lifestyle choices
all contributed to the economic hardships
that account for most of these cases. The
generation born between 1964 and 1980,
commonly referred to as Generation X, often
received more years of financial support from
parents than earlier generations enjoyed.
Further research will be needed to determine
if this trend continues.

Comments

F. The full title is centered on the top of the page beneath the running head. Double-space between the title and the first line of text (as in MLA style).

G. At the beginning of paragraph 2, Harton explains what "RYA" means. Thereafter, she uses the abbreviation without explanation. According to the APA *Publication Manual:*

> To maximize clarity, APA prefers that authors use abbreviations sparingly. Although abbreviations are sometimes useful for long, technical terms in scientific writing, communication is usually garbled rather than clarified if, for example, an abbreviation is unfamiliar to the reader. (p. 80)

The APA therefore recommends:

> A term to be abbreviated must, on its first appearance, be written out completely and followed immediately by its abbreviation in parentheses. Thereafter, the abbreviation is used in the text without further explanation (do not switch between the abbreviated and written-out forms of a term). (p. 83)

Generation X: Moving Back Home   F

1   Jim and Carole Wilson appear to be a comfortable couple in their 50s, married for 30 years. The Wilsons own a home, drive nice cars, and were able to pay for a college education for all three of their children. The Wilsons deviate from the stereotypical couple, though, because one of their college-educated children has moved back home. Scott, the oldest child, quit his temporary job (waiting tables "while I look for something better") and resumed residence in his old bedroom. Unfortunately for parents like the Wilsons, this scenario has become increasingly common. Grown children are returning to the nest or sometimes never leaving at all. The primary impetus for this phenomenon is economic: Young adults are moving back home because they find it more convenient to live with their parents than to live on their own. By moving back home, they are able to pursue an education, find refuge when unemployed, save money so that they can pay off student loans, or simply enjoy a higher level of comfort than they can provide for themselves.

2   The Returning Young Adult (RYA)   G
phenomenon is a family development syndrome looked at as circular in the family's attempt to "launch" the young adult members into independence. The young adult leaves home to experience adult independent living, returns home, hopefully to leave again, this time successfully. The adults in question are

usually in their 20s. According to Natalie Schwartzberg (1991),

> American family young adulthood can be defined as usually beginning in the early twenties . . . when the young person is launched from the family of origin, and ending sometime in the early thirties, when the young adult is firmly ensconced in a job and is capable of intimacy. (p. 77)

As this quote suggests, emotional stability is often linked to financial stability. Unfortunately, many young adults have difficulty achieving financial independence. When they fail to attain a secure and satisfying job, these adults choose to return to what they perceive as the safety of their parents' home. As a result, what Peck (1991) defines as the "launching stage" becomes "one of the most complex stages of the family's life cycle" (p. 150).

3   Before analyzing the financial reasons why people in their 20s are returning to their parents' homes, researchers first determine the characteristics of this group. Burnett and Smart (1994) define RYAs: "To be a true RYA, both the individual and parents expected the child to leave home, the child actually did leave home but, because of the need for economic support, returned" (p. 255). The RYA phenomenon is also called the crowded nest or "boomerang effect." The number of children in the RYA generation who return to live with their parents seems

surprisingly high. "About 40 percent of young adults return to their parents' home at least once. Men and women are equally likely to return home until age 25, but men are more likely to return after that age" ("Boomerang age," 1990, p. 26). With almost half of the 20-something generation moving home, a family with two or more children can almost surely anticipate an RYA. Another intriguing statistic is that males "are more than twice as likely as females to live with their parents" (Burnett & Smart, 1994, pp. 257-258). Over 70% of those male RYAs have a yearly income of less than $10,000, also. From the data, researchers can typify the RYA as a male in his early 20s with a low-paying job or no job.

4   Determining the characteristics of the RYA's family is another important control. The RYA family often has an above-average income (Burnett & Smart, 1994, p. 254), which actually helps influence adult children to move home since most of them have not accumulated all the material comforts their parents have attained. Parents of young adults actually wield great influence in determining whether or not children become an RYAs. However, the economic circumstances of RYAs are almost always the deciding factor in moving back home. These characteristics of RYAs and their families suggest the need for further research on financial considerations, including the growing challenge of financing a higher education.

5   Education affects young adults in two ways with regard to moving home. Either the RYA is attending college and cannot afford to live on his or her own, or the RYA chose not to further his or her education and cannot be self-sustaining on the paycheck alone. In the first case, research shows that more young adults are going to college, and almost half of first-year college students have a job ("Boomerang age," 1990, p. 30). Furthermore, many students start at 2-year colleges and so take longer to finish, and students also now take longer to choose a major. Such statistics show that young adults are spending more time in college than ever before. Living with one's parents effectively decreases a student's financial burden. Holtz (1995) claims, "The average college undergraduate was taking more than six years to earn a degree; fewer than half graduated after the traditional four years of study" (p. 124). An economic chain reaction exists for college students living at home. "Because people are delaying marriage, they are living with their parents longer. They are delaying marriage because they're going to school. They're going to school because most well-paying jobs now require a college degree" ("Boomerang age," p. 26). Of course, these RYAs have sound reasons for living with their parents, but what about the RYAs who are not continuing their education?

6   Some RYAs simply cannot afford to live away from home on a small salary. The

typical 25-year-old working man has a median income less than the poverty level for a single person (Holtz, 1995, p. 158). Obviously, returning to one's childhood home makes sense whether the young adult is trying to save money or to maintain a particular lifestyle. Although long-term prospects for the educated RYA are more promising, the average income for males without a college degree has fallen (Levy & Michel, 1991, p. 45). Many RYAs do not even have jobs. Whether RYAs' unemployment is a result of attending college or of lacking proper education, the best financial decision to make is to move home with Mom and Dad. As one RYA explained in an online discussion: "I thought that I was being practical by studying business, but business life bores me. I need time to figure out what I really want" (J. Shaw, personal communication, November 18, 1999).

7   Jobs obviously affect the economic situations of young adults. Some RYAs hold jobs and some do not, but for both groups, the dilemma is not having enough money to maintain a desired lifestyle and pay the bills too. One study notes, "As the U.S. economy shifts from manufacturing to services, it sharply reduces the number of entry-level jobs available to people who don't have much schooling" ("Boomerang age," 1990, p. 30). Another problem can be traced to the challenge of choosing a major in college. As the business and technology

sectors grow faster than areas grounded in liberal arts, college students can increase their chances for long-term job security by selecting a marketable major. But unemployment can occur in any field, hence the frequency with which RYAs rely on the parental safety net, as illustrated by E. L. Klingelhofer (1989):

> The inability to find appropriate work has not been as catastrophic a burden as it once might have been because the parents were able to support the child, to help out, to tide him or her over. And, as the individual quest for work wore on and eventually, wore out, what had been thought of as a temporary arrangement imperceptibly became a permanent one. (p. 86)

Whereas unemployment once meant failure and embarrassment, now it seems to be an opportunity to return home.

8   Even for young adults with jobs, moving home can be a solution to financial problems. RYAs change careers with great frequency. As research reveals, "Young adults have the highest rate of occupational mobility. Thirty percent of employed men aged 16 to 19, and 22 percent of those aged 20 to 24, changed occupations," compared with 10% for all workers ("Boomerang age," 1990, p. 52). Apparently, grown children choose to live with their parents to find some stability during professional uncertainty.

Furthermore, the jobs that young adults,
even when college educated, obtain may not
yield enough money to survive away from
home. A college education can be very
expensive, especially over 6 years. Some
young adults who shoulder their entire
college debts cannot afford to live away
from home while paying student loans
(Kuttner, 1995, p. M5). Regardless of whether
an RYA has a job or not, the economic sense
of moving back home exceeds the need for
independence.

9   The final financial reason why grown
children are returning to the nest
encompasses personal lifestyle decisions:
delayed marriage and middle-class comfort.
The average age of marriage has steadily
increased since the 1970s. Littwin (1986)
concludes:

> Commitment to a relationship is just as
> difficult for them as commitment to a
> career or point of view. It is one act
> that might define them and therefore
> limit their potential. Besides, it is
> difficult to be in a relationship when
> you still don't know who you are.
> (p. 219)

10   With the option of moving home, young
adults do not feel the pressure or the
necessity to marry early. Even when people
do marry early and divorce, research shows
that many young adults return to their
parents' homes to recover and stabilize

Comments

H. Harton cites the personal communication from Coles in paragraph
11 in the text but, as with other nonrecoverable sources such as
personal letters, e-mail, and bulletin board postings, does not list
it in the references on page 233.

I. Harton's concluding paragraph (see **3b(2)**) follows the traditional
model of summarizing the preceding points and suggesting a direction for future study.

J. The reference list is organized alphabetically and begins on a new
page. The last name is always given first, and initials are provided
for first and middle names. The date of publication is always given
parenthetically, immediately after the author's name. (See **7h(1)**.)

K. Observe the use of periods and commas, the style of capitalization
for book and article titles, and the different capitalization style for
journal titles. Underline book and journal titles, and carry continuous underlining of periodical titles through the volume number.

L. If Harton had used a copy manuscript format, which is required
when submitting work for publication, she would have indented
the first line of each entry five spaces. The first two entries would
look like this:

```
    Boomerang age. (1990). American
Demographics, 12, 25-30.
    Burnett, J., & Smart, D. (1994).
Returning young adults. Psychology and
Marketing, 11, 253-269.
```

(Klingelhofer, 1989, p. 86). RYAs can opt to
live with their families as an alternative
to marriage or to reestablish themselves
after a divorce. In either scenario, the RYA
is more financially stable than if he or she
lived alone.

11   Some RYAs return to the nest to attain
the material comforts of a middle- to
upper-class home that they enjoyed and
expected as dependents. Adult children
now receive allowances, their own rooms,
telephones, cars, personal freedom. Why
should they leave the nest? For
wealthier families, adult children moving
home is a particular problem. Littwin
(1986) says:

> The affluent, perfect parent is the
> ideal target for rebellion-and-rescue.
> . . . The young adult resents that
> he has been given so much that he
> cannot give himself. He has been
> cared for too well and too
> conscientiously. (p. 140)

A potential RYA, still a student at a
private university and for whom his parents
pay all expenses, recently complained about
the constraints his full-time summer job
placed on his lifestyle: "I don't see how
you and Dad have any fun when you are
working at least 50 hours a week. I want to
enjoy my life" (L. Coles, personal
communication, November 15, 1999). In an
instant-gratification-seeking generation,

returning to the nest is just easier than earning comfort.

12   In conclusion, young adults are moving back home for a variety of reasons. Of course, people of the 20-something generation would not be able to return home without parental acquiescence. Future research will reveal if RYAs develop a pattern of adult dependence on their parents and whether this pattern will hold true for children born after 1980 (sometimes called Generation Y) since this generation is coming of age in a stronger economy. But for now, research proves that grown children are moving back home for a myriad of financial considerations. And as one Gen X'er bemoans: "We as a generation have yet to produce any defining traits, except perhaps to show a defeatist belief that we will do worse than our parents" (Janoff, 1995, p. 10).

References

Boomerang age. (1990). <u>American Demographics,</u> <u>12,</u> 25-30.

Burnett, J., & Smart, D. (1994). Returning young adults. <u>Psychology and Marketing,</u> <u>11,</u> 253-269.

Holtz, G. T. (1995). <u>Welcome to the jungle:</u> <u>The why behind "Generation X."</u> New York: St. Martin's Griffin.

Janoff, J. B. (1995, April 24). A gen-x Rip Van Winkle. <u>Newsweek, 127,</u> 10.

Klingelhofer, E. L. (1989). <u>Coping with your</u> <u>grown children.</u> Clifton, NJ: Humana Press.

Kuttner, R. (1995, June 25). The new elite: Living with mom and dad. <u>The Los</u> <u>Angeles Times,</u> p. M5.

Levy, F., & Michel, R. C. (1991). <u>The</u> <u>economic future of American families:</u> <u>Income and wealth trends.</u> Washington, DC: Urban Institute.

Littwin, S. (1986). <u>The postponed generation:</u> <u>Why American youth are growing up later.</u> New York: William Morrow.

Peck, J. S. (1991). Families launching young adults. In F. H. Brown (Ed.), <u>Reweaving</u> <u>the family tapestry: A multigenerational</u> <u>approach to families</u> (pp. 149-168). New York: Norton.

Schwartzberg, N. (1991). Single young adults. In F. H. Brown (Ed.), <u>Reweaving the</u> <u>family tapestry: A multigenerational</u> <u>approach</u> (pp. 77-93). New York: Norton.

Chapter 8

Writing under Pressure

This chapter focuses on how to write well under the pressure of time constraints. It includes advice on

- managing deadlines (**8a**),
- overcoming writer's block (**8b**), and
- taking essay tests (**8c**).

It is not always possible to engage in a writing process that stretches over a period of weeks or even days. Sometimes writers must respond within a day or an hour, and almost all students are faced at some point with essay examinations that must be written in two hours or less. The key to succeeding in such situations is to use the time you have as efficiently as possible.

8a Make deadlines work for you.

Because you will almost always be working with deadlines, both in your academic life and afterward, learning to manage your time on in-class writing assignments and essay exams will help you demonstrate your writing ability or your knowledge of any subject.

Preparing ahead of time always helps. Although an essay exam may not occur until midterm, preparation should begin on the first day of class. Pay attention to indications that your instructor considers certain material especially important. Ask questions whenever you are uncertain. Be sure to read the instructions and questions carefully. Take notes on readings and lectures and regularly exercise your own writing skills in a journal to build fluency.

If you are writing a paper that is due in one, two, or more weeks, it is especially important to start early. Establish your topic as soon as you can, and set deadlines for writing a first paragraph and a first draft; set a third deadline for revising and editing. Be aware that you will probably alter what you write first or abandon it in your final paper. Just the act of writing, however, will generate ideas.

8b There are strategies for overcoming writer's block.

The only difference between your writer's block and that of experienced writers is that they have developed their own strategies for overcoming it. Here are some suggestions:

- Step away from the work. Although you may not be aware of it, your mind will continue to develop ideas for your writing.
- Plan your time carefully. The stress that results from a looming deadline can be a major contributor to writer's block.
- Don't strive for perfection. Remember that perfection is a goal that even experienced writers seldom reach.
- Prioritize your responsibilities and assign time for each activity.
- Set up regular writing habits; write at the same time and the same place whenever possible.
- In an out-of-class assignment, do not worry about getting the wording exactly right in the first draft. You can revise later.
- Do not stop the flow of your writing by worrying about mechanical problems (spelling or punctuation) in your first draft. You can check such errors later.
- In an essay exam try to sit in the same place in the classroom where you have sat all semester.

8c Essay tests require special preparation.

(1) Setting up a schedule

Check the number of questions on the exam and the number of points for each question and then figure what percentage of the time you should allot to each question. When no points are specified, you can tell which questions the instructor considers important if he or she recommends spending more time on one than on another. If one question will count more heavily than the others, pace yourself with this fact in mind.

When you have used up the time you have allotted for a question, leave room on the page to complete it later and go on to the next whether you are finished or not. Even if you cannot complete every question, partial answers to every question will usually gain you more points than complete answers to only some of the questions. It is a good idea to allow some time at the end for revising and proofreading your answers. You can also use this time to put the finishing touches on any incomplete answers.

(2) Reading instructions and questions carefully

Students who normally write well sometimes do poorly when writing in-class essays and essay exams because they are in such a rush to begin writing that they hurry through the instructions without reading them carefully or, if there are choices, they do not adequately consider which question best suits them. Before you start writing, read the instructions carefully and note specific directions.

Another good idea is to reframe the question in your own words. Does your version match the question? If so, you can feel confident that you understand what is demanded of you and go ahead. If not, you have probably missed the point and will need to rethink your approach.

When you are asked to demonstrate your mastery of the information being tested, it is a good idea to know exactly what approach your instructor expects. Most essay examinations contain a sentence that begins with a word that tells you what you are to do and ends with a reference to the information you are to demonstrate your grasp of.

- **Compare (and contrast)** means you should examine the points of similarity (compare) and difference (contrast) between two stated things. See **2e(5)**.
- **Define** asks you to state the class to which the item to be defined belongs (see **2e(7)**) and what distinguishes it from the others of that class.
- **Describe** requires you to use details in a clearly defined order to sketch the item that you are asked to describe. See **2e(2)**.
- **Discuss** gives you wide latitude to address the topic in a variety of ways—examine, analyze, evaluate, state pros and cons—and is thus more difficult to handle than some of the others, because you must choose your own focus. It is also the term that appears most frequently. See **2d** and **2e**.
- **Evaluate** asks you to appraise the advantages and disadvantages of the topic. See **9b(3)**.
- **Explain** means you must clarify, make plain, and interpret the topic (see **2d(1)**), reconcile differences, or state causes (see **2e(4)**).
- **Illustrate** requires you to offer concrete examples or, if possible, figures, charts, and tables to explain the topic. See **2d(1–2)**.
- **Summarize** involves stating the main points in a condensed form; omit details, and curtail examples. See **7c(4)**.
- **Trace** means you should narrate a sequence of events, describe progress, or explain a process. See **2e(1–4)**.

(3) Organizing your response

Find time to draft a plan for your work (see **2c**). Identify the thesis you will offer; then list the most important points you plan to cover. These might occur to you randomly, and you might subsequently decide to rearrange them, but the first step is to create a list that does justice to your topic. When you have finished the list, you should review it and delete any points that seem irrelevant or not important enough to discuss in the time allowed. Then number the remaining points in a logical sequence determined by chronology (reporting events in the order in which they occurred), by causation (showing how one thing led to another), or by order of importance (going from the most important point to the least important).

Here is an example of an edited list quickly jotted down in response to the following question: "Some readers believe that *Huckleberry Finn* is racist. Discuss the treatment of race in this novel. Do you think the book is racist? If so, why? If not, why not?"

THESIS: Huckleberry Finn is not racist. The best character in the book is black, and a white boy comes to understand this.

tie together

5. use of racist language
1. treatment of Jim
4. Huck's go to hell speech
~~Jim in jail~~
6. reproducing authentic dialogue → *mention the snake bite*
3. Jim protects Huck in the storm
7. the scene where the slaves get sold ← *if time allows*
2. Jim as Huck's true father

The language of an assignment sometimes tells you how to organize it. For example, consider the following task.

Discuss how the building of railroads influenced the development of the American West during the second half of the nineteenth century.

At first glance, this assignment might seem to state the topic without indicating how to organize a discussion of it. To *influence,* however, is to be responsible for certain consequences. In this case, the building of railroads is a cause, and you are being asked to identify its effects (see 2e(4)). Once you have recognized this, you might decide to discuss different effects in different paragraphs.

(4) Stating main points clearly

Instructors who read essay exams and in-class essays are usually looking to see how well students have understood assigned material. Stating your main points clearly will help them make that evaluation. Make your main points stand out from the rest of the essay by identifying them somehow. For instance, you can use transitional expressions such as *first, second, third;* you can underline each main point; or you can create headings to guide the reader. Use your conclusion to summarize your main points.

(5) Sticking to the question

Always answer the exact question as directly as you can. Do not wander from the question being asked to answer the question you wish had been asked. Similarly, make sure that you follow your thesis as you answer the question; do not include irrelevant material. If you move away from your original thesis because better ideas have occurred to you as you write, go back and revise your thesis (see 2b). If you drift into including irrelevant material, draw a line through it.

(6) Revising and proofreading

Save a few minutes to reread your answer. Make whatever deletions and corrections you think are necessary. If time allows, think about what is not on the page by asking yourself if there is anything you have left out that you can still manage to include. Unless you are certain that your instructor values neatness more than competence, do not hesitate to make corrections and do not use your valuable time just to make your answer look neat. Make sure, however, that your instructor will be able to read your changes. Clarify any illegible scribbles. If you have added ideas in the margins, in each case draw a line to a caret (ʌ) marking the exact place in the text where you want additions or corrections to be placed. Finally, check spelling, punctuation, and sentence structure (see **4d**).

Chapter 9 Writing about Literature

This chapter will help you understand

- vocabulary used for discussing literature (9a),
- personal responses to literature (9b(1)),
- essays about fiction (9c),
- essays about drama (9d), and
- essays about poetry (9e).

9a Understanding literary terms helps writers discuss literature thoughtfully.

Like all specialized fields, literature has its own vocabulary. Learning it will help you understand literature and write about it effectively.

(1) The elements of literature

Setting

Setting involves place—not only the physical setting, but also the atmosphere created by the author. It also involves time. A story set in San Francisco in 1876 will have a different setting from one set there in 2001 because the city has changed.

Plot

The sequence of events that happen to characters is the **plot.** Plot is usually an important aspect in both fiction and drama, and it can also be an element of poetry, especially in long poems, such as *Paradise Lost.*

Characters

The **characters** carry the plot forward and usually include a main character, called a **protagonist,** who is in conflict with another character, with an institution, or with himself or herself. Characters can be understood by paying close attention to their appearance, language, and actions.

Allusion

An **allusion** is a brief, unexplained reference to a work, person, place, event, or thing (real or imaginary) that serves to convey meaning compactly. Writing about the way she came to see her father, Sylvia Plath describes him in "Daddy" as a "man in black with a Meinkampf look." *Mein Kampf,* German for "my struggle," is the title of Hitler's political manifesto. Although Plath does not directly compare her father to Hitler, she links the two by making an allusion.

Symbols

A **symbol** is an object, usually concrete, that stands for something else, usually abstract. On one level, it is what it is; on another level, it is more than what it is. (For an example, see pages 249–50.) When you write about a particular symbol, first note the lines in which it appears. Then think about what it could mean. When you have an idea, trace the incidents in the work that reinforce that idea.

Theme

The main idea of a literary work is its **theme.** Depending on how they interpret a work, different readers may identify different themes. When you believe you have identified a theme, state it as a sentence and be precise. A theme conveys a specific idea; it should not be confused with a topic.

Topic	family conflict
Vague theme	*King Lear* is about family conflict.
Specific theme	*King Lear* reveals a conflict between a father who yearns for respect and daughters who have lost confidence in his judgment.

For additional definitions of terms, see **9a(2)** and **9c–e**.

(2) Purpose

An interpretation that attempts to explain the meaning of one aspect of a work is called an **analysis.** To analyze a work of literature, divide it into elements, examine such elements as setting and characters, and determine how one element contributes to the overall meaning. An analysis focuses on a scene, symbol, theme, or character. An interpretation that attempts to explain every element in a work is called an **explication** and is usually limited to poetry.

An **evaluation** of a work determines how successful the author is in communicating meaning to readers. The most common types of evaluation are book, theater, or film reviews. Like other interpretations, evaluation is a type of argument in which a writer cites evidence to persuade readers to accept a clearly formulated thesis. (See chapter 5.) An evaluation of a literary work should consider both strengths and weaknesses, if there is evidence of both.

CAUTION Although **summarizing** a literary work can be a useful way to make sure you understand it, do not confuse summary with analysis, interpretation, or evaluation. Those who have read the work are unlikely to benefit from reading a summary of it. Do not submit one unless your instructor has asked for it.

9b Reading carefully and thinking critically about what you read will help you discover and develop your topic.

Begin the process of writing about literature by reading carefully and noting your personal response. Think critically about these impressions and be open to new ideas as you plan your essay.

(1) Personal response

As you read, trust your own reactions. What characters do you admire? Did the work remind you of any experience of your own? Did it introduce you to a different world? Were you amused, moved, or confused? These first impressions can provide the seeds from which strong essays will grow. You may find, however, that you need to modify your initial impressions as you study the work more closely or as writing takes you in a direction you did not originally anticipate.

You can facilitate this engagement by **annotating** the texts you own—marking key passages and raising questions that occur as you read (see 7b). You can also benefit from **freewriting** about your first impressions or by keeping a journal in which you record your reactions to and questions about reading assignments (see 1b(2)). These methods of exploring a subject can help you discover what you think or what you want to understand. In addition to generating topics for writing, they provide a useful method for identifying questions you could raise in class. When you use these methods, write whatever comes to mind without worrying about whether you are correct.

When reflecting on your personal response to a work of literature, you can clarify your thinking by considering how it could be shaped by the factors that make you who you are. For example, if you find yourself responding positively or negatively to a character in a novel or play, you could ask yourself whether this response has anything to do with your

- political beliefs,
- social class,
- geographic region,
- religion,
- race,
- gender, or
- sexual orientation.

Thinking along these lines can help you decide how to focus your paper.

(2) Topics

If your instructor asks you to choose your own topic, your first step should be to reflect on your personal response (see **9b(1)**). Reviewing your response may enable you not only to choose a topic, but also to formulate a tentative thesis. Also, try some of the methods suggested in **2a** to explore the work you plan to discuss.

Readers are usually interested in learning what *you* think. If you choose an easy topic, you may find yourself repeating what many others have already said. Try to avoid writing the obvious, but do not let the quest for originality lead you to choose a topic that would be too hard to develop adequately.

Apply strategies of development, singly or in combination (see **2e**). You might **define** why you consider a character heroic, **classify** a play as a comedy of manners, or **describe** a setting that contributes to a work's meaning. Perhaps you could **compare and contrast** two poems on a similar subject or explore **cause-and-effect** relationships in a novel. Why, for example, does an apparently intelligent character make a bad decision? Or you could combine two or more strategies when you have a clear focus. For example, you could show how the description of a family's house defines that family's values or reveals the effects of an underlying conflict.

(3) Rereading a work

Not only does a literary work provoke different responses from different readers, but also you can have a significantly different response when rereading a work—even a work you think you understand already. If its length makes rereading impractical, at least reread the chapters or scenes that impressed you as especially important or problematic.

If you have a tentative thesis, rereading a work will help you find the evidence you need to support it. You are likely to find evidence that you did not notice on your first reading or that will require you to modify your thesis. To establish yourself as a credible source (see **1f**), use evidence appropriate for your purpose (see **5e**) and present it fairly.

(4) Research

Both writers and readers often favor papers that are focused on a person's individual response, analysis, interpretation, or evaluation. But by reading criticism that reveals what other readers think of a given literary work, you can engage in a dialogue. When you draw on the ideas of other people, however, remember that you must use those sources responsibly (see **7c–d**) and that even when you incorporate them you must still advance a position that is clearly your own.

When you read criticism, remember that a work rarely has a single meaning. Three different critics may offer three radically different interpretations. Your responsibility is not to determine who is right but to determine the extent to which you agree or disagree with these differing views. Read critically (see chapter **1**) and formulate your own thesis (see **2b**).

Chapter **6** explains how to do research. To locate material on a specific writer or work, consult your library's catalog (see

6d(1)) and the *MLA Bibliography,* an index of books and articles about literature. An essential resource for literary studies, the *MLA Bibliography* can be consulted in printed volumes, through an online database search, or through access to a CD-ROM covering several years. (See pages 122–26.)

Your college or community library is also likely to have a number of reference books that provide basic information on writers, books, and literary theory. Works such as *Contemporary Authors, The Oxford Companion to English Literature,* and *The Princeton Handbook of Poetic Terms* can be useful when you are beginning your research or when your research has introduced you to terms you need to clarify.

For an example of a paper that incorporates research about literature, see the essay by Dieter Bohn in 7f.

CAUTION Research is not appropriate for all assignments. Your instructor may want only your own response or interpretation. If your instructor has not assigned a research paper, ask whether one is acceptable.

9c Essays about fiction help readers see that a good story has many dimensions.

Although the events have not happened and the characters may never have existed, serious fiction expresses truth about the human condition through such components as **setting, character,** and **plot** (see 9a(1)). Experienced readers consider how these components are tied together. The questions generated by the **pentad** (see pages 32–33) can be helpful in this respect. For example, you might ask how a character has been shaped by the setting in which she lives or how a key element of the plot is closely tied to this setting.

When thinking about the characters in a work of fiction, you can also benefit from considering whether they are **static** or **dynamic.** A static character remains the same, whereas a dynamic character changes in some way. Works of fiction could include both types. Often, however, the main character, or **protagonist,** is transformed by experience. Other characters may change as well. Being alert to how characters may be changing, and why, can help you understand the **theme** (see **9a(1)**). You must also consider how the story is being presented to you.

Point of view

The position from which the action is observed—the person through whose eyes the events are seen—is the **point of view.** It may be that of a single character within the story or of a narrator who tells it. Many works of fiction are told from a single point of view, but some shift the point of view from one character to another. Readers sometimes assume that the author of a work of fiction is the person who is telling the story when it is actually being presented by one or more of the characters.

When a piece of fiction is conveyed by one of its characters, the point of view is **partially omniscient**—that is, partially all-knowing. A narrator who knows the thoughts of all characters is **omniscient.** A story told by a character who refers to herself or himself as "I" employs the **first-person** point of view. (Do not confuse this character with the author.)

When the narrator does not reveal the thoughts of any character, the work is being told from the **dramatic** or **objective** point of view.

9d **Essays about drama help readers understand texts that are written for public performance.**

Drama has many of the same elements as fiction. In particular, both involve character, plot, and setting (see **9a(1)**). The primary difference is the method of presentation. In a novel you may find long descriptions of characters and setting, as well as passages revealing what characters are thinking. In a play, you learn what a character is thinking when he or she shares thoughts with another character or presents a **dramatic soliloquy** (a speech delivered to the audience by an actor alone on the stage).

Dialogue

Dialogue is the principal medium through which we understand the characters when reading a play. Examine dialogue to discover motives, internal conflicts, and relationships among characters. In Ibsen's *A Doll's House,* for example, Nora's development can be traced through her speech. The play opens with her reciting lines like "Me? Oh, pooh, I don't want anything." It concludes with her deciding to leave her husband and declaring, "I must educate myself." In writing about drama, pay close attention to dialogue.

Stage direction

Plays are written to be performed, and when you see a performance all you have to do is watch and listen. When you read a play, however, you need to imagine what a performance would be like. Reading **stage directions**—which are usually in italics, especially at the beginning of an act or a scene—will help you. The playwright may have described the setting, called for specific props, indicated how the actors should be dressed, and positioned actors on different parts of the stage. As the play unfolds, directions will also indicate when an actor enters or leaves the stage. If you read only the dialogue, skipping over the directions, you can easily lose track of who is on stage and why.

Paying attention to dialogue and stage direction can help you understand a play's theme as well as the symbols that help convey that theme (see 9a(1)). For example, at the beginning of *A Streetcar Named Desire,* by Tennessee Williams, one of the characters buys a paper lantern to cover a naked light bulb. During the play, she frequently talks about light, emphasizing her preference for soft, attractive lighting. Eventually another character tears off the lantern, and still another character tries to return the ruined lantern to her as she is being taken away to a mental hospital. Anyone seeing this play performed, or reading it carefully, would note that the lantern is a symbol. It is what it is (a real paper lantern), but it also stands for something more than it is (a character's determination to avoid harsh truths).

9e   Essays about poetry help readers understand the power of compressed language.

Poetry shares many of the components of fiction and drama. It, too, may contain a narrator with a point of view. Dramatic monologues and narrative poems may have plot, setting, and characters. But poetry is primarily characterized by its concentrated use of connotative diction, imagery, allusions, figures of speech, symbols, sound, and rhythm. Before starting to write a paper about a poem, try to capture its literal meaning in a sentence or two; then analyze how the poet transfers that meaning to you through the use of the following devices.

Speaker

The first-person *I* in a poem is not necessarily the poet. It is more likely to be a character, or **persona,** that the poet has created to speak the words. In some poems, there may be more than one speaker. Although there are times when the poet may be the speaker, you usually need to distinguish between the two when writing about poetry.

Diction

The term **diction** means "choice of words," and the words in poetry convey meanings beyond the obvious denotative ones.

(See 24a(2).) As you read, check definitions and derivations of key words in your dictionary to find meanings beyond the obvious ones. How do such definitions and derivations reinforce the meaning of the poem? How do the connotations contribute to that meaning?

Simile

A **simile** is a comparison using *like* or *as* to link dissimilar things. (See 24a(4).)

> you fit into me
> like a hook into an eye
>
> a fish hook
> an open eye

In these lines, Margaret Atwood uses sewing and fishing items to describe a disturbing personal relationship.

Metaphor

A comparison that does not use *like* or *as,* **metaphor** is one of the figures of speech most frequently used by poets. (See 24a(4).) In the following example from "Walking Our Boundaries," Audre Lorde uses a metaphor to describe how it feels to wait for a lover's touch.

> my shoulders are
> dead leaves
> waiting to be burned to life.

Imagery

The **imagery** in a poem is conveyed by words describing a sensory experience. Notice the images in the following lines from the poem "Meeting at Night," by Robert Browning, about a lover journeying to meet his sweetheart.

Then a mile of warm sea-scented beach;
Three fields to cross till a farm appears;
A tap at the pane, the quick sharp scratch
And a blue spurt of a lighted match,
And a voice less loud, through its joys and fears,
Than the two hearts beating each to each!

The heat and smell of the beach; the sounds of the tap at the window, the scratch of a match being lighted, the whispers, and the hearts beating; and the sight of the two lovers embracing— all of these images convey the excitement and anticipation of lovers meeting in secret.

Personification

The attribution to objects, animals, and ideas of characteristics possessed only by humans is called **personification.** In the following lines, Emily Dickinson personifies death, portraying it as a man driving a carriage.

Because I could not stop for Death—
He kindly stopped for me—
The Carriage held but just Ourselves—
And Immortality.

Sound

Sound is an important element of poetry. **Alliteration** is the repetition of initial consonants, **assonance** is the repetition of vowel sounds in a succession of words, and **rhyme** is the repetition of similar sounds either at the end of lines (end rhyme) or within a line (internal rhyme). When you encounter such repetitions, analyze their connection to each other and to the meaning of a line, stanza, or poem. For instance, notice how the repetition of the *w* and the *s* sounds in the following lines from Elinor Wylie's "Velvet Shoes" sounds like the soft whisper of walking in a snowstorm.

Let us walk in the white snow
In a soundless space [. . .].

Whenever possible, read poetry aloud so you can hear it.

Rhythm

The regular occurrence of accent or stress that we hear in poetry is known as **rhythm,** which is commonly arranged in patterns called **meters.** Such meters depend on the recurrence of stressed and unstressed syllables in units commonly called **feet.** The most common metrical foot in English is the **iambic,** which consists of an unstressed syllable followed by a stressed one (prŏceéd). A second common foot is the **trochaic,** a stressed syllable followed by an unstressed one (fíftў). Less common are the three-syllable **anapestic** (ŏvĕr-coḿe) and the **dactylic** (párăgrăph). A series of feet make up a line to form a regular rhythm, as exemplified in the following lines from Coleridge's "Frost at Midnight."

Thĕ Frŏst pĕrfoŕms ĭts śecřet mínĭstrý,
Ŭnhelpĕd bў ánў wínd. Thĕ ówleťs cŕy
Cămĕ loúd — ańd hárk, ăgáin! loúd aš bĕfóre.

Note the changes in rhythm and their significance—the ways in which rhythm conveys meaning. The second line contains a pause (**caesura**), which is marked by the end of the sentence and which adds special emphasis to the intrusion of the owlet's cry.

9f **Using proper form shows your audience that you have written your paper carefully.**

Writing about literature follows certain conventions.

Tense

Use the present tense when discussing literature, because the author is communicating to a present reader at the present time. (See **17c(1)**.)

In "A Good Man Is Hard to Find," the grandmother reaches out to touch her killer just before he pulls the trigger.

Similarly, use the present tense when reporting how other writers have interpreted the work you are discussing.

As Henry Louis Gates has shown. . . .

Documentation

When writing about literature, use MLA-style documentation. (See 7e–f.) References to short stories and novels are by page number; references to poetry are by line number; and references to plays are usually by act, scene, and line number. This information should be placed in the text in parentheses directly after the quotation, and the period or comma should follow the parentheses. (See 30f and 7e(1).)

Poetry

For **poems** and **verse plays,** type quotations of three lines or less in the text and insert a slash (see 31h) with a space on each side to separate the lines.

```
"Does the road wind uphill all the way? /
Yes, to the very end"--Christina Rossetti
opens her poem "Uphill" with this two-line
question and answer.
```

Quotations of more than three lines should be indented one inch (or ten spaces) from the left margin, with double-spacing and without slashes between them. (See page 156.)

Author references

Use the full name in your first reference to the author of a work and only the last name in all subsequent references. Treat men and women alike: *Dickens* and *Cather,* not *Dickens* and *Willa* or *Charles Dickens* and *Miss Cather.*

CHECKLIST for Analyzing Literature

- What is your personal response to this work?

- What is the main idea you see in this work?

- How does the setting of this work contribute to its meaning?

- Are ideas or people in conflict in this work? If so, what does that conflict reveal?

- Are there any symbols in this work? Is one symbol especially significant?

- Have specific images helped you to understand this work?

- When you frame a thesis statement, will you be able to support it with sufficient evidence from the work in question?

Chapter

10   Writing for Work

Effective business communication requires a strong sense of audience (see **1g(2)**), an ability to write clearly and efficiently (see chapter **25**), and an understanding of business conventions. These conventions are changing as technology redefines the workplace. Thanks to fax machines and e-mail, for example, many business people find themselves writing more than ever. They also have to take responsibility for their own writing. Although there are still some executives who dictate a letter for someone else to edit and type, most business people are expected to write for themselves.

This chapter will help you understand how to

- use e-mail appropriately in the workplace (**10a**),
- write a memo (**10b**),
- format a business letter (**10c**),
- write a letter of application (**10d**), and
- compose a résumé (**10e**).

 10a **E-mail provides efficient communication.**

Because e-mail is a less formal medium than the traditional business letter or memo, you need to balance its implicit informality with a businesslike attention to detail. The tone (see **3a(3)**) of your e-mail should be suited to a business environment, that is, neither coldly formal nor overly familiar. Furthermore business e-mail tends to be used for brief comments or requests, whereas longer documents such as responses to reorganization plans and employee evaluations are generally still handled by letter or memo.

Be aware, also, that e-mail is not really private. Not only may your recipient keep your message in a file, print it out, or forward it to someone else, but also it may remain on the company's main computer. Most businesses operate e-mail on their own networks, so the system administrator also has access to what you have written.

Take care to spell your recipient's name correctly at the *To:* prompt, and be sure to enter an accurate and descriptive subject line. Busy people use the subject line to identify those messages they need to respond to immediately and those they can postpone. Send copies to anyone who is mentioned in your message or who has some other legitimate reason for being included, but do not send out copies of your messages indiscriminately. (See also 4c(1).)

CHECKLIST for Business E-Mail

- Does the subject line describe the content of your message?

- Have you sent a copy to everyone who needs to receive one? To anyone who need not?

- Do you sound like the kind of person you want or need to be while at work?

- Is your content clear, concise, focused, and accurate?

- If you need a response, have you established the kind of response you need and when you need it?

- Are you respecting the privacy of others, or are you forwarding a personal message without permission?

- Have you proofread you message to eliminate typographical errors?

10b Memos are useful when you want colleagues to study information or bring it to a meeting.

Although e-mail is ideal for sending brief announcements and requests for information, many business writers prefer the memo when communicating detailed information such as policy directives, activity reports, and monthly action reports. Although the length of a memo varies according to its purpose, the basic format is relatively standard. The names of the person or persons to whom the memo is addressed appear in the first line, the person who wrote it in the second, the date in the third, and the subject in the fourth.

If the memo is long, it sometimes begins with a statement of purpose and then gives a summary of the discussion. This summary helps busy people decide which memos to read carefully and which to skim. The discussion is the main part of the memo and may benefit from the use of headings to highlight key parts. If appropriate, the memo closes with recommendations for action to be taken. You should clearly state in this part of the memo who is to do what and when. In the following example, excerpted from a longer memo, you can see how the writer opens with a statement of purpose.

An example of memo format

To: Regional Sales Managers
From: Alicia Carroll, National Sales Director
Date: January 26, 2000
Re: Performance review

Now that we have final sales figures for 1999, it is clear that sales are growing in the South and West, but declining in the

Northeast and Midwest. These results can be traced to numerous factors and should not be seen as a reflection of individual performance. Each of you will soon receive a confidential evaluation of your work. The purpose of this memo is to share information and to outline goals for the coming year.

10c Business letters convey formal communication, especially between a representative of a company and someone outside the company.

A business letter has six parts: (a) heading; (b) inside address; (c) salutation; (d) body; (e) closing, which consists of the complimentary close and signature; and (f) added notations. In letters to organizations or to persons whose name and gender you do not know, use the office or company name.

Dear Registrar: Dear Mobil Oil:

Check to see whether your company or organization has a policy about letter format. Most companies use a block format for regular correspondence (see pages 260–61), although an indented format (see pages 262–63) is sometimes used for personal business correspondence. In block format, double-space between paragraphs without indenting them. See the following example.

Model business letter (block format)

WDS WILLCOX, DAVERN, AND SMITH 529 LAKE SIDE BOULEVARD
CHICAGO, IL 60605
312-863-8916

↖ Letterhead containing
return address

September 6, 2000

Dr. Elizabeth Boroughs ⎤
Fairchild Clinic   ⎥   Inside
1710 Sheridan Ave.   ⎥   address
Lakewood, IL 60045   ⎦

Dear Dr. Boroughs: ⎤   Salutation

I have just given final approval to several organizational
changes designed to ensure closer attention to the individual
needs of our clients. Everyone here is excited about these
changes, and I am writing to advise you of the one that will
affect you most directly.

As you probably know, tax laws have changed considerably in
recent years. The new codes are complex, and interpretation
continues to evolve. Given the complexity of the codes, the
importance of guiding clients through effective tax planning,
and the availability of highly trained personnel, accountants in
our company will henceforth work within one of three
divisions: corporate, small business, and individual.

Richard Henderson, who has prepared your taxes for the past
three years, will now be working exclusively with individual
clients. I have reviewed your tax records with him, and we
agree that Grace Yee, one of our new associates, will give the
Fairchild Clinic the best help we can offer. Although she is

new to our staff, she comes to us with twelve years of experience, working mostly with medical groups.

You can expect to hear separately from both Rick and Grace, but I wanted to let you know myself that Willcox, Davern, and Smith remains committed to serving you and your business.

Sincerely,   } Complimentary close

Ted Willcox   } Signature

Edward Willcox   } Typed name

President   } Title

EW/nfd } Notation

10d Writing a good application letter can persuade a busy person to pay attention to your résumé.

Writing a letter of application is an essential step in applying for a job. This letter usually accompanies a résumé (see 10e), and it should do more than simply repeat information that can be found there. Your letter provides you with the chance to sound articulate, interesting, and professional.

Whenever possible, address your letter to a specific person or department. Then, in your opening paragraph, state the position you are applying for, how you learned about it, and—in a single sentence—why you believe you are qualified to fill it. Devote the paragraphs that follow to describing the experience that qualifies you for the job. If your experience is extensive, you can establish that fact and then focus on how you excelled in one or two specific situations. Mention that you are enclosing a résumé, but do not summarize it. Your goal is to get a busy person to read the résumé.

In addition to stating your qualifications, you might indicate why you are interested in this particular company. Demonstrating that you already know something about it will help you appear to be a serious candidate.

Instead of closing with "I hope to hear from you soon," tell your reader how and where you can be reached and mention any relevant information about your schedule during the next few weeks. Indicate that you are available for an interview and would enjoy the opportunity to exchange information.

Model application letter (indented format)

> 431 Felton Ave.
> St. Paul, MN 55102
> April 19, 2000

Mr. Thomas Flanagan
Tristate Airlines
2546 Ashton Ave.
Bloomington, MN 55121

Dear Mr. Flanagan:

I am writing to apply for the position of Assistant Director of Employee Benefits in the Human Resources Department of Tristate, as advertised in this morning's *Star Tribune*. My education and experience are well suited to this position, and I'd welcome the chance to be part of a company that has shown so much growth during a period when other airlines have been operating at a loss.

As you can see from my résumé, I majored in Business Administration with an emphasis in human resources. Whenever possible, I have found campus activities and jobs that would give me experience in working with people. As an assistant in the Admissions Office at the University of Southern Minnesota, I worked successfully with students, parents, alumni, and faculty. The position required both a knowledge of university regulations and an understanding of people with different needs.

I also benefited from working as an administrative intern last summer in the personnel division of Central Bank & Trust, a department that handles the benefits for almost three thousand employees. When I was working there, new computers were installed for the division. Because I have extensive experience with computers, I was able to help other employees make the transition. More important, I improved my knowledge of state law on health insurance and learned procedures for monitoring health benefits that are easily transferable.

I am very much interested in putting my training to use at Tristate and hope that we can schedule an interview sometime during the next few weeks. I will be here in St. Paul except for the week of May 7, but I will be checking my messages daily when I am out of town, and you should have no difficulty reaching me.

Sincerely,
Marcia Baumeister
Marcia
Baumeister

enc.

10e Writing an effective résumé can persuade employers to interview you.

A résumé is a list of a person's qualifications for a job and is enclosed with a letter of application. It is made up of four categories of information.

- Personal data: name, mailing address, telephone number, e-mail address, and (if available) fax number
- Educational background
- Work experience
- References

Employers usually appreciate clearly written and well-organized résumés.

Make your résumé look professional. It is a form of persuasion designed to emphasize your qualifications for a job and get you an interview. Because there is usually more than one applicant for every job, your résumé should make the most of your qualifications. If you keep your résumé in a computer file, you can easily tailor it to each job you apply for so you can present your qualifications in the best light.

Writing a résumé requires planning and paying attention to detail. First, make a list of the jobs you have had, the activities and clubs you have been part of, and the offices you have held. Amplify these items by adding dates, job titles and responsibilities, and a brief statement about what you learned from each of them. Delete any items that seem too weak or tangential to be persuasive. (See 2a(2).)

One way to organize a résumé is to list experience and activities in reverse chronological order, so that your most recent experience comes first. This is a good plan if you have a relevant job history, without gaps that are hard to explain. An alternative way to organize a résumé is to list experience in terms of job skills rather than jobs held. This way is especially useful when your work history is modest or you are applying for a position in a new field but know you have the skills for the job.

Software programs that will prompt you to select the kind of résumé you need and then provide prompts for completing the different sections of it are available. When using a computer to write your résumé, you can also view it in its entirety on your screen and redesign it if necessary.

Although résumés have always been expected to look professional, an unprofessional-looking résumé is even less likely to gain favorable attention now that electronic resources facilitate effective presentation. Use good-quality paper (preferably white or off-white) and a laser printer. Use boldface to mark divisions and experiment with different fonts. Resist the impulse to make your format unnecessarily complicated. When in doubt, choose simplicity. For a sample résumé, see pages 266–67.

CHECKLIST for Résumé Writing

- Make sure to include your name, address, and telephone number; an e-mail address or fax number could also be useful.

- Identify your career objective simply, without elaborating on future goals. Try to match your qualifications to the employer's needs.

- Mention your degree, college or university, and pertinent areas of special training.

- Do not include personal data such as age and marital status.

- Whenever possible, make clear the relationship between jobs you have had and the job you are seeking.

- If you decide to include the names and addresses of references, include their phone numbers as well. List people who have agreed to write or speak on your behalf. Make sure these individuals understand the nature of the position you are seeking.

- To show that you are efficient, well organized, and thoughtful, use a clean, clear format.

- Make sure the résumé is correct by proofreading it carefully.

Chronological résumé (reverse order)

Marcia Baumeister
431 Felton Ave.
St. Paul, MN 55102
(651) 228-1927
Marciab4@hotmail.com

CAREER OBJECTIVE:
A management position specializing in the administration of employee benefits.

WORK EXPERIENCE:
Intern, Central Bank & Trust, June–August 1999.
Provided information to new employees, helped the personnel department get online with new information technology, and entered data for changes in medical benefits.

Student Assistant, Admissions Office, University of Southern Minnesota, January 1998–May 1999.
Responded to queries from parents and prospective students, conducted campus tours, planned orientation meetings, and wrote reports on recruitment efforts.

Tutor, University Writing Center, September 1997–May 2000.
Tutored students in business writing for six hours a week and worked as needed with other clients. Provided computer assistance, including ways to access information on the World Wide Web.

EDUCATION:

University of Southern Minnesota, B.S. with honors, 2000. Majored in Business Administration with an emphasis in Human Resources. Minors in Economics and Communications. Recipient of the 1999 Grable Award for university service.

Active in Management Club, Yearbook, Alpha Phi Sorority.

References available on request.

Grammar

Grammar

Chapter
11 Sentence Essentials

English sentences make statements (**declarative**), ask questions (**interrogative**), give commands or make requests (**imperative**), and make exclamations (**exclamatory**).

Declarative	He answered a hard question. [statement]
Imperative	Answer the question now. [request or command]
Interrogative	Did he answer the hard question? He answered, didn't he? He answered it? [questions]
Exclamatory	What a hard question you asked! And he answered it! [exclamations]

Careful study of this chapter will give you a clearer understanding of

- the essential parts of a sentence (**11a**);
- verbs and predicates (**11b**);
- subjects, objects, and complements (**11c**); and
- the importance of word order (**11d**).

For explanations of any unfamiliar terms, see the Glossary of Terms.

11a A sentence must contain a subject and a predicate.

An English sentence divides into two parts.

COMPLETE SUBJECT	+	COMPLETE PREDICATE.
The **plate**	+	**is** clean.
Gabriel	+	**replaced** the bulb in the lamp.
Our former **dean,** Professor George Smithers,	+	**donated** his entire library to the university.

The **subject** is what the sentence is about and answers the question *Who?* or *What?* The **predicate** says something about the subject (see **11b–c**) and contains a word that expresses action or state of being—a verb. The pattern is **SUBJECT + PREDICATE,** which is the usual order of English sentences.

11b Verbs form the essential part of the predicate of a sentence.

A verb is a word that expresses action or state of being and that often, but not always, ends in *-s* or *-ed.*

Chandra **writes.** [verb by itself]

Chandra **writes** clearly. [verb plus a word that describes, limits, or qualifies (modifies) the verb]

Verbs can be compound, that is, composed of more than one verb.

Chandra **writes** and **speaks** clearly.

Phrasal verbs Verbs that combine with words such as *at, in, out, up,* and the like (often called **particles**) function in the same ways that single-word verbs or verbs with auxiliaries do. However, the meaning of the combined verb is different from that of the single-word verb. For example, the meaning of the verb *turned* is different from the meaning of the combination *turned out.*

> Martha **turned** the car **out of the way.** [prepositional phrase modifying the verb *turned*]
>
> Nothing **turned out** the way she expected. [phrasal verb meaning *happened*]

Some examples of phrasal verbs are *look up, burn down, phase out, turn off, watch out, put off, try on.* A phrasal verb can sometimes be separated from its accompanying preposition.

> She **looked up** the word in the dictionary. [The parts of a phrasal verb are usually side by side.]
>
> She **looked** the word **up** in the dictionary. [The word the verb acts on may come between the parts of the phrasal verb.]
>
> OR
>
> She **looked** it **up** in the dictionary.

The meanings of phrasal verbs can be found in a good ESL dictionary, such as *The Longman Dictionary of Contemporary English.* This type of dictionary will also tell you whether the phrasal verb can be separated.

Sometimes a verb has a helping verb, an additional verb often called an **auxiliary** or **verb marker.** The verbs *have* and *be* are auxiliaries and follow the pattern of **AUXILIARY + VERB.** (See chapter **17** for a complete discussion of verbs.)

> The film **had started** by then.
>
> She **will be arriving** at noon.
>
> Mara **should go** now.

Other words sometimes come between the auxiliary and the verb.

> I **have** not **bought** my ticket.
>
> Television **has** still not completely **replaced** radio.

Verbals are words derived from verbs but used as nouns, adjectives, or adverbs. A **gerund** is a verbal noun ending in *-ing*. It functions like any other noun. An **infinitive** is a verbal signaled by *to* and used as a noun, an adjective, or an adverb. A **participle** is a verbal adjective ending in *-ing* or *-ed*.

> **Using** a computer is simple. [gerund]
>
> I love **to run.** [infinitive]
>
> I stop at **blinking** lights. I bought a **used** computer. [participles]

11c Subjects, objects, and complements can be nouns, pronouns, or word groups serving as nouns.

Nouns such as *sister, school, computer, democracy,* or *puppy* name persons, places, things, ideas, animals, and so on. **Pronouns** stand for nouns.

> **Russell** sent a **check** to the **Alzheimer's Foundation.**
>
> **He** sent **it** to **them.** [Pronouns substituted for the nouns in the previous sentence.]

Groups of words such as *father-in-law, Labor Day,* and *swimming pool* generally refer to a single thing and so are classified as *compound nouns.*

 Count/Noncount Nouns (See 26a(1) for the use of articles.)

Count nouns are words that represent individual items that can be counted and cannot be viewed as a mass, such as *book, child,* or *atom.* Count nouns can be either singular or plural. (See **26a(1).**)

Noncount nouns, such as *humor* or *furniture,* represent an abstract concept, a mass, or a collection. They cannot usually be plural. Use *a* and *an* only with count nouns. Use *the* with either.

Nouns also appear in expressions that are grammatically independent of the rest of the sentence (absolute expressions) and in expressions directing speech to particular persons (direct address).

> **All protests aside,** he will repay the loan immediately. [absolute phrase]
>
> **Arlese,** have you seen my sister? [direct address]

(1) Subjects of verbs

Grammatically complete sentences contain a subject. Except for commands or requests (imperatives) in which the subject, *you,* may be understood, those subjects take the form of nouns, pronouns, or groups of words serving as nouns.

> **Georgia** *produces* delicious peaches.
>
> *Does* **South Carolina** also *produce* peaches?

Subjects of verbs may be compound.

> **Georgia** and **South Carolina** produce peaches. [compound subject]

In commands or requests, the subject is often understood.

> [**You**] *Take* my luggage to my room. [command]
>
> [**You**] Please *come* to see me when you're in town. [request]

To identify the grammatical subject of a sentence, find the verb and then use it in a question beginning with *who* or *what,* as shown in the following examples.

The runner leaped the hurdle.	The book was read by Nan.
Verb: **leaped**	Verb: **was read**
WHO leaped? **The runner** (not the hurdle) **leaped.**	WHAT was read? **The book** (not Nan) **was read.**
Subject: **runner**	Subject: **book**

Subjects usually come before verbs in sentences. In questions, however, and after the words *there* and sometimes *it* (these are called **expletives**—words that fill out a sentence without altering its meaning), the subject comes after the verb.

> **Was** the **book** interesting? [verb + subject—a question]
>
> There **were** no **refusals.** [*there* (expletive) + verb + subject]

(2) Objects of verbs

Normally, nouns, pronouns, or groups of words serving as nouns that come after the verb and that are influenced by it or complete its meaning are called **objects** or **complements.**

Direct objects

Verbs that express action often require a noun or a pronoun—a **direct object**—to receive or show the result of the action. (See 17a(4).)

> Martin bought three **books.** [direct object: *books*]

To identify a direct object, find the subject and the verb and then use them in a question ending with *whom* or *what*.

Juana silently took his hand.

Subject and verb:	**Juana took**
Juana took WHAT?	**hand**
Direct object:	**hand**

Direct objects in sentences like the following are directly affected by the action of the verb.

Hurricane Andrew ravaged Miami. [The subject, *Hurricane Andrew,* acts. The object, *Miami,* receives the action.]

Indirect objects

Sometimes an **indirect object**—a word that shows to whom or for whom the action occurred—comes between the verb and the direct object.

Martin bought **me** three **books.** [indirect object: *me;* direct object: *books*]

Like the subjects of verbs, direct and indirect objects can be nouns, pronouns, or groups of words used as nouns.

Some verbs (such as *bring, buy, give, lend, offer, sell, send,* and *take*) can have both a direct object and an indirect object.

Linda gave Felipé a new bicycle. [subject + verb + direct object: **Linda + gave + bicycle.**]

Linda gave a bicycle TO WHOM? **Felipé** [indirect object: **Felipé**]

Direct and indirect objects of verbs can be compound.

He eats only **vegetables** and **fruit.** [compound direct object]

We offered **Elena** and **Octavio** a year's membership. [compound indirect object]

Sentence Essentials

(3) Subject and object complements

A **subject complement** refers to, identifies, or qualifies the subject and helps complete the meaning of the forms of *be* (*am, is, are, was, were, been*), linking verbs (such as *become, seem*), and sensory verbs (such as *feel, look, smell, sound, taste*). These verbs are often called **intransitive verbs.** (See **17a(4)**.)

> Leilani is my **sister.** [*Sister,* a noun, identifies *Leilani,* the subject.]
>
> Violence became **inevitable.** [*Inevitable,* an adjective, describes or qualifies *violence,* the subject.]
>
> The rose smelled **sweet.** [*Sweet,* an adjective, describes *rose.*]

An **object complement** refers to, identifies, or qualifies the direct object. Object complements help complete the meaning of verbs such as *call, elect, make, name,* and *paint.*

> Today, we call Einstein a **genius.** [*Genius,* a noun, is an object complement renaming *Einstein.*]
>
> The benefits make the job **desirable.** [*Desirable,* an adjective, is an object complement describing *job.*]

11d Word order determines the meaning of a word in a sentence.

Becoming thoroughly aware of English word order—usually **SUBJECT + VERB + OBJECT** or **COMPLEMENT**—will help you recognize subjects, objects, and complements. The five most common sentence patterns show how important word order is and how a change in word order results in a change in meaning.

Pattern 1	SUBJECT + VERB.

s *v*
Most parents worry.

s *v*
The air in the room smelled.

Pattern 2	SUBJECT + VERB + OBJECT.

s *v* *do*
My cat terrorizes their dog.

s *v* *do*
Their dog terrorizes my cat.

Pattern 3	SUBJECT + VERB + INDIRECT OBJECT + DIRECT OBJECT.

s *v* *io* *do*
Lissa showed Aaron her prize.

s *v* *io* *do*
Professor Crowl taught me physics.

Pattern 4	SUBJECT + LINKING VERB + SUBJECT COMPLEMENT.

s *v* *sc*
Joe DiMaggio was a hero.

Pattern 5	SUBJECT + VERB + DIRECT OBJECT + OBJECT COMPLEMENT.

s *v* *do* *oc*
Marcus named his son Derek.

s *v* *do* *oc*
We called Joe DiMaggio a hero.

Chapter

12 Phrases and Clauses

Sentences are composed of combinations of elements—phrases and clauses—and we have a number of customs that tell us what can be combined and how those combinations must be arranged. (For explanations of any unfamiliar terms, see the *Glossary of Terms*.) Careful study of this chapter will give you a clearer understanding of

- how to recognize and use phrases (**12a**),
- how to recognize and use clauses (**12b**), and
- how to recognize different forms of sentences (**12c**).

12a A phrase is a group of words that can function as a single part of speech.

A word group that does not have a subject or a predicate and that functions as a single part of speech (noun, verb, adjective, adverb) is a **phrase.** (See **15a–b.**)

(1) Noun phrases

The heavy frost killed **fruit trees.** [subject and object]

They elected Alexandra **vice president.** [subject, object, and object complement]

(2) Verb phrases

The flowers **have wilted.** [predicate]

Have you **watered** them? [predicate]

(3) Verbal phrases

Although **verbals** are much like verbs because they have different tenses, can take subjects and objects, and can be modified by adverbs, they can serve only as modifiers or noun phrases. **Gerund phrases** are always used as subjects or objects, and **infinitive phrases** often are (although they can also function as modifiers). **Participial phrases** generally modify nouns.

> Students **standing around** did not ask questions. [participial phrase, *standing around,* modifying the noun *students*]
>
> Some organizations serve their communities by **picking up trash** on nearby highways. [gerund phrase, *picking up trash,* serving as the object of the preposition *by*]
>
> **To graduate early** had become a necessity for Marissa. [infinitive phrase, *to graduate early,* serving as the subject of the sentence]

 CAUTION Infinitives, participles, and gerunds cannot function as the verb in a sentence.

(4) Prepositional phrases

Prepositions set up relationships, and they have objects, usually a noun or a pronoun.

> Parking **on campus** is prohibited. [adjectival phrase]
>
> We were racing **against time.** [adverbial phrase]

The preposition establishes a relationship such as space, time, accompaniment, cause, or manner between the object of the preposition and another part of the sentence. A preposition combined with its object (and any modifiers) is called a **prepositional phrase.** Prepositional phrases are modifiers.

> **With great feeling,** Martin Luther King, Jr., expressed his dream **of freedom.** [*With great feeling* tells us about King's manner, and *of freedom* makes the kind of dream specific.]

A prepositional phrase can also occasionally serve as a subject. ("*After supper* is too late!")

Some Common Prepositions

about	beneath	in	regarding
above	beside	inside	round
across	between	into	since
after	beyond	like	through
against	by	near	to
among	concerning	of	toward
around	despite	off	under
as	down	on	unlike
at	during	out	until
before	except	outside	up
behind	for	over	upon
below	from	past	with

Some prepositions, called **phrasal prepositions,** can contain more than one word.

Except for the last day, it was a wonderful trip.

Phrasal Prepositions (Two or More Words)

according to	by way of	in spite of
along with	due to	instead of
apart from	except for	on account of
as for	in addition to	out of
as regards	in case of	up to
as to	in front of	with reference to
because of	in lieu of	with regard to
by means of	in place of	with respect to
by reason of	in regard to	with the exception of

Until indicates a continuing situation that will come to an end at a definite time in the future. *By* indicates an action that will happen at or before a particular time in the future. *Besides* means *with* or *plus* and usually "includes," whereas *except* means *without* or *minus* and usually "excludes."

I will finish my work **by** six o'clock.

I will be away **until** next Tuesday.

Besides a salad, we had soup and crackers.

We had everything we wanted **except** a salad.

(5) Appositive phrases

Appositives identify, explain, or supplement the meaning of the words they refer to.

Johnnycake, **a kind of cornbread,** is a New England specialty.

(6) Absolute phrases

The lunch having been packed, we were ready to go. [sentence modifier]

12b Recognizing clauses helps in analyzing sentences.

A clause is a group of related words that contains a subject and a predicate.

(1) Independent clauses

An **independent clause** has the same grammatical structure as a simple sentence; both contain a subject and a predicate. They can be combined with other independent clauses or with dependent clauses to form sentences. In the example below, the independent clauses are in bold.

> **The boy chased the dog,** but **he couldn't catch him.** [two independent clauses]

(2) Subordinate clauses

A **subordinate clause** is a group of related words that contains a subject and a predicate but cannot stand alone.

> Maria received the gold medal **because her performance was flawless.**

Subordinate clauses provide additional information about the independent clause and establish the relationship between the additional information and the independent clause. A subordinate clause is grammatically dependent and functions within a sentence as a modifier or as a subject or object.

> I needed to get to the meeting early **because I wanted to pick my seat.** [clause modifying the entire independent clause *I needed . . . early*]
>
> Astronomers don't know **what black holes really are.** [clause serving as the direct object of *know*]

A subordinate clause begins with a conjunction such as *after, when, because, although* that introduces, connects, and relates the clause to other words in the sentence. (See pages 286–87 for a list of subordinating conjunctions.)

Subordinate clauses used as subjects or objects

Nouns	Noun Clauses
The **testimony** may not be true.	**What the witness said** may not be true. [subject]

| We do not understand their **motives**. | We do not understand **why they did it.** [direct object] |
| Send the money to **charity**. | Send the money to **whoever needs it most.** [object of the preposition] |

That before a noun clause can often be omitted.

Subordinate clauses used as modifiers

Two types of subordinate clauses—adjectival clauses and adverbial clauses—serve as modifiers.

Adjectival clauses   Adjectival clauses, which nearly always follow the words they modify, usually begin with a relative pronoun but may sometimes begin with words such as *when, where,* or *why* and answer the questions *Which one?, What kind of?,* or *How many?*

Adjectives	**Adjectival Clauses**
The newly **renovated** student union opens today.	The student union, **which has been renovated,** opens today.
My sister lives in a **peaceful** town.	The town **where my sister lives** is peaceful.

Adverbial clauses   An adverbial clause usually answers the questions *Where?, When?, How?,* and *In what condition?,* and is ordinarily introduced by a subordinating conjunction.

Adverbs	**Adverbial Clauses**
As a result, the company hired six new writers.	**Because its annual report was criticized,** the company hired six new writers.
He packed for his vacation **quickly**.	He packed for his vacation **after he called a taxi.**

(3) Coordinating and subordinating conjunctions

Conjunctions are words such as cars *and* trucks; *neither* Martha *nor* Debbie; *after* Lisa graduated, and *why* the dog ran away.

Conjunctions are connectors. **Coordinating conjunctions** and **correlatives** join sentence elements (single words, groups of words lacking a subject or predicate—phrases—or groups of words having a subject and a predicate—clauses). (See **20c**.)

in the boat **or** on the pier

will try **but** may lose

neither Ana **nor** Miguel

Subordinating conjunctions join subordinate clauses to independent clauses. (See **12b(2)**.)

I worked **because** Dad needed money.

The river rises **when** the snow melts.

Coordinating Conjunctions

and, but, for, nor, or, so, yet

Correlative Conjunctions

both—and, either—or, neither—nor, not only—but also, whether—or

Subordinating Conjunctions

after	as if	before
although	as though	even if
as (far/soon) as	because	even though

how	now that	till
if	once	unless
in case	provided (that)	until
in that	since	when, whenever
inasmuch as	so that	where, wherever
insofar as	supposing that	whether
lest	than	while
no matter how	though	why

Adverbial conjunctions (words like *consequently, however, nevertheless, then,* and *therefore*—see page 299) sometimes link independent clauses.

> Olivia had begged to register for the class; **therefore,** it was odd that she was often absent.

12c Sentences may be analyzed by form.

The form of a sentence is identified by the number and kinds of clauses it contains.

(1) Simple sentences

> **I** [subject] **totaled my car.** [A simple subject is followed by a predicate containing a verb and a direct object.]

(2) Compound sentences

> **I totaled my car,** so **I bought a new one.** [A comma and a coordinating conjunction (*so*) link the two independent clauses.]

(3) Complex sentences

Because I totaled my car, I bought a new one. [A subordinate clause—signaled here by *because* and ended by a comma (see 27b)—precedes the independent clause.]

(4) Compound-complex sentences

I totaled my car, so I bought a new one, even though I had planned to wait. [*So* connects the two independent clauses; *even though* signals the subordinate clause.]

Chapter 13

Sentence Fragments

The information in this chapter can help you

- recognize fragments and
- revise fragments resulting from incorrectly punctuated phrases (13a) and clauses (13b).

A **fragment,** an incomplete sentence starting with a capital and ending with a period, is usually avoided in college and professional writing. Fragments lack a subject or verb, or both, but can still be difficult to recognize within the context of surrounding sentences.

> He enjoys flowers and shrubs. **Which help screen his yard from the street.**
>
> **Having driven across the desert.** We enjoyed the cool weather.

Fragments are often phrases or clauses beginning with a word (subordinating conjunction or relative pronoun) that marks them as subordinate. Fragments can be corrected by substituting *they* for the subordinator to make an independent sentence or by connecting the phrase to an adjoining sentence.

> He enjoys flowers and shrubs. **They help screen his yard from the street.**
>
> **Having driven across the desert,** we enjoyed the cool weather.

CAUTION Since fragments are generally considered errors in college writing, it is safer not to use them at all. You often see fragments in books and magazines because professional writers sometimes deliberately use them for literary emphasis, in dialogue, as answers to questions, as transitions, and as exclamations. Fragments are also characteristic of advertising.

> **Understand? Unbelievable! No pain, no gain.** [colloquial use of question with an implied subject (*you*), of exclamation, and of phrases]
>
> I don't remember a world without language. From the time of my earliest childhood, there was language. **Always language, and imagination, speculation, utters of sound. Words, beginnings of words.** —SIMON J. ORTIZ [literary use of phrases]

Because grammar checkers identify fragments by matching noun and verb phrases, they occasionally identify some phrases as sentences, or if the group of words contains a word the checkers do not recognize as a verb, checkers may identify some sentences as fragments. You need to be able to identify fragments yourself.

Four Steps to Finding Fragments

Step 1   **Find the verb or verbs in the sentence.** Words that end in *-ing* are seldom verbs (*sing, ring,* and other such verbs are the exceptions). You can test for a verb by adding *-s* or *-ed*.

Step 2   **Find the subject of the sentence.** Test for it by asking *Who?* or *What?*

Step 3   **If you do not have a subject-verb pair, you have a fragment.** A sentence must have at least one subject-verb pair. If a verb or a subject is left over, you are probably dealing with a compound subject or predicate. A connector like *and* or *but* (coordinating conjunction) must link those compound elements.

Step 4   **Do any sentences begin with a subordinating
conjunction or relative pronoun (*which, that*)?**
See **12b(3)**. If so, make sure another clause
follows. You must have one more pair of subjects
and verbs than you have conjunctions.

13a You can revise phrases mistakenly punctuated as sentences in at least two ways.

Verbal phrases, prepositional phrases, appositives, parts of compound predicates, and other word groups without subjects and predicates are sometimes mistakenly written as fragments.

Fragments can be revised in one of the ways listed below.

1. *Make the phrase into a sentence by supplying the missing subject and/or verb. This method elevates the importance of the fragment.*

   Archeologists excavating ancient cities carefully brush dirt from the artifacts. _{They use} **Using paintbrushes for that purpose.**

   Later, Raymond began to tap out the rhythm. _{He tapped first} **First on the table and then on the counter.**

   My department is looking for a new teacher. _{We prefer} **Preferably a writing teacher.**

   Mai was the first woman to be elected president of her class. _{She was also} **And tapped for Mortar Board.**

   I am interested only in the properties of citrus fruits. _{Examples are} **Such as lemons, oranges, and grapefruit.**

2. *Attach the fragment to a related sentence. This method establishes a relationship between the fragment and the sentence it is attached to.*

Archeologists excavating ancient cities carefully brush dirt from the artifacts, using ~~Using~~ paintbrushes for that purpose.

Later, Raymond began to tap out the rhythm, first ~~First~~ on the table and then on the counter.

My department is looking for a new teacher, preferably ~~Preferably~~ a writing teacher.

Mai was the first woman to be elected president of her class, and ~~And~~ tapped for Mortar Board.

I am interested only in the properties of citrus fruits, such ~~Such~~ as lemons, oranges, and grapefruit.

13b You can revise subordinate clauses mistakenly punctuated as sentences in at least three ways.

1. *Attach the fragment to a related sentence.*

They tried to understand Arturo's objections, which ~~Which~~ were unreasonable.

Arturo discovered that he had made serious mistakes, when ~~When~~ he forgot to deposit a large payment from a customer and when he wrote a check for more money than he had in the bank.

OR

Arturo discovered that he had made serious mistakes. **When he forgot to deposit a large payment from a customer, and ~~when~~ he wrote a check for more money than he had in the bank.** [The colon (**31d**) serves as a coordinator, so the subordinating conjunctions are deleted.]

2. *Remove the subordinating word and supply the missing elements.*
   They tried to understand Arturo's objections. *The objections* ~~Which~~ were unreasonable.

   Arturo discovered that he had made serious mistakes. *He* ~~When he~~ forgot to deposit a large payment from a customer, and ~~when~~ he wrote a check for more money than he had in the bank.

3. *Reduce the fragment to a modifier and include it in the related sentence.*
   They tried to understand Arturo's *unreasonable* objections. ~~Which were unreasonable.~~

   Arturo discovered that *forgetting to deposit payments and writing overdrafts were* ~~he had made~~ serious mistakes. ~~When he forgot to deposit a large payment from a customer and when he wrote a check for more money than he had in the bank.~~

Chapter 14

Comma Splices and Fused Sentences

A fused sentence and a comma splice are both composed of two (or more) improperly joined independent clauses. A fused sentence results from joining two independent clauses without using punctuation or a conjunction. A comma splice results from joining two independent clauses with a comma. This chapter will help you

- recognize a comma splice or a fused sentence and
- know when to separate clauses and when to join them.

Grammar checkers are somewhat better at finding comma splices than they are at finding fragments and considerably better than they are at finding fused sentences.

A fused sentence (often called a "run-on sentence") or a comma splice (often called a "comma fault") occurs only when you are writing compound or compound-complex sentences. (See **12c**.) Not recognizing where a sentence begins and ends leads to these very similar problems.

Fused	The current was swift he swam to shore.
Comma splice	The current was swift, he swam to shore.

Both comma splices and fused sentences can be corrected by separating the clauses with a semicolon or a period or by joining them with a conjunction.

To separate independent clauses:	Examples:
1. Place a period after each clause.	The current was swift. **He** swam to shore.
2. Place a semicolon between clauses.	The current was swift; he swam to shore.
To link independent clauses:	Examples:
A comma can be inserted before *and, but, or, nor, for, so,* or *yet.*	The roads were icy, **so** they decided not to drive.
To relate clauses by subordination:	Examples:
1. One clause can be subordinated to the other.	**Because the roads were icy,** they decided not to drive.
2. One clause can become an introductory phrase.	**Because of the icy roads,** they decided not to drive.

When the clauses are short, parallel in form, and unified in thought, a comma (instead of a semicolon or a period) can link independent clauses not joined by a coordinating conjunction.

They came, they fought, they died.

Ways to recognize independent clauses and distinguish them from phrases and subordinate clauses are explained in chapter 12, especially 12a and 12b.

CHECKLIST for Comma Splices and Fused Sentences

Most of the time the following advice will help you find comma splices and fused sentences. They generally occur

1. with transitional phrases such as *however, therefore, for example;*

2. when an explanation or example occurs in the second clause;

3. when a positive clause follows a negative first clause;

4. when a pronoun is the subject of the second clause; or

5. when a series of ideas is phrased as connected clauses.

You can identify a comma splice or a fused sentence by noticing how many pairs of grammatical subjects and verbs (see 11a–c) are in the sentence. Match the verbs to the subjects.

1. If no punctuation separates the pairs, you have a fused sentence.

2. If a comma instead of a coordinating conjunction separates the pairs, you have a comma splice.

To fix comma splices and fused sentences

1. link clauses with a comma and a coordinating conjunction,

2. separate the clauses by using a semicolon,

3. separate the clauses by punctuating each as a sentence,

4. subordinate one clause to the other,

5. reduce one clause to an introductory phrase, or

6. rewrite the sentence integrating one clause into the other.

14a A fused sentence or a comma splice may be revised in one of three ways.

Fused sentences and comma splices may be revised by

- linking the clauses with a comma followed by *and, but, or, for, nor, so,* or *yet* (coordinating conjunctions);
- separating the clauses with a semicolon (see **28a**) or a period; or
- making one clause subordinate to the other.

Fused	She didn't know what to say to his announcement she was not at a complete loss for words, either.
Comma splice	She didn't know what to say to his announcement, she was not at a complete loss for words, either.
Revised	She didn't know what to say to his announcement, **nor** was she at a complete loss for words, either. [Note the shift in the word order of subject and verb after the coordinating conjunction *nor.*]
OR	She was **neither** ready with a response to his announcement **nor** at a complete loss for words. [This simple sentence has a compound complement.]
OR	She didn't know what to say to his announcement; she was not at a complete loss for words, either. [A semicolon separates the independent clauses.]
OR	She didn't know what to say to his announcement. She was not at a complete loss for words, either. [The clauses are punctuated as separate sentences.]
OR	**Despite not knowing** what to say to his announcement, she was not at a complete loss

for words. [One clause is reduced to a verbal phrase; see **22b**.]

Fused   She wrote him a love letter he answered it in person.

Comma splice   She wrote him a love letter, he answered it in person.

Revised   She wrote him a love letter, **so** he answered it in person. [The coordinating conjunction *so* is added after the comma; see **27a**.]

OR   She wrote him a love letter; he answered it in person. [Independent clauses are separated by a semicolon; see **28a**.]

OR   She wrote him a love letter. **H**e answered it in person. [Each independent clause is written as a sentence.]

OR   **When** she wrote him a love letter, he answered it in person. [The addition of *when* makes the first clause subordinate.]

A comma, however, is used to separate a statement from an attached question used for emphasis.

You took the test, didn't you? He plays the bassoon, doesn't he? They couldn't be wrong, could they—not all those millions!

—WILLIAM GOLDING

14b Independent clauses may also be separated by using a semicolon with a word such as *however, therefore,* and the like (conjunctive adverb). (See 28a.)

Fused   A century ago the wild West was tamed therefore, the stories it produced were no longer tales of cowboys and bandits.

Comma splice	A century ago the wild West was tamed, therefore, the stories it produced were no longer tales of cowboys and bandits.
Revised	A century ago the wild West was tamed; **therefore,** the stories it produced were no longer tales of cowboys and bandits. [independent clause; conjunctive adverb, independent clause]

Unlike a coordinating conjunction, which has a fixed position between the independent clauses it links, many conjunctive adverbs and transitional phrases either begin the second independent clause or take another position inside it.

She believed that daily exercise has many benefits, **but** she couldn't fit it into her schedule.

She believed that daily exercise has many benefits; **however,** she couldn't fit it into her schedule.

She believed that daily exercise has many benefits; she couldn't, **however,** fit it into her schedule.

Conjunctive Adverbs

also	however	next
anyhow	incidentally	otherwise
anyway	indeed	similarly
besides	instead	still
consequently	likewise	then
finally	meanwhile	therefore
furthermore	moreover	thus
hence	nevertheless	

Transitional Phrases

after all	at any rate	by the way
as a result	at the same time	even so

for example	in other words	on the other hand
in addition	in the second place	
in fact	on the contrary	

14c Divided quotations can trick you into making a comma splice. (See chapter 30.)

Comma splice   "Who won the Superbowl?" he asked, "what was the final score?"

Revised   "Who won the Superbowl?" he asked. "What was the final score?"

Comma splice   "Injustice is relatively easy to bear," says Mencken, "it is justice that hurts."

Revised   "Injustice is relatively easy to bear," says Mencken; "it is justice that hurts."

Chapter 15 Modifiers

Adjectives and adverbs are modifiers; that is, they qualify, restrict, or intensify the meaning of other words. They also describe degrees of comparison. This chapter will help you

- recognize adjectives and understand how to use them (**15a**),
- recognize adverbs and understand how to use them (**15b**),
- use the comparative and superlative forms correctly (**15c**),
- know when to use a group modifier (**15d**),
- place modifiers near the words they modify (**15e**),
- avoid dangling modifiers (**15f**), and
- revise double negatives (**15g**).

Adjectives modify nouns and pronouns; **adverbs** modify verbs, adjectives, and other adverbs.

Adjectives	Adverbs
a **quick** lunch	eat **quickly**
She looked **angry.**	She looked **angrily** at me.

In traditional grammar, the articles *a, an,* and *the* are often classified as adjectives.

Because both adjectives and adverbs work as modifiers, often look very much alike, and generally occur near one another, they can be difficult to tell apart. To determine whether a word is an adjective or an adverb, you must consider its form and its function in a particular sentence.

15a Adjectives modify nouns, groups of words functioning as nouns, or pronouns. They may function as subject or object complements.

Adjectives answer the questions *What kind?, How many?,* or *Which ones?*

young children   **several** men   **writing** class

The English language does not allow adjectives to be pluralized. Thus, the same word can modify both a singular and a plural noun.

sour oranges   a sour lemon

---

(1) Identifying adjectives

Because many adjectives are formed from other parts of speech, you can often determine that a word is an adjective by looking at its ending; *-able, -al, -ful, -ic, -ish, -less,* and *-y* are commonly used to make an adjective from a noun or a verb.

accept**able**	angel**ic**	effort**less**
rent**al**	yellow**ish**	sleep**y**
event**ful**		

Certain adjectives formed from nouns have the *-ly* ending (*cost, costly*). Sometimes a verbal serves as an adjective: for instance, an infinitive or a participle ending in *-ing* or *-ed.*

a determin**ing** factor   a determin**ed** effort   a chicken **to eat**

In English, adjectives are customarily used in the following order, and having more than three adjectives is considered awkward: determiner, evaluator, physical descriptor (size, shape, age, color), origin, material, purpose.

> a fascinating old village
>
> two large green Brazilian parrots
>
> that ugly brick building
>
> a round Italian pizza pan

(2) Adjectives used as subject or object complements

An adjective used as a subject complement completes the meaning of the verb by describing the subject of the sentence. A common error is to use an adverb as a subject complement.

The actor looked ~~**angrily.**~~ *angry* [explains something about *actor*]

The actor looked up ~~**angry.**~~ *angrily* [explains something about *looked up*]

Adjectives that modify the direct object in sentences with such verbs as *call, consider, elect, find, make, name* are **object complements.**

They found Collette **trustworthy.**

CAUTION Do not omit the *-d* or *-ed* of a past participle used as an adjective. (See 17a, page 323.)

The dog was too frighten*ed* to go to him.

15b Adverbs modify verbs, adjectives, and other adverbs.

Adverbs answer the questions *How?, When?,* or *Where?*

> Leela played her part **perfectly.** I wanted to go home **early.** I put the cat **outside.**

Adverbs that modify verbs commonly describe how (manner), when (time), or where (place) the action occurred.

Manner	We walked **quietly.**
Time	We arrived **later.**
Place	We walked **home.**

The *-ly* ending is usually associated with adverbs formed from adjectives. A few adverbs have two acceptable forms (*quick, quickly; slow, slowly*). When in doubt, consult the dictionary for the label *adv.* and any usage notes.

Infinitives can also serve as adverbs.

| studied **to pass** | happy **to leave** | afraid **to speak** |

A number of words can function as either adjectives or adverbs—for example, *fast, well.* When in doubt, consult your dictionary for the labels *adj.* and *adv.* and any usage notes.

Most dictionaries still label the following as colloquial, meaning that you may hear it in conversation but should avoid it in writing: *sure* for *surely, real* for *really,* and *good* for *well.*

| **Conversational** | The Broncos played **real good** during the first quarter. |
| **Written** | The Broncos played **very well** during the first quarter. [appropriate in both written and conversational usage; see **23b(1)**.] |

15c **Many adjectives and adverbs change form to show relative quality, quantity, or manner (the degree of comparison).**

Generally, one-syllable adjectives and adverbs and two-syllable adjectives with the stress on the first syllable form the comparative by adding *-er* and the superlative by adding *-est*. Other longer adjectives and most adverbs form the comparative by using *more* (or *less*) and the superlative by using *most* (or *least*).

tall, taller, tallest [one-syllable adjective]

fast, faster, fastest [one-syllable adverb]

pretty, prettier, prettiest [two-syllable adjective with stress on the first syllable]

quickly, more/less quickly, most/least quickly [two-syllable adverb]

fortunate, more/less fortunate, most/least fortunate [three-syllable adjective]

rapidly, more/less rapidly, most/least rapidly [three-syllable adverb]

A few common modifiers have irregular forms.

little, less, least

good/well, better, best

bad/badly, worse, worst

(1) The comparative

Make sure to complete the comparison, and always make clear what the item is being compared with. In the examples, the conjunction *than* signals the second element being compared.

The city is much **bigger** now **than** it was five years ago.

Dried apples are **more** nutritious per pound **than** fresh apples.

Note that the comparison may be implied by the context.

> She wrote **two** papers, and the instructor gave her a **better** grade on the second.

The comparative form used with *other* sometimes refers to more than two.

> Bert can run **faster** than the *other* players can.

(2) The superlative

> Bert is the **fastest** of the three runners.
> OR
> Bert is the **fastest** runner of all.

(3) The incorrect double comparative or superlative

> Our swimming hole is much ~~more~~ shallower than Crystal Lake.
> That was the ~~most~~ funniest movie I have seen.

15d Using a word group or a noun as a modifier can be awkward or ambiguous.

Many word groups or nouns effectively modify other nouns (as in *reference* manual, *House Ways and Means* Committee). Avoid such forms, however, when they are awkward or confusing.

Awkward	Many candidates entered the president race.
Better	Many candidates entered the presidential race.

15e Placing modifiers near the words they modify clarifies meaning.

The meaning of the following sentences changes according to the position of the modifiers.

Natasha went out with **just** her coat on.

Natasha **just** went out with her coat on.

Just Natasha went out with her coat on.

A grammar checker will often catch split infinitives (which are now generally regarded as acceptable), but it does not catch dangling or misplaced modifiers.

---

(1) Modifiers such as *almost, even, hardly, just, merely, nearly,* and *only*

These modifiers come immediately before the words they modify.

The truck ~~only~~ *only* costs $2,000.

He ~~even~~ *even* works during his vacation.

(2) Prepositional phrases

Arne says that he means to leave the country *in the first paragraph* ~~in the first paragraph.~~

(3) Adjectival clauses

I put the chair in the middle of the room *that I had recently purchased* ~~that I had recently purchased.~~

(4) "Squinting" constructions

I agreed ~~the next day~~ to help him.
The next day ^

OR

I agreed ~~the next day~~ to help him.
the next day ^

(5) Split infinitives

A split infinitive occurs when a word comes between *to* and the verb: *to carelessly purchase.*

The jury was unable ~~to~~, under the circumstances, convict the
to ^
defendant.

Today, even the most conservative authorities generally agree that splitting an infinitive is occasionally not only natural but also desirable.

He forgot to **completely** close the gate. [COMPARE He forgot **completely** to close the gate.]

15f Modifiers that refer to no particular word in the sentence need revising.

Dangling modifiers are primarily verbal phrases that do not modify any particular words or phrases in the sentence.

Dangling *Tuning the television to CNN,* the State of the Union speech reached millions of voters.

Revised *Tuning the television to CNN,* **millions** of voters listened to the State of the Union speech.

Dangling	The afternoon passed very pleasantly, *lounging* in the shade and *reminiscing* about our childhood.
Revised	**We** passed the afternoon very pleasantly, *lounging* in the shade and *reminiscing* about our childhood.
Dangling	On *entering* the stadium, the size of the crowd surprised Theo.
Revised	On *entering* the stadium, **Theo** was surprised at the size of the crowd.
Dangling	*When only a small boy,* my father took me with him to Chicago.
Revised	*When* **I was** *only a small boy,* my father took me with him to Chicago.

15g A double negative is incorrect.

The term **double negative** refers to the use of two negatives within a sentence or clause to express a single negation.

He did**n't** keep ~~no~~ *any* records. OR He ~~didn't~~ *Kept* keep **no** records.

Because *hardly, barely,* and *scarcely* already denote severely limited or negative conditions, using *not, nothing,* or *without* with these modifiers creates a double negative.

I could**n't hardly** quit in the middle of the job. OR I could**n't** ~~hardly~~ quit in the middle of the job.

Chapter

16 Pronouns

This chapter explains

- what the various kinds of pronouns (personal, relative, indefinite, and so on) are and how to use them (**16a**);
- how the forms of pronouns are determined by case (**16b**);
- how to handle case with compound constructions, *who* and *whom,* and other problem situations (**16c**);
- how to make sure pronouns agree with the nouns they replace (**16d**); and
- how to ensure clear reference to those nouns (**16e**).

Case refers to the form of a noun or pronoun that shows how it relates to other words in a sentence; for instance, in the phrase, *Martin's cat,* the possessive case of *Martin's* shows that Martin owns the cat. Most of what there is to say about case in English applies primarily to pronouns because a pronoun changes form to show this relationship.

He [the subject] wants **his** [modifier showing possession] cousin to help **him** [direct object].

Pronouns also have singular and plural forms.

They [plural subject] want **their** [plural modifier showing possession] cousins to help **them** [plural direct object].

Grammar checkers perform poorly when checking for case errors. They can find most reflexive pronoun errors and some *who/whom* errors, but checkers sometimes incorrectly identify other errors and even suggest erroneous "corrections."

16a Understanding the various kinds of pronouns helps writers use them correctly.

Although English has several kinds of pronouns, the important categories for studying case are *personal, relative, interrogative,* and *reflexive* pronouns.

(1) Personal pronouns

The first-person pronoun (*I, we*) identifies the speaker, the second-person pronoun (*you*) identifies the person spoken to, and the third-person pronoun (*he, she, it, they*) identifies the person or thing spoken about. Personal pronouns change form to reflect their relationship to other words in the sentence.

Person	Subjective		Objective		Possessive	
	Singular	**Plural**	**Singular**	**Plural**	**Singular**	**Plural**
First person	I	we	me	us	my mine	our ours
Second person	you	you	you	you	your yours	your yours
Third person	he she it	they	him her it	them	his hers its	their theirs

(2) Relative pronouns

Relative pronouns (*who, whom, whoever, whomever, which, whose,* and *that*) introduce clauses that refer to a noun in the main clause.

Julieta, who is my sister, lives in Atlanta.

Who, whose, and *whom* ordinarily refer to people; *which* to things; and *that* to either. The possessive pronoun *whose* (in place of the awkward *of which*) sometimes refers to things.

> The poem, **whose** author is unknown, has recently been set to music.

CAUTION Do not confuse *who's* and *whose*. *Who's* is a contraction for *who is,* and *whose* indicates possession.

(3) Interrogative pronouns

The **interrogative** pronouns *who* and *whom* ask questions and change form to reflect their grammatical use in the sentence.

> **Who** asked the question? [subjective case for the subject of the sentence]

Which does not change form.

(4) Reflexive/intensive pronouns

The reflexive pronouns *myself, ourselves, yourself, himself, herself, itself,* and *themselves* refer to the subject of the clauses in which they appear. Intensive pronouns are used primarily for emphasis and are indistinguishable in form from the reflexives.

> Jake saw a picture of **himself.** [reflexive]
>
> Jake, **himself,** brought it here. [intensive]

CAUTION Do not use *myself* or *me* in place of *I* in a compound subject.

> Jake and ~~myself~~ I brought it here.
>
> ~~Me and Jake~~ Jake and I brought it here.

Hisself and *theirselves* are not accepted in college or professional writing.

James and Jerry painted the house by *themselves* ~~theirselves~~.

16b Pronouns change form to indicate the subjective, objective, or possessive case.

(1) Subjects and complements

A subject complement is a word that renames the subject. A linking verb is a form of *be* (*am, is, are, was, were*), a word expressing the senses (*look, sound, feel, taste, smell*), or a condition (*become, grow, prove, remain, seem, turn*). It relates the subject to the subject complement. (See **11c(3)**.) Pronouns that are the subjects of sentences use the subjective form.

Russell and ~~me~~ *I* were in charge.

The ones in charge were *he and I* ~~him and me~~.

Although many languages include the subject pronoun in the verb, in English it must be stated except with certain imperatives. See **11c(1)**.

(2) Objects

When a pronoun is a direct or an indirect object or the object of a preposition, it takes the objective case.

Direct object   Miguel loves **her.**
Indirect object   Miguel gave **her** his love.

Object of a   Miguel cares deeply for **her.**
preposition

(3) Modifiers

Modifiers that indicate ownership or a comparable relationship
are in the **possessive case.**

> That book is **mine.** [COMPARE That book is my book.]

CAUTION *Their* and *they* can be confused in spoken English. See the
Glossary of Usage for confusion among *their, there,*
they're, and *there're.*

16c The case of a pronoun is determined by the pronoun's use in its own clause.

(1) Compound constructions

Multiple *subjects* or *subject complements* are in the subjective
case.

> I thought **he or Dad** would come to my rescue.
>
> It was **Maria and I** who solved the problem.
>
> **She and her father** buy groceries on Saturday morning.

The first-person pronoun *I* occurs last in a compound construction.

> $\overset{and\ I}{\text{Me and}}$ Ricardo are good friends.

Multiple *objects of prepositions* are in the objective case.

> between Merrill and $\overset{me}{\text{I}}$ with Amanda and $\overset{him}{\text{he}}$

Multiple *objects of verbs* or *verbals* and *subjects of infinitives*
are in the objective case.

Clara may appoint **you or me.** [direct object]

They lent **Tom and her** ten dollars. [indirect object]

You can test the case of any pronoun in a compound construction by eliminating the accompanying noun or pronoun and the conjunction.

They elected (George and) me to the board.

Gabriel gave it to (Edwyn and) me.

To test the case of a pronoun with an appositive (a word that renames a noun or pronoun), remove the appositive.

~~Us~~ *We* students need this.

The director told ~~we~~ *us* extras to go home.

(2) *Who* or *whom*

The case form of *who* or *whoever* is determined by its grammatical function in its own clause. The subject of a verb in a subordinate clause takes the subjective case, even if the whole clause is used as an object.

I remembered **who** won the Academy Award that year. [*Who* is the subject of the clause *who won the Academy Award that year.*]

She offered help to **whoever** needed it. [*Whoever* is the subject of the clause *whoever needed it.*]

When the pronoun is the direct object or the object of a preposition, *whom* is *always* the correct form. See **11c(2)**.

They helped the people ~~who~~ *whom* they liked. [direct object]

Gabriel happily greeted ~~whoever~~ *whomever* he met that day. [direct object]

(3) *Who* or *whom* before interpolated expressions

Such expressions as *I think, he says, she believes,* and *we know* can follow either *who* or *whom.* The case still depends on the grammatical function of *who* or *whom* in its own clause. To make sure you have used the correct form, delete the intervening phrase.

> Walter picked Jan, **who** (he knows) speaks well. [*Who* is the subject of the verb *speaks.*]

> Walter picked Jan, **whom** (he knows) we all respect. [*Whom* is the object of the verb *respect.*]

(4) The case of a pronoun after *than* or *as*

In sentences with implied (rather than stated) elements, the choice of the pronoun form is important to meaning.

> She likes Clarice more than **I.** [subjective case, meaning "more than I like Clarice"]

> She likes Dana more than **me.** [objective case, meaning "more than she likes me"]

(5) Objective form with infinitives and gerunds (a verb form ending in *-ing* and used as a noun)

The subject or the object of the infinitive or gerund is always in the objective case.

> They wanted Dave and me to help **him.** [object of the infinitive in the objective case]

> Their guide tried steering **them** around the dangerous rapids. [object of the gerund in the objective case]

The possessive form of the pronoun is used before a gerund.

> I appreciated ~~him~~ his helping Denise.

The *-ing* ending marks both gerunds and participles. A participle is a verbal used as an adjective.

The man **sitting** (participle modifying *man*) at the desk annoyed us. [The participle tells us more about which man annoyed us.]

16d Pronouns agree with their antecedents (nouns that pronouns refer to).

When a pronoun has an antecedent, these two words usually agree in number.

Singular   A **wolf** has **its** own language. [*wolf—its*]
Plural   **Wolves** have **their** own language. [*wolves—their*]

A pronoun also agrees with its antecedent in gender (masculine, feminine, or neuter).

the **boy** and **his** sister [masculine antecedent]
the **girl** and **her** brother [feminine antecedent]
the **garden** and **its** weeds [neuter antecedent]

No currently available grammar checker can identify problems with pronoun-antecedent agreement. You need to rely on your own knowledge to recognize that a singular pronoun does not agree with a plural noun.

---

(1) Agreement with generic nouns or indefinite pronouns

Everybody has to live with ^*himself or herself* **themselves.** [Rephrased using a plural: *People have to live with themselves.*]

Each student has the combination to *his or her* ~~their~~ own locker. [singular compound phrase]

Singular   A lawyer represents **his or her** clients.

Plural   Lawyers represent **their** clients.

When the gender of the antecedent is clear, use the appropriate personal pronoun.

Masculine   John represents **his** clients.

Feminine   Mary represents **her** clients.

When the gender of the antecedent is not clear or when the noun could refer to either men or women, rewrite the sentence to make the noun plural or use a form of *his or her* or *himself or herself.*

College students who support themselves have little free time. [COMPARE A college student who supports *himself* or *herself* . . .]

When referring to a word such as *student,* which can include both men and women, you can avoid agreement problems by dropping the pronoun, by making the sentence passive, or by making the antecedent plural.

Each student has the combination to a private locker. [no pronoun]

The combination to a private locker is issued to each student. [passive]

Students have the combinations to their private lockers. [plural]

In spoken language a sentence such as the following is considered easy and natural; in college and professional writing, however, it is still not accepted.

Everyone *who* was invited to dinner~~, but they~~ had already eaten. [sentence revised to avoid the agreement problem]

CAUTION Be careful not to introduce errors into your own writing because you are trying to avoid sexist usage. (See **23d**.)

(2) Words joined by *and* or by *or* or *nor*

Mark and Gordon lost **their** enthusiasm.

Did **Mark or Gordon** lose **his** enthusiasm?

If one of two antecedents joined by *or* or *nor* is singular and the other is plural, the pronoun usually agrees with the nearer antecedent.

Neither the **president nor** the **senators** had announced **their** decision. [*Their* is closer to the plural antecedent *senators*.]

(3) Collective noun antecedents

When the antecedent is a collective noun, special care should be taken to avoid treating it as both singular and plural in the same sentence.

The choir **is** writing ~~**their**~~ its own music. [Because the choir is working as a unit, it is regarded as singular.]

The group of students disagree on methods, but **they** unite on basic aims. [Because the students in the group are behaving as individuals, the group is regarded as plural.]

See **23d** for ways to avoid sexist language.

16e A pronoun must refer clearly to a specific antecedent.

Clarity involves making sure that pronoun references or usage is not

- ambiguous or unclear (**16e(1)**),
- remote or awkward (**16e(2)**),
- broad or implied (**16e(3)**), or
- impersonal (**16e(4)**).

(1) Ambiguous or unclear pronoun references

When a pronoun could refer to either of two possible antecedents, there are two ways to make the antecedent clear: rewrite the sentence or replace the pronoun with a noun.

Quinn pointed out ~~to Roy that since his~~ *that because Roy's* cat was shedding, ~~he~~ *Roy* had cat hair all over his suit.

The books *that* were standing on the shelf ~~that~~ needed sorting.

A pronoun may sometimes clearly refer to two or more antecedents.

Jack and Jill met **their** Waterloo.

(2) Remote or awkward references

Rewriting a sentence to bring a pronoun and its antecedent closer together or substituting a noun for an obscure pronoun will clarify meaning.

Remote	The *sophomore* found herself the unanimously elected president of a group of animal lovers, *who* was not a joiner of organizations.
Better	The **sophomore, who** was not a joiner of organizations, found herself the unanimously elected president of a group of animal lovers.
Obscure	Before Ellen could get to the jewelry store, **it** was all sold.
Better	Before Ellen could get to the jewelry store, all the **jewelry** was sold.
Awkward	The Kiwanis Club sells tickets for the **fireworks** on the Fourth of July **that** it sponsors.
Better	The Kiwanis Club sells tickets for the fireworks that it sponsors on the Fourth of July.

(3) Broad or implied references

Pronouns such as *it, such, this, that,* and *which* may refer to a specific word or phrase or to the sense of the whole clause, sentence, or paragraph.

> Some people think that the fall of man had something to do with sex, but *that*'s a mistake. —C. S. LEWIS [*That* refers to the sense of the whole clause.]

When used carelessly, broad references can interfere with clear communication. Make each pronoun refer to a specific word.

> When class attendance is compulsory, some students feel that
> education is being forced on them. This *perception* is not true.

Express the idea referred to rather than merely implying it.

> He wanted his teachers to think he was above average, as he could
> have been if he had used *his intelligence* it to advantage.

(4) Impersonal *it*

Awkward	It was no use trying.
Revised	**There was** no use trying.
OR	**Trying was** useless.

Chapter
17 Verbs

Being able to use verbs competently is an important part of being able to write clear and effective sentences. This chapter

- identifies the various kinds of verbs (**17a**);
- identifies the various forms of verbs (**17b**);
- explains the time relationships between verbs (**17c**);
- shows the relationship between the verb and the subject as well as the ways commands, possibilities, or wishes are expressed (**17d**);
- explains agreement of subjects and verbs (**17e**);
- offers advice about *lie/lay, sit/set,* and *rise/raise* (**17f**); and
- suggests ways to avoid confusing inconsistencies with verbs (**17g**).

You will, of course, encounter many terms as you work with the various forms and functions of verbs, but understanding the following five terms is basic to understanding explanations about verbs.

Tense refers to the form of the verb that indicates time—for example, present or past.

Person refers to whether the subject of the sentence is speaking (*I, we*—first person), spoken to (*you*—second person), or spoken about (*he, she, it, one, they*—third person).

Number refers to whether the subject of the sentence is one person or thing (singular) or more than one (plural).

Voice refers to the form of the verb that defines the relationship between the subject and the action (or state) of the verb.

Mood refers to the way a speaker or writer regards an assertion—as a statement, a command, or a condition not reflected in fact.

Grammar checkers cannot detect the subtle differences in the ways we use verbs. They catch some missing verbs, some helping verbs mismatched with main verbs, and some verbs lacking *-ed* endings, but they miss at least as many as they find. They can also identify some misused infinitives but seldom other verbals (see **17c(2)**). They cannot distinguish between true passive verbs such as *have been seen* and a form of *be* followed by an adjective such as *have been healthy* and so frequently incorrectly flag passive constructions. Furthermore, they cannot tell when a passive construction is appropriate and so generally advise writers to "correct" them. They cannot find problems with improper tense forms or conditional sentences, and they occasionally flag properly used subjunctives as agreement errors.

17a Verbs change form depending on what kind of verbs they are and how they are used.

Verbs may be regular or irregular, or they may be helping verbs (auxiliaries). Verbs may be used as transitive or intransitive, or as linking verbs.

Regular and irregular verbs express action, occurrence, or existence (state of being): Claudia **studies**.

Auxiliary verbs are forms of *be, have,* or *do* that combine with a verb to indicate voice, tense, or mood: Claudia **has** studied all night.

Modal auxiliary verbs—*will, would, may, might, shall, should, can, could, must, ought, dare, need, let*—are also considered auxiliaries and shade the meaning of the verb (its aspect): Claudia **must** study all night.

Transitive verbs take a direct object: Claudia **has studied** history. [direct object]

Intransitive verbs do not take an object: Claudia **studies** hard.

Linking verbs relate the subject and a word referring to the subject (the complement). A linking verb may be a form of *be* (*am,* are, is, was, were), a verb referring to the senses (*feel, look, smell, sound, taste*), or a verb that expresses existence or becoming (*appear, become, get, grow, prove, remain, seem, stay, turn*): Claudia **is** studious. She **sounds** authoritative. She **seems** responsible.

(1) Regular and irregular verbs

Regular verbs form the past tense by adding a suffix that contains a *-d* or a *-t: laugh, laughs, laughed; build, builds, built.*

Irregular verbs do not take the *-d* or *-ed* ending. They form their past tense by changing internally: *run, ran; speak, spoke; think, thought.*

(2) Auxiliary verbs

Auxiliary verbs (helping verbs) combine with other verbs to express time or emphasis or action in progress. The present form of a verb may also be combined with another special kind of auxiliary verb, called a **modal auxiliary,** to make requests, give instructions, and express certainty, doubt, necessity, obligation, possibility, or probability: *we shall overcome, you can dream, she must sleep, they should laugh,* and so on.

CHECKLIST of Auxiliary Verbs			
Auxiliary Verbs		**Modal Auxiliary Verbs**	
be	have	shall	may
am	has	should	might
is	had		must
are			
was	do	will	can
were	does	would	could
been	did		
being			

Although the auxiliary always precedes the basic verb, other words may intervene.

Have the members **paid** their dues?

Television **will** never completely **replace** newspapers.

(3) The forms of *be*

The most irregular verb in the English language is *be*. Following is a list of forms of *be* used with various subjects in the present and past tenses.

	First Person	Second Person	Third Person
Present	I am	you are	he/she/it is [singular]
	we are	you are	they are [plural]
Past	I was	you were	he/she/it/ was [singular]
	we were	you were	they were [plural]

CAUTION Some dialects use *be* in place of *am, is,* or *are* (the present forms of *be*). Some also use *be* with the present participle (see **17a(2)**) to indicate habitual action. College writing and professional writing require the conventional forms of *be*, as shown in the list above.

She ⁀*be* a fine hockey player. [*be* instead of *is*]
   is

He ~~be walking~~ to class. [Habitual action—he always walks to class.]
   walks

He ⁀walking to class today. [Simple action—his walking today was unusual.]
   is

In constructions where the subject is equivalent to a complement, do not omit the verb.

Siriphan *is* very homesick.

(4) Transitive, linking, and intransitive verbs

A noun or a pronoun follows a **transitive verb** and completes its meaning (a direct object). A transitive verb can also be made passive. (See **17b(1)**.)

The hammer **bent** the nail. [*Nail,* the direct object, receives the action of *hammer.*]

An **intransitive verb** does not accept a direct object, and it cannot be made passive.

The bell **tolled** repeatedly. [The adverb *repeatedly* modifies the verb.]

One kind of intransitive verb, a **linking verb,** uses a noun, pronoun, or adjective to complete its meaning, but it cannot be made passive. (See the *Glossary of Terms.*)

The bell **looks** fragile. [The subject complement, *fragile,* refers to *bell.*]

Some verbs can be transitive or intransitive, depending on the sentence.

Transitive	Darlene **studies** the book. [*book*—direct object]
Intransitive	Darlene **studies** all night. [complete—no object or complement]

A dictionary will indicate whether a verb is transitive or intransitive, or whether it can be either.

17b The conjugation of a verb is based on its principal parts.

A **conjugation** is a table of the various forms of a verb.

(1) The complete conjugation of a verb

The following conjugation of the verb *see* shows the relationships among tense, person, voice, and mood. (See **17c–d.**) It also shows how auxiliary verbs help make a verb passive and form the perfect tenses.

Indicative Mood

		Active Voice		Passive Voice	
		Singular	*Plural*	*Singular*	*Plural*
Present tense	**1st**	I see	we see	I am seen	we are seen
	2nd	you see	you see	you are seen	you are seen
	3rd	one (he/she/it) sees	they see	one (he/she/it) is seen	they are seen
Past tense	**1st**	I saw	we saw	I was seen	we were seen
	2nd	you saw	you saw	you were seen	you were seen
	3rd	one (he/she/it) saw	they saw	one (he/she/it) was seen	they were seen
Future tense	**1st**	I shall (will) see	we shall (will) see	I shall (will) be seen	we shall (will) be seen

		Active Voice		Passive Voice	
		Singular	*Plural*	*Singular*	*Plural*
	2nd	you will see	you will see	you will be seen	you will be seen
	3rd	one (he/she/it) will see	they will see	one (he/she/it) will be seen	they will be seen
Present perfect tense	**1st**	I have seen	we have seen	I have been seen	we have been seen
	2nd	you have seen	you have seen	you have been seen	you have been seen
	3rd	one (he/she/it) has seen	they have seen	one (he/she/it) has been seen	they have been seen
Past perfect tense	**1st**	I had seen	we had seen	I had been seen	we had been seen
	2nd	you had seen	you had seen	you had been seen	you had been seen
	3rd	one (he/she/it) had seen	they had seen	one (he/she/it) had been seen	they had been seen
Future perfect tense (seldom used)	**1st**	I shall (will) have seen	we shall (will) have seen	I shall (will) have been seen	we shall (will) have been seen
	2nd	you will have seen	you will have seen	you will have been seen	you will have been seen
	3rd	one (he/she/it) will have seen	they will have seen	one (he/she/it) will have been seen	they will have been seen

Imperative Mood

	Active Voice	Passive Voice
	see	be seen

Subjunctive Mood

	Active Voice	Passive Voice
	see	see

The subjunctive is difficult to distinguish from other forms of a verb except for the subjunctive forms of *be.* (See **17d(2)**.)

If I **were** you, I would quit. [See **17d(2)**.]

(2) The principal parts of verbs

The three principal parts of verbs are the base form—or simple present—(*see*), which is the same as the infinitive (*see*); the past form (*saw*); and the past participle (*seen*). (A participle is a verb form that can function as an adjective. The *to* in *to see* is an infinitive marker, not precisely part of the infinitive.) Some consider the present participle (*seeing*) to be a fourth principal part. (See *principal parts* in the *Glossary of Terms*.)

CHECKLIST of the Principal Parts of Verbs		
Part I: Principal Parts of Verbs Sometimes Misused		
Present	**Past**	**Past Participle**
arise	arose	arisen
ask	asked	asked

Present	Past	Past Participle
attack	attacked	attacked
bear	bore	borne/born
begin	began	begun
blow	blew	blown
break	broke	broken
bring	brought	brought
burst	burst	burst
choose	chose	chosen
cling	clung	clung
come	came	come
do	did	done
drag	dragged	dragged
draw	drew	drawn
drink	drank	drunk
drive	drove	driven
drown	drowned	drowned
eat	ate	eaten
fall	fell	fallen
fly	flew	flown
forgive	forgave	forgiven
freeze	froze	frozen
give	gave	given
go	went	gone
grow	grew	grown
happen	happened	happened
know	knew	known
ride	rode	ridden
ring	rang	rung
rise	rose	risen

Present	Past	Past Participle
run	ran	run
see	saw	seen
shake	shook	shaken
speak	spoke	spoken
spin	spun	spun
spit	spat	spat
steal	stole	stolen
sting	stung	stung
swear	swore	sworn
swim	swam	swum
swing	swung	swung
take	took	taken
tear	tore	torn
throw	threw	thrown
wear	wore	worn
weave	wove	woven
wring	wrung	wrung
write	wrote	written

Part II: Verbs with Options for the Past or Past Participle

Present	Past	Past Participle
awaken	awakened OR awoke	awakened
dive	dived OR dove	dived
get	got	got OR gotten
hang (things)	hung	hung
hang (people)	hanged	hanged
shrink	shrank OR shrunk	shrunk OR shrunken
sing	sang OR sung	sung
sink	sank OR sunk	sunk

Present	Past	Past Participle
spring	sprang OR sprung	sprung
stink	stank OR stunk	stunk
strive	strove OR strived	striven OR strived
wake	woke OR waked	woken OR waked

Part III: Principal Parts of Troublesome Verbs

Present	Past	Past Participle	Present Participle
lay	laid	laid	laying [*to put down; transitive*]
lead	led	led	leading
lie	lay	lain	lying [*to recline; intransitive*]
loosen	loosened	loosened	loosening
lose	lost	lost	losing
pay	paid	paid	paying
set	set	set	setting [*to place; transitive*]
sit	sat	sat	sitting [*to rest on the buttocks;* intransitive]
study	studied	studied	studying

(3) Participles

Participles such as *rising* or *shrunk* are never used alone as the verb of a sentence. When an *-ing* or an *-en* form or an irregular participial form such as *shrunk* is part of the verb, it always has at least one helping verb. Whether the *-ed* form is a verb or a past participle depends on the context. Both the past and present participles can work as modifiers, and they can also form part of the verb.

Sentences with Participles	Sentences with Simple Verbs
We could see heat waves *rising* from the road. [present participle]	Heat waves *rise* from the road. [simple present tense verb]
We ate pastries *baked* yesterday. [past participle]	We *baked* pastries yesterday. [simple past tense verb]

Be especially careful not to confuse nouns modified by participles with actual sentences. (See **13a.**)

CAUTION Although it is easy to remember a clearly pronounced *-d* or *-ed* (*added, repeated*), it is sometimes harder to remember a needed *-d* or *-ed* in such expressions as *supposed to* or *used to* when the sound is not emphasized in speech. (See **15a.**)

     asked   *prejudiced*
Yesterday, I ~~ask~~ myself if the judge was ~~prejudice~~.

  used
He ~~use~~ to smoke.

    supposed
I am not ~~suppose~~ to be the boss.

  talked
She ~~talk~~ to Ellen yesterday.

17c Verb tense makes time relationships clear.

Verbs usually change form to show whether an action happened in the present, the past, or the future. This change of form is called **tense,** and through tense a verb can show, for example, that one action began yesterday and is still going on but that another action began yesterday and ended yesterday. Tenses are based on primary forms called principal parts (*ask, asked, asked*). (See **17b.**)

Verbs

Simple Tenses

Present	We often write letters. [based on the base form *write*]
Past	After graduation, we wrote letters. [change of form to show past tense]
Future	We will write letters after graduation. [future time expressed using an auxiliary]

Perfect Tenses

Present	We have written letters since graduation. [time expressed using an auxiliary with the past participle]
Past	We had written letters after graduation. [time expressed using an auxiliary with the past participle]
Future	We will have written letters before graduation. [time expressed using an auxiliary with the past participle]

(1) Tense forms

Tense is not the same as time. Although tenses refer to time (see page 333), the tense forms often do not reflect divisions of actual time. For instance, as the following examples show, the present tense form is certainly not restricted to present time.

Present tense (timeless or habitual present, now)

Dana **uses** common sense. [habitual action]

Blind innocence **sees** no evil. [timeless truth]

The new supermall **opens** tomorrow. [present with an adverb denoting the future]

In 1939 Hitler **attacks** Poland. [historical present]

Joseph Conrad **writes** about what he **sees** in the human heart. [literary present]

Past tense (before now)

They **played** a good game. [action completed in the past]

Adolpho **played** well in those days. [action contained in the past]

We **were learning** to use a computer. [continuing action in the past]

Future tense (at a future time, after now)

We **will see** the movie. [some time after now]

We **will be spending** June in the mountains. [continuing action in the future]

Present perfect (up to now)

She **has used** her savings wisely.

I **have seen** the movie.

Past perfect (before a specific time in the past)

Terese **had planned** to meet with me before class.

Future perfect (a specific time in the future)

Our bumpers **will have rusted** by the time he changes his mind.

(2) Logical sequence of tense forms

Combinations of tense forms can make very fine distinctions in relation to actual time.

When the speaker **finished**, everyone **applauded**. [Both actions took place at the same definite time in the past.]

When I **had been** here for two weeks, I **learned** that my application for financial aid **had been denied**. [The first *had* before *been* indicates a time before the action described by *learned*. The second *had been* indicates action completed before that indicated by *learned*.]

17d Verbs have voice and mood.

(1) Voice

Active voice emphasizes the subject as the *doer* of the action. **Passive voice** deemphasizes the doer of the action and makes the subject the *receiver*. (See **21d(1)** and the *Glossary of Terms*.) To make an active verb passive, use the appropriate form of *be* with the base verb. **Intransitive verbs** are used only in the active voice.

Active	The interviewer rejected Tom's application. [The subject *interviewer* acts on the object *application*.]
Passive	Tom's application was rejected by the interviewer. [The subject *application* is acted upon.]

Most writers choose the active voice because it is clearer, more precise, more concise, and more vigorous than the passive. Many also prefer the active voice because, unlike the passive, it allows people to take responsibility for their actions. Careful writers generally reserve the passive voice for occasions when the agent (the person or thing doing the act) is unknown or unimportant, or when the action itself is more important than the agent. This use of the passive is reflected in scientific writing, where the experiment is more important than the experimenter. (See **21d(1)**.)

(2) Mood

The **indicative mood** makes statements—a definite attitude; the **imperative mood** issues commands or requests—an insistent attitude; and the **subjunctive mood** expresses situations that are hypothetical or conditional—a tentative attitude.

Indicative	Dannice calls me every day.
Imperative	Call me every day, Dannice!
Subjunctive	It is important that Dannice call me every day.

The subjunctive mood, though rare, still occurs in certain fixed expressions, such as *God bless you,* and is also used with certain verbs, to express wishes, and with certain other hypothetical meanings.

I wish I **were** in Ashville.

17e Verbs must agree with their subjects.

Agree means that the subject and verb match. That is, if a subject is plural, the verb must have a plural form, and if the subject is singular, the verb must have a singular form. The following subsections give guidance on how to handle common trouble spots:

- when words come between the subject and verb (**17e(1)**) or when the endings are not clear (**17e(2)**);
- when the subject is compound (**17e(3–4)**);
- when the sentence is inverted (**17e(5)**);
- when the subject is a relative or indefinite pronoun (**17e(6–7)**), a collective noun (**17e(8)**), or *what* with a linking verb (**17e(9)**); and
- when the subject is a noun that is plural in form but singular in meaning, a word used as a word, or a title (**17e(10)**).

A singular subject takes a singular verb, and a plural subject takes a plural verb. Except for forms of *have* or *be,* the only verbs that change form to indicate the number and person of their subjects are present tense verbs. For that reason, most problems with subject-verb agreement occur when present tense is used.

	Present Tense	**Past Tense**
Singular	A young professional **works** long hours to be successful.	A young professional **worked** long hours to be successful.

Plural	Many young professionals **work** long hours to be successful.	Many young professionals **worked** long hours to be successful.

It is easy to confuse the endings of *verbs* (where -*s* indicates **singular**) with those of *nouns* (where -*s* indicates **plural**).

Subject + *s*	Verb + *s*
The **students need** attention.	The **student needs** attention.
Zinnias bloom best in the sun.	A **zinnia blooms** best in the sun.

If the subject of your sentence is singular but is not *I* or *you,* the verb needs the -*s* ending.

That talk show host asks silly questions. [The sound of the -*s* may be masked in speech if the word that follows begins with an *s.*]

Grammar checkers only occasionally flag agreement errors and frequently suggest bizarre "corrections." If you understand subject-verb agreement, you may find a grammar checker useful for finding errors you have overlooked in proofreading. If, however, you are not confident about subject-verb agreement, using a grammar checker can be risky.

(1) Words coming between the subject and the verb

The **rhythm** of the pounding waves **is** calming. [*Waves* is the object of a prepositional phrase, not the subject.]

Phrases such as *accompanied by, along with, as well as, in addition to, including, no less than, not to mention,* and *together with* generally introduce a prepositional phrase and do not affect the number of the subject.

> Her **salary** together with tips **is** just enough to live on.

> **Tips** together with her salary **are** just enough to live on.

(2) Subject and verb endings not clearly sounded in rapid speech

> **Economists seem** concerned. [might sound like "Economist seem" concerned, but the former is correct]

> She ~~ask~~ asks Sybil first.

(3) Compound subjects joined by *and*

> My two best **friends** and my **fiancé hate** each other.

> The **coach** and the **umpire were** at home plate.

> **Writing on a legal pad** and **writing with a computer are** not the same at all. [gerund phrases—COMPARE Two actions are not the same.]

A compound subject that refers to a single person or unit takes a singular verb.

> The **writer and director** of *The Thin Red Line* **is** Terence Malik.

(4) Subjects joined by *either . . . or*

> Either Patty or Tom **was** asked to preside.

If one subject is singular and one is plural, the verb agrees with the subject closer to the verb.

> Neither the basket nor the **apples were** expensive.

> Neither the apples nor the **basket was** expensive.

(5) Inverted word order or *there* + verb constructions

Hardest hit by the subzero temperatures and snow **were** the large **cities** of the Northeast.

There **are** several **ways** to protect yourself from a tornado.

(6) Relative pronouns (*who, which, that*) as subjects

It is the **doctor who** often **suggests** a diet.

Those are the **books that are** out of print.

The Starion is the only **one** of the new models **that includes** air conditioning as standard equipment. [*That* refers to *one*.]

(7) Indefinite pronouns

Each, either, everybody, one, and *anyone* are considered singular and so require singular verbs.

Either of them **is willing** to shovel the driveway.

Everybody in our apartment building **has** a parking place.

Other indefinite pronouns such as *all, any, some, none, half,* and *most* can be either singular or plural, depending on whether they refer to a unit or quantity (singular) or to a collection of individuals (plural).

Wendy collects comic books; **some are** very valuable.

The bank would not take all the money because **some was** foreign.

Singular subjects that are preceded by *every* or *each* and that are joined by *and* agree with a singular verb.

Every cat and dog in the county **has** to be vaccinated.

Each fork and spoon **has** to be polished.

Placing *each* after a plural subject does not affect the verb form.

The cat and the dog **each have** their good points.

(8) Collective nouns and phrases

Collective nouns and phrases refer to a group of individual things. Whether they require a singular or a plural verb depends on whether the sentence refers to the group as a whole or to the individual items in the group.

Singular (Regarded as a Unit)	Plural (Regarded as Individuals or Parts)
Ten million gallons is a lot of oil.	**Ten million gallons** of oil **were spilled.**
The **majority is** very large.	The **majority** of us **are** in favor.
The **number is** very small.	A **number were** absent.

In American English, nouns that refer to a group as a whole (collective nouns) are not treated as plural.

The committee ~~are~~ is meeting tonight.

Although the use of *data* and *media* as singular nouns (instead of *datum* and *medium*) has gained currency in conversational English, treat *data* and *media* as plural in college writing.

The media **have** shaped public opinion.

The data **are** in the appendix.

(9) Linking verbs with *what*

Because the pronoun *what* is singular or plural depending on whether the word (or word group) it refers to is singular or plural, the verb agrees with its complement in sentences such as the following.

> What I think **is** my own **business.**
>
> What tastes best **is different** for each of us.
>
> What our parents gave us **were memories** to be cherished.

(10) Titles of single works, words spoken of as words, and nouns plural in form but singular in meaning

Nouns that look like they are plural but are treated as singular include *economics, electronics, measles, mumps, news,* and *physics.*

> Economics **is** important for a business major.

Some nouns (such as *athletics, politics, series, deer,* and *sheep*) can be either singular or plural, depending on the meaning.

> Statistics is an interesting subject.
>
> Statistics are often misleading.

Four Steps to Subject-Verb Agreement

Step 1   **Is the verb present tense?** If yes, check the subject.

Step 2   **Is the subject a singular noun such as *book, tree,* or *hope*?** If yes, use the form of the verb with *-s.*

Step 3   **Is the subject a singular pronoun?** If yes, check to see if it is third person.

Step 4   **Is the pronoun third-person singular?** If yes, use the form of the verb with *-s.*

17f Sit and set, lie and lay, and rise and raise are often confused.

You can *set, lay,* or *raise* something, but you yourself *sit, lie,* or *rise.*

Intransitive (see 17a(4))

Sit **down. You** sat **up. Sitting** down, I thought it over.
Lie down. He **lay** there for hours. It **has lain** next to the shed for months. **Lying** down, I fell asleep.
I **rise** before daybreak. I **rose** even earlier yesterday. I **have** always **risen** at seven. I am **rising** earlier each day.

Transitive (see 17a(4))

I **set** the clock. I **set** it down. It had been **set** there. We were **setting** the pieces on the tray.
We **lay** those aside. I **laid** the pencils next to the pads. She **was laying** our tests next to our seats.
I **raise** the window each night. I **raised** the window last night. I am **raising** the window to clear the smoke.

Thinking of these verbs in pairs and learning their principal parts can help you remember which form to use. *Sit, lie,* and *rise* are intransitive; *set, lay,* and *raise* are transitive. *Set, lay,* and *raise* mean "to place or put something somewhere." For example, to *set* the table means to *lay* the silverware next to the plates. *Sit, lie,* and *rise,* the intransitive verbs of the pairs, mean "be seated," "get into a horizontal position," and "get up." For example, *you sit down* or *lie down* or *rise up.*

17g Unnecessary shifts in tense or mood can confuse readers.

Writers deliberately use a variety of tenses when they write about actions or events happening at different times. In other situations, however, changing tenses, mood, or voice can be distracting to the reader. Most shifts occur with literary or historical topics. Literary action occurs in fictional time and by convention is referred to in the present tense. Historical events may be referred to in the historical present. (See 17c(1).) Shifts can make reading a passage difficult.

The *Padshahnama* ~~was~~ *is* [It still exists.] an ancient manuscript that is owned by the ~~Royal~~ Library at Windsor Castle. This manuscript ~~will detail~~ *details* [the literary present] the history of Shah-Jahan, the ~~Muslim ruler~~ who has [The action was completed many years ago.] commissioned ~~the~~ building of the Taj Mahal during his reign in India. Battles, court scenes, and the adventures of Shah-Jahan's sons are among the significant events depicted in the *Padshahnama*. Shah-Jahan ~~is~~ *was* imprisoned [Use of the literary present here conflicts with the past tense later in the sentence.] for the last eight years of his life by his son, Awrangzeb, who was the new Mughal ruler.

Effective Sentences

Effective Sentences

Chapter 18

Sentence Unity: Consistency

Good writing is unified and sticks to its purpose. Consistent throughout, it has no shifts in grammatical structure, tone, style, or viewpoint. This chapter can help you understand how to revise

- unrelated ideas (**18a**),
- a series of details into a clear sequence (**18b**),
- mixed metaphors and constructions (**18c**), and
- faulty predication (**18d–e**).

18a Relating ideas clearly in a sentence helps the reader.

An endangered species, tigers live in India, where ~~there are many~~ *their natural habitat is shrinking because of population pressures* ~~people.~~ [The added phrase clarifies the cause-and-effect relationship between the tigers' habitat and their endangerment.]

18b Arranging details in a clear sequence makes your point clear.

Although detail usually makes writing more interesting, too much of it can be distracting. Do not include details that are not necessary to develop your point.

When I was only sixteen, I left home to attend a college that was nearby ~~and that my uncle had graduated from twenty years earlier.~~ [If the detail about the uncle is important, include it in another sentence. If not, delete it.]

18c Careful writers avoid mixed metaphors and mixed constructions.

(1) Mixed metaphors

Mixed metaphors combine different images and create illogical comparisons.

If you are on the fast track *to a brilliant corporate career* ~~up the corporate ladder,~~ it is best to keep working as hard as you can.

(2) Mixed constructions

A sentence that begins with one kind of construction and shifts to another is a **mixed construction.** (See **18d–e.**) Mixed constructions often omit the subject or the predicate.

When Simon plays the didgeridoo *it* sounds like a wounded cow.

BETTER Simon's playing makes the didgeridoo sound like a wounded cow.

18d Faulty predication can lead to problems.

Faulty predication occurs when the subject and predicate do not fit together logically.

One kind of prejudice is a salesclerk~~,~~ 's ignoring ~~especially after she or he has ignored~~ an elderly customer. [The ignoring of the customer, not the salesclerk, is an example of prejudice.]

18e Faulty predication in definitions is illogical.

(1) Constructing definitions logically

Constructions combining *is* with *when, where,* or *because* are often illogical because forms of *to be* signify identity or equality between the subject and what follows.

The ~~reason the~~ package arrived so late ~~is~~ because he didn't mail it soon enough.

The Internet ~~is when~~ allows you to look at text and images from across the world.

People go to a ~~A~~ grocery store ~~is where people go~~ to buy food.

(2) Defining words precisely (see 2e(7))

A short dictionary definition may be adequate when you need to define a term or convey a special meaning that may be unfamiliar to the reader.

Here *galvanic* means "produced as if by electric shock." (See 30d.)

Giving an example of a synonym or two may clarify the meaning of a term. Such synonyms are often used as appositives.

Machismo, confidence with an attitude, is described in the article.

Many homophones (*be* and *bee, in* and *inn, see* and *sea*) are not spelling problems.

To set the terms of the discussion, make clear to the reader which meaning you are using or formulate your own definitions of the concepts you wish to clarify.

In this paper, I use the word *communism* in the Marxist sense of social organization based on the holding of all property in common.

Knowledge is seasoning for the mind's palate.

Clichés could be defined as thoughts that have hardened.

A formal definition first states the term to be defined and puts it into a class, then differentiates it from other members of its class.

A *phosphene* [term] is a luminous visual image [class] that results from applying pressure to the eyeball [differentiation].

Chapter

19   Subordination and Coordination

Subordination and coordination clarify structural relationships among ideas and help readers follow your train of thought. (See 12b and 13b.) This chapter offers advice on revising

- short, choppy sentences (19a),
- long, stringy sentences (19b), and
- faulty or excessive subordination (19c).

Subordinate means "being of lower structural rank." Subordinate structures such as phrases, appositives, or subordinate clauses make the ideas they express appear less important than the ideas expressed in independent clauses, whether those ideas are really less important or not. In the following sentences, subordinate clauses are italicized, and the independent clauses are boldfaced.

Subordinate Clause	Main Clause
After they ran the obstacle course,	**they splashed water on their faces.**
After they splashed water on their faces,	**they ran the obstacle course.**

Reversing the clauses changes the meaning of the sentence. In the following sentence, the subordinate clause contains the vital information; the independent clause simply gives it a context.

The weather service announced *that a tornado was headed straight for town.* [The subordinate clause is the direct object of the sentence.]

Coordinate means "being of equal structural rank." Two grammatically equal ideas are expressed in coordinate structures such as two independent clauses.

> **They ran the obstacle course,**
> and
> **they splashed their faces with water.**

Coordination also gives ideas equal structural emphasis.

> a **stunning** and **unexpected** conclusion [coordinate adjectives]
> **in the attic** or **in the basement** [compound prepositional phrases]

19a Careful subordination can combine a series of related short sentences into longer, more effective units.

Choppy I was taking eighteen hours of course work. I wanted to graduate in three years. It turned out to be too much. I also had a full-time job at the newspaper. I just couldn't do both.

Revised I was taking eighteen hours of course work because I wanted to graduate in three years, but it turned out to be too much. Since I already had a full-time job at the newspaper, I just couldn't do both.

Use some of the following subordinate structures to relate the other ideas to the main one.

(1) Adjectives and adjectival phrases

~~The road was slick~~ with ice, ~~it looked~~ shiny and black.~~ It was very treacherous.

Slick the , road (handwritten insertions)

(2) Adverbs and adverbial phrases

~~Season~~ the ground beef with garlic and Italian herbs. ~~Use a lot of garlic. Go lighter on the herbs.~~ ~~Brown~~ it over low heat.

After seasoning heavily lightly with , brown slowly (handwritten insertions)

OR

Season the ground beef **heavily** with garlic and **lightly** with Italian herbs, and brown it **slowly.**

(3) Appositives and contrasting elements

Philip's meanness ~~was~~ a small-minded act.~~ It was noticed.~~ ~~But it was~~ not criticized.

but (handwritten insertion)

(4) Subordinate clauses

Subordinate clauses are linked and related to main clauses by subordinating conjunctions and relative pronouns. These subordinators signal whether a clause is related to the base sentence by **time** (*after, before, since, until, when, while*), **place** (*where, wherever*), **reason** (*as, because, how, so that, since*), **condition** (*although, if, unless, whether*), or **additional information** (*that, which, who, whose*). (See pages 286–87 and 311–12 for a list of these subordinators.)

~~The~~ thunderstorm ended.~~ Then~~ we saw a rainbow.~~ It~~ seemed to promise a pleasant evening.

When the , which (handwritten insertions)

19b Using subordination and coordination is preferable to stringing several main clauses together.

Do not overuse coordinating connectives like *and, but, however, or, so, then*, and *therefore*. For ways to revise stringy or loose compound sentences, see **22c**. Methods of subordination that apply to combining two or more sentences also apply to revising faulty or excessive coordination in a single sentence.

(1) Subordination

Stringy	**I can't float. I just sink. I even hold my breath.** [three loosely related sentences]
Better	*Even though I hold my breath,* **I seem to sink rather than float.** [one subordinate clause and one independent clause]

(2) Coordination

The tornado hit, and the town was leveled. [equal grammatical emphasis on *the tornado* and *the town*]

COMPARE The town was leveled when the tornado hit. [Subordinating *the tornado* emphasizes *the town*.]

OR The tornado hit, leveling the town. [Subordinating *the town* emphasizes *the tornado*.]

(3) Logical connections

When
∧I slammed the car door on my hand, ~~and~~ I broke three fingers.

[Subordinate to show a cause-and-effect relationship between ideas.]

OR

I broke three fingers because I slammed the car door on my hand.

CAUTION When introducing a single adjectival clause, do not use *but* or *and* before *which, who,* or *whom.*

Leela is a musician ~~and~~ who can play several instruments.

19c Faulty or excessive subordination can confuse the reader.

Although
Chen was only a substitute pitcher, ~~winning~~ *he won* half of his games. [*Although* establishes the relationship between the ideas.]

insecure, idle
Some people ~~who are not busy and who are insecure when they are involved in personal relationships~~ worry ~~all the time~~ about whether their friends truly love them.

Chapter

20 Parallelism

Parallelism contributes to ease in reading by making ideas that are parallel in meaning parallel in structure. It also provides clarity and rhythm. This chapter comments on

- balancing similar grammatical elements (**20a**),
- clarifying parallel structure (**20b**), and
- dealing with correlative constructions (**20c**).

Parallel elements appear in lists or series, in compound structures, in comparisons, and in contrasting elements.

I like to swim, to dance, and ~~having~~ fun. [*to have* written above]

In the following examples, verbals used as subjects and complements are parallel in form.

> **To define** flora is **to define** climate. —*NATIONAL GEOGRAPHIC*
>
> **Seeing** is **believing.**

20a Similar grammatical elements need to be balanced.

For parallel structure, balance nouns with nouns, prepositional phrases with prepositional phrases, and clauses with clauses.

(1) Parallel words and phrases

The Africans carried with them a pattern of kinship
that emphasized ‖ **collective survival,**
‖ **mutual aid,**

cooperation,
mutual solidarity,
interdependence,
and ‖ responsibility for others.

—JOSEPH L. WHITE

She had ‖ no time to be human,
‖ no time to be happy.

—SEAN O'FALLON

(2) Parallel clauses

I remember Iyatiku's sister, Sun Woman,
‖ who held so many things in her bundle,
‖ who went away to the east. —PAULA GUNN ALLEN

(3) Parallel sentences

‖ When I stepped up with my left foot, I squelched.
‖ When I stepped up with my right foot, I gurgled.

20b Parallel structures need to be clear to the reader.

Repeating a preposition, an article, the *to* of the infinitive, or the introductory word of a phrase or clause can make parallel structure clear.

The reward rests not ‖ **in** the task
but ‖ **in** the pay. —JOHN KENNETH GALBRAITH

I was happy in the thought
‖ **that** our influence was helpful
and ‖ **that** I was doing the work I loved
and ‖ **that** I could make a living out of it. —IDA B. WELLS

To establish a relationship among sentences, the first three sentences in the following paragraph are parallel, all beginning with a subordinate clause starting with *when*.

When you're three years old and stick mashed potatoes up your nose, that's expected. **When you're six** and make your bed but it looks like you're still in it, you deserve some credit for trying. **When you're nine** and prepare the family meal but the casserole looks worse than the kitchen, you should be applauded for your effort. But somewhere along the line, some responsible adult should say, "You're too old for this nonsense."

—DAN KILEY, *The Peter Pan Syndrome: Men Who Have Never Grown Up*

20c Conjunctions such as *both . . . and* (correlatives) require parallel structures.

Correlatives (*both . . . and, either . . . or, neither . . . nor, not only . . . but also, whether . . . or*) link sentence elements that are always parallel.

Whether at home or at work, he was always busy.

The team not   practices
~~Not only~~ ~~practicing~~ at 6 a.m. during the week, but ~~the team~~ also scrimmages on Sunday afternoons.

OR

does the team practice   *it*
Not only ~~practicing~~ at 6 a.m. during the week, but ~~the team~~ also scrimmages on Sunday afternoons.

Chapter
21 Emphasis

You can emphasize ideas by using subordination and coordination (chapter **19**), parallelism (chapter **20**), and exact word choice (chapter **24**) and also by writing concisely (chapter **25**). This chapter presents additional ways to emphasize material, such as

- placing words at the beginnings or ends of sentences (**21a**),
- using periodic sentences (**21b**),
- arranging ideas in climactic order (**21c**),
- using forceful verbs (**21d**),
- repeating words (**21e**),
- inverting sentence order (**21f**), and
- varying sentence length (**21g**).

21a Placing words at the beginning or end of a sentence emphasizes them.

~~In today's society, most~~ *Good* good jobs ~require a college education~ *today* ~~as part of the background you are supposed to have.~~

Traffic roared
~I could hear the roar of traffic~ outside my hotel room in Chicago~ ~~when I was there.~~

The colon and the dash often precede an emphatic ending. (See also **31d** and **31e**.)

In short, the freedom that the American writer finds in Europe brings him, full circle, back to himself, with the responsibility for his development where it always was: in his own hands.

—JAMES BALDWIN

Until fairly recently, the pattern was that the father and sons worked, and, to whatever extent their earnings allowed, the mothers and daughters were supposed to display culture, religion, luxury, and other assorted fine feelings of society—in addition to seeing that the housework got done.   —JUDITH MARTIN

21b A periodic sentence surrounded by cumulative sentences is emphasized.

In a **cumulative sentence,** the main idea (the independent clause or sentence base) comes first; less important ideas or details follow. In a **periodic sentence,** however, the main idea comes last, just before the period.

> **Cumulative**   History has amply proved that large forces can be defeated by smaller forces superior in arms, organization, morale, and spirit.
>
> **Periodic**   That large forces can be defeated by smaller forces superior in arms, organization, morale, and spirit is one important lesson of history.

Both types of sentences can be effective. Because cumulative sentences are more common, however, the infrequently used periodic sentence is often the more emphatic.

21c When ideas are arranged from least to most important, the last idea receives the most emphasis.

> They could hear the roar of the artillery, the crash of falling timbers, the shrieks of the wounded.

Violating this principle can achieve a humorous effect, appropriate only when a writer intends to be humorous.

Contemporary man, of course, has no such peace of mind. He finds himself in the midst of a crisis of faith. He is what we fashionably call "alienated." He has seen the ravages of war, he has known natural catastrophes, he has been to singles bars. —WOODY ALLEN

21d Active, forceful verbs can add emphasis to sentences.

(1) Active voice (see 17d(1))

Active voice emphasizes the *doer* of the action by making the doer the subject of the sentence. **Passive voice** emphasizes the *receiver* of the action, minimizes the role of the doer, and results in wordier sentences.

Active   All citizens should insist on adequate medical care.

Passive   Adequate medical care should be insisted on by all citizens.

Because whoever or whatever is responsible for the action is no longer the subject, sentences in the passive voice are often less precise. The passive voice is appropriate, however, when the doer of an action is unknown or unimportant.

Passive   The television set was stolen. [The thief is unknown.]

When reporting research or scientific experiments, writers often choose to use the passive voice to preserve their objectivity and to emphasize the work being done on a project rather than who is doing it.

Passive   The experiment was conducted under carefully controlled conditions over several months.

Unless they have a strong reason to use the passive voice, good writers prefer the active voice.

(2) Action verbs and forceful linking verbs

Forms of *have* or *be* rob your writing of energy and forceful-ness. The real action often lies in a verbal phrase or in the object or complement.

Our college ~~is~~ always *wins* ~~the winner of~~ the conference. [The subject complement—*winner*—contains the real action conveyed more forcefully by the verb *win*.]

The meat *smells* ~~has a~~ rotten ~~smell~~. [The action needs to come in the verb—*smells*—rather than in the noun serving as subject complement—*smell*.]

21e Repeating important words gives them emphasis.

Although good writers avoid *unnecessary* repetition (see chapter 25), they also understand that *deliberate* repetition emphasizes an idea central to their purpose.

> We forget all too soon the things we thought we could never forget. We forget the loves and the betrayals alike, forget what we whispered and what we screamed, forget who we are.
>
> —JOAN DIDION

21f Inverting the standard word order of a sentence gives it emphasis.

> At the feet of the tallest and plushiest offices lie the crummiest slums. —E. B. WHITE [COMPARE The crummiest slums lie at the feet of the tallest and plushiest offices.]

21g A short sentence following one or more long ones is emphasized.

In the last two decades there has occurred a series of changes in American life, the extent, durability, and significance of which no one has yet measured. No one can.   —IRVING HOWE

Chapter
22   Variety

Varying the kinds of sentences you use can make your writing lively and distinctive, but relying too heavily on a few familiar structures often makes writing predictable. Some of the ways to vary sentence structure that are covered in this chapter are

- combining choppy sentences (**22a**);
- varying sentence beginnings (**22b**);
- avoiding stringy compound sentences (**22c**);
- inserting words or phrases between the subject and the verb (**22d**); and
- using questions, commands, or exclamations instead of statements (**22e**).

Both of the following paragraphs express the same ideas in virtually the same words, both use acceptable sentence patterns, and both are grammatically correct. Variety in sentence structure and length, however, gives one paragraph a stronger rhythm than the other.

Not Varied

The land is small, subdued. Its colors are low in key. The salt marshes and the low houses at their margins have a comforting dimension, and the woods beyond, the hidden ponds, and the suddenly revealed harbors do, too. You should, however, look outward. The sea is always there. The sea is a great presence, for it is fraught with sublimity. You may in some places not actually see the ocean, but you can sense its proximity and catch whiffs of its tang. You hear or seem to hear its distant roar and rut. [five simple sentences and three compound ones]

Varied

The land is small, subdued; its colors are low in key. The salt marshes, the low houses at their margins, the woods beyond, the hidden ponds, the suddenly revealed harbors have a comforting dimension. But look outward and there is always the sea, a great presence fraught with sublimity. Even where you cannot actually see the ocean, you sense its proximity, catch whiffs of its tang, hear or think you hear its distant roar and rut. —EDWARD B. GARSIDE [This paragraph contains four sentences of varying length and structure: one simple, two compound, and one complex. The sentences begin with subjects, a coordinating conjunction, and an adverb.]

If you have difficulty distinguishing between various types of sentence structure, review the fundamentals treated in chapter 11, as well as those in 12b.

22a A series of short, simple sentences sounds choppy. (See 21g.)

You can lengthen some sentences by showing how the ideas are subordinate or coordinate. (See chapter 19.)

Choppy   The Maine coast and the Oregon coast look very much alike. The houses by the water, however, are different. It's a matter of architectural style.

Effective   Although the Maine coast and the Oregon coast look very much alike, the architectural style of the houses by the water is different. [use of subordination to combine sentences]

22b Writing sounds monotonous when too many sentences begin the same way.

Most writers begin more than half their sentences with the subject—far more than any other construction. Although this pattern is normal for English sentences, relying too heavily on it can make your writing dull. Experiment with the following alternatives for beginning sentences.

(1) Adverb or adverbial clause

Finally, an ancient rattling, clanking pickup rounded the corner and lurched down the street toward us. [adverb]

Although the rules of the game have not changed much, basketball is a faster, rougher game than it was when Wilt Chamberlain played. [adverbial clause]

(2) Prepositional or verbal phrase

Out of necessity they stitched all of their secret fears and lingering childhood nightmares into this existence.   —GLORIA NAYLOR [prepositional phrase]

Looking north from the summit of Quandary Peak, we see a serrated pattern of snowcapped summits marching toward the Canadian border. [participial phrase]

(3) Sentence connectives—coordinating conjunctions, conjunctive adverbs, transitional phrases

In the following examples, each sentence connective shows the relationship between the ideas in each set of sentences. (See also **3d.**)

Difficulty in finding a place to park is one of the factors keeping people from shopping downtown. **Moreover,** public transportation has become too expensive. [conjunctive adverb]

This legislation will hurt the economy. **In the first place,** it will cost thousands of jobs. [transitional phrase]

(4) Appositive, absolute phrase, introductory series (see 19a)

A town of historic interest, Santa Fe also has many art galleries. [appositive]

His fur bristling, the cat attacked. [absolute phrase]

Light, water, temperature, minerals—these affect the health of plants. [introductory series; see **31e(3)**]

22c **Stringing simple sentences together to make a compound sentence is less effective than experimenting with structure.**

If you normally write short, simple sentences and then revise by just linking those sentences with *and* or *but*, your writing will still lack variety. To revise, use one of the following methods.

(1) Compound-complex sentences

Compound	Seafood is nutritious, and it is low in fat, and it has become available in greater variety.
Complex	Seafood, which is nutritious and low in fat, has become available in greater variety.

(2) Compound predicates in simple sentences

Compound	She deftly trapped the kitten, and then she held it so that its legs were against her palm, and next she strapped a tiny collar around its neck.
Simple	She deftly trapped the kitten, held it so that its legs were against her palm, and strapped a tiny collar around its neck.

(3) Appositives

Compound	J. P. Webb was an old-fashioned construction engineer, and he built two of the most spectacular roads in Summit County.
Simple	J. P. Webb, an old-fashioned construction engineer, built two of the most spectacular roads in Summit County.

(4) Prepositional or verbal phrases

Compound	The snow was thick, and we could not see where we were going.
Simple	In the thick snow, we could not see where we were going.
Compound	The town is near the interstate, and it attracted commuters, and its population grew rapidly.
Simple	The town, located near the interstate, attracted commuters and grew rapidly in population.

22d Occasionally using words or phrases to separate the subject and verb can vary the conventional subject-verb sequence.

Although it is usually best to keep the subject next to the verb so that the relationship between them is clear (see **11b**), breaking this pattern on occasion can lead to variety. In the following examples, subjects and verbs are in boldface.

Subject-verb	**Great Falls was** once a summer resort, but **it has become** a crowded suburb.
Varied	**Great Falls,** once a summer resort, **has become** a crowded suburb.

22e When surrounded by declarative sentences, a question, an exclamation, or a command adds variety.

What was Shakespeare's state of mind, for instance, when he wrote *Lear* and *Antony and Cleopatra*? It was certainly the state of mind most favourable to poetry that there has ever existed. —VIRGINIA WOOLF [Woolf's answer follows the initial question.]

Now I stare and stare at people, shamelessly. Stare. It's the way to educate your eye. —WALKER EVANS [A one-word imperative sentence provides variety.]

Diction

Diction

Chapter 23 **Good Usage**

A writer's indispensable tool for finding information about the acceptable uses of language is a good college dictionary. Whereas a thesaurus can alert you to possible synonyms and is an important aid to writing, a dictionary furnishes the meaning of a word, its pronunciation, and its part of speech, as well as the word's plural forms and verb tenses. Although a dictionary includes words appropriate in colloquial as well as in college and professional writing (often referred to as edited American English or EAE), it also includes usage labels and short usage paragraphs to distinguish between the two. Words labeled **dialect, slang,** or **nonstandard,** as well as words no longer in common use labeled **archaic** or **obsolete,** are usually inappropriate for college and professional writing. If a word has no label, it is acceptable. (See the Glossary of Usage.)

In this chapter, you will learn about

- dictionaries (**23a**);
- language for different audiences and occasions (**23b**);
- clear, simple style (**23c**); and
- inclusive writing (**23d**).

Dictionaries

Because language is constantly changing, it is important to choose a desk dictionary, not a pocket dictionary, with a recent copyright date. Many are available, either in paperback or on CD-ROM; both usually include the same information. Pocket dictionaries, which are useful for spelling and quick definitions, omit important information on usage and derivation. Reliable dictionaries include:

> *The American Heritage Dictionary*
> *Funk & Wagnall's Standard College Dictionary*
> *Merriam-Webster's Collegiate Dictionary*
> *The Random House Dictionary*
> *Webster's New World Dictionary*

Occasionally, you may need to refer to an unabridged dictionary.

> *The Oxford English Dictionary.* 2nd ed. 20 vols. 1989–.
>   CD-ROM. 1994.
> *Webster's Third New International Dictionary of the English*
>   *Language.* 1995.

CAUTION When using a thesaurus, do not merely substitute one word for another without understanding subtle distinctions in meaning. In listing synonyms, dictionaries often point out such distinctions.

23a Dictionaries provide information beyond the definition of a word.

Reading the introductory material and noting the meaning of any special abbreviations will help you understand the information your dictionary provides. The following sample entry from the tenth edition of *Merriam-Webster's Collegiate Dictionary* provides important information. Almost all desk dictionaries provide the same information, although possibly in a different order. *Answer* is listed twice in the following entries— first as a noun and then as a verb.

Part of speech

Pronunciation

Syllabication

Origin

Spelling — ¹**an·swer** \'ant(t)-sər\ *n* [ME, fr. OE *andswaru* (akin to ON *ands-var* answer); akin to OE *and-* against, *swerian* to swear—more at ANTE-] (bef. 12c)   **1 a** : something spoken or written in

Date of first occurrence — reply to a question   **b** : a correct response   **2** : a reply to a legal charge or suit : PLEA; *also* : DEFENSE   **3** : something done in response or reaction ⟨his only ~ was to walk out⟩—**4** : a — Usage of definition #3

solution of a problem   **5** : one that imitates, matches, or corresponds to another ⟨television's ~ to the news magazines⟩

vb. forms — ²**answer** *vb* **an·swered; an·swer·ing** \'an(t)s-riŋ, 'an(t)-sə-\ (bef. 12c)   **1** : to speak or write in reply   **2 a** : to be or make oneself responsible or accountable   **b** : to make amends : ATONE   **3** : to be in conformity or correspondence ⟨~ed to the description⟩   **4** : to act in response to an action performed elsewhere or by another   **5** : to be adequate : SERVE ~ *vt*   **1 a** : to speak or write in reply to   **b** : to say or write by way of reply   **2** : to reply in rebuttal, justification, or explanation   **3 a** : to correspond to ⟨~s the description⟩   **b** : to be adequate or usable for : FULFILL   **4** *obs* : to atone for   **5** : to act in response to ⟨~ed the call to arms⟩   **6** : to offer a solution for; *esp* : SOLVE—**an·swer·er** \'an(t)-sər-ər\ *n*

syn ANSWER, RESPOND, REPLY, REJOIN, RETORT mean to say, write, or do something in return. ANSWER implies the satisfying of a question, demand, call, or need ⟨*answered* all the questions⟩. RESPOND may suggest an immediate or quick reaction ⟨*responded* eagerly to a call for volunteers⟩. REPLY implies making a return commensurate with the original question or demand ⟨an invitation that requires you to *reply*⟩. REJOIN often implies sharpness or quickness in answering ⟨"who asked you?" she *rejoined*⟩. RETORT suggests responding to an explicit charge or criticism by way of retaliation ⟨he *retorted* to the attack with biting sarcasm⟩.

Synonyms and distinctions with usage examples

Spelling, syllabication, and pronunciation

Dictionaries enable you to check spelling and word division (syllabication) as well as the pronunciation of unfamiliar words. A key to sound symbols appears at the bottom of the entry pages and also in the introduction. Alternative pronunciations usually represent regional differences.

Parts of speech and inflected forms

Labels such as *tr. v.* and *adj.* identify the various forms that nouns, verbs, and modifiers take to indicate number, tense, and comparison.

Word origin/etymology

The origin of a word—also called its derivation or etymology—can be useful in understanding its meaning and appreciating the many cultures that have influenced the English language.

Date of first occurrence

The date (*bef. 12c*) in parentheses in the sample is the first known occurrence of the word in written English.

Definitions

Definitions are listed in different order in different dictionaries. The sample lists the oldest meaning first. Often, meanings are ordered according to how common they are.

Usage

Most dictionaries discuss usage to show how a word has been used in context.

Synonyms

Dictionaries always list synonyms, sometimes with detailed explanations of subtle differences in meaning. Used in conjunction with a thesaurus, such discussions are extremely helpful. The entry for the word *answer* lists five one-word synonyms.

The entry for each synonym has a cross-reference to the entry for *answer*.

23b Language varies according to the audience, the place, and the purpose.

There is a difference between the words used in conversation (colloquialisms) or informal writing, such as a personal journal (see **1b(2)**), and the more formal language appropriate for college and professional writing. In any case, it is important to select words that are meaningful to your audience.

The words you choose will vary from situation to situation, place to place, and occupation to occupation. These are differences of register—the variety of language used in specific social contexts. The language used for college or professional writing is almost always appropriate.

(1) Colloquial (or conversational) words

Common in speech, words labeled **colloquial** (or **conversational**) are used by writers in dialogue and informal writing. In academic writing, unlabeled words are generally preferred.

Although contractions, such as *it's* and *aren't,* are common in English, many instructors consider them inappropriate for college writing.

(2) Slang

Slang is usually defined as words that belong to a particular age group, locality, or profession or that are variously considered breezy, racy, excessively informal, facetious, or taboo. Sometimes they are newly coined or highly technical. Slang is easily dated and may be misunderstood, so it is usually avoided in college writing.

(3) Regionalisms

Because their meaning may not be widely known, regional or dialectal usages, such as *tank* for *pond,* are normally avoided in writing to an audience outside the region where they are current. Speakers and writers can safely use regional words known to the audience they are addressing, however.

(4) Nonstandard usage

Words and expressions labeled **nonstandard** should not be used in college and professional writing, except possibly in direct quotations. For example, *ain't* should not be used for *am not,* nor should "He done ate" be used for "He has already eaten."

(5) Archaic and obsolete words

All dictionaries list words (and meanings for words) that have long since passed out of general use. Such words are still found in dictionaries because they occur in our older literature and so must be defined for the modern reader, but they should not be used.

(6) Technical words

Jargon is technical language tailored specifically for a particular occupation, as when one physician writes to another. Technical language can be an efficient shortcut for specialized concepts, but you should use jargon only when you can be sure that both you and your readers understand it.

23c A clear, straightforward style is preferable to an ornate one.

An ornate or flowery style slows reading and calls attention to your words rather than your ideas. Although different styles are appropriate for different situations—depending, for example, on purpose, audience, and context (see 1g)—you should usually keep your writing simple and straightforward.

Ornate   The majority believes that society's approbation derives primarily from diligent pursuit of allocated tasks.

Simple   Most people believe success results from hard work.

23d Writing should be inclusive and not stereotype groups according to race, class, age, orientation, or gender.

Make sure that you choose language that includes all the members of your audience. Take care, as well, to use the terms preferred by various groups. You can get some guidance by looking at reputable regional newspapers, prestigious national magazines, and recent dictionaries or by asking people of various ages (and, if possible, various regions) who belong to that particular group.

Good sources for information about African American English and nonsexist language can be found on the Internet at http://www.cal.org/ebonics/ and http://www.stetson.edu/~history/nongenderlang.html.

---

(1) Sexist language

Making language inclusive (that is, avoiding sexist terms) means treating men and women equally. For example, many feel that women are excluded when *man* is used to refer to both men and women.

Man's achievements in the twentieth century are impressive.

Sexist language has a variety of sources. Easiest to spot is the kind that results from true contempt for the opposite sex—not simply vulgar terms, but also language that denigrates, such as referring to people by their body parts. More difficult to recognize is the sexist language that results from stereotyping, such as referring to a male teacher or a woman lawyer. We are less likely to notice the kind of stereotyping that occurs from such statements as "*room mother* for the third grade" or "The *drunk* couldn't find *his* car." Most difficult to recognize is sexist usage embedded in the language itself—the use of *he* to refer to both men and women and terms such as *mankind.*

You will gain the approval of your audience by being alert for possible uses of sexist language and knowing how to find it and revise it. As the following list illustrates, revising to remove sexist language is relatively straightforward.

- **Generic *he:*** A doctor should listen to *his* patients.

    A doctor should listen to **his or her** patients. [use of the appropriate form of *he or she*]

    Doctors should listen to **their** patients. [use of plural forms]

    Listening to patients **is important for** doctors. [eliminating the pronoun by revising the sentence]

- **Occupational stereotype:** Glenda, a female engineer at Howard Aviation, won the best-employee award.

    Glenda, an engineer at Howard Aviation, won the best-employee award. [removal of the unnecessary gender reference]

- **Terms such as *man* or those with *-ess* or *-man* endings:** Labor laws benefit the common *man*. *Mankind* benefits from philanthropy. The *stewardess* brought me some tomato juice. The *fireman* rescued the kitten from the tree.

  Labor laws benefit **working people.** [A neutral term replaces the stereotype.]

  Everyone benefits from philanthropy.

  The **firefighter** rescued the kitten from the tree.

- **Patronizing labels:** The CEO said he would ask his *girl* to schedule the appointment.

  The CEO said he would ask his **secretary** (or **assistant**) to schedule the appointment.

- **Stereotyping gender roles:** I was told that the university offers free tuition to faculty *wives*.

  The university offers free tuition to faculty **spouses.**

- **Inconsistent use of titles:** *Mr. Holmes* and his *wife* Mary took a long trip to China.

  Mr. and Mrs. Holmes took a long trip to China.

  Peter and Mary Holmes-Wolfe took a long trip to China. OR **Peter Holmes** and **Mary Wolfe** took a long trip to China.

- **Unstated gender assumption:** Have your *mother* make your costume for the school pageant.

  Have your **parents** provide you with a costume for the school pageant.

(2) References to race and ethnicity

Stereotyping is harmful whether it occurs in a racial or ethnic context or not. Even positive stereotypes can be harmful because they exclude those to whom the stereotype does not apply. All Native Americans are not concerned about the land, nor are all Asian Americans exceptional engineering students or all African Americans talented athletes. Similarly, not everyone who has a talent for organization is German, nor are all good cooks Italian, or all racists White. In most situations, identifying someone's race or ethnicity is just as unnecessary as making gender-specific references.

Further, because language changes, the terms used to refer to various racial and ethnic groups also change from time to time and from place to place. Although people of African descent are no longer referred to as *colored* or *Negro,* those terms persist in the names of important organizations such as the National Association for the Advancement of Colored People and the United Negro College Fund. And today, whether to refer to *African Americans* or *Blacks* is sometimes a question of which generation your audience belongs to. People of Spanish-speaking descent in different parts of the nation have different preferences about whether to say *Latino/Latina, Chicano/Chicana,* or *Hispanic, Latin American, Mexican American,* or *Puerto Rican.* Many descendants of indigenous peoples prefer *Native American* to *American Indian,* and *Asian American* has supplanted *Oriental.* Use the term the group itself prefers.

(3) Ability, age, class, religion, occupation, and orientation

Although referring to persons with physical disabilities as *handicapped* may be demeaning, being overly cautious about references to disabilities is equally demeaning. Older people may respond positively when they are called *mature,* but many dislike being called *senior citizens* as much as young people would dislike being called *junior citizens.*

Statements such as "We celebrate the major holidays—Christmas, Easter, the Fourth of July" with no mention of Yom Kippur or Ramadan are insensitive and exclusionary. Terms such as *faggot* or *dyke* perpetuate hate. Although some attempts to enhance the prestige of manual labor—such as the fictitious term *deforestation technician* to describe a member of a logging team—could be considered elitist and patronizing, using legitimate, inclusive terms for various occupations such as *housekeeper* instead of *maid* shows sensitivity. Labels such as *soccer mom*, *yuppie*, or *redneck* are clearly class references that reduce individuals to types. In all instances, avoid the stereotyping that uncritical use of language can create: people with cancer are not *victims*, a *long-time companion* may or may not be a partner in a same-sex relationship, and *inner-city residents* are just as likely to be the rich and famous as members of a particular ethnic group.

Chapter

24   Exactness

Good writing often consists of short, familiar, carefully chosen
words. When drafting (see chapter **2**), choose words that express your ideas and feelings. When revising (see chapter **3**),
make those words exact, fresh, and natural. Use the words you
already know effectively, but add to your vocabulary to increase
your options for choosing the exact word that suits your purpose, audience, and occasion.

Make new words your own by

- mastering their denotations and connotations and by writing clear
  definitions (**24a**);
- understanding how to use idioms (**24b**); and
- using fresh, clear expressions (**24c**).

24a Accurate and precise word choice conveys meaning efficiently.

(1) Accuracy

The **denotation** of a word indicates what it names, not what it
suggests. For example, the noun *beach* denotes a sandy or peb-
bly shore, not suggestions of summer fun. Inaccurate usage mis-
states your point, inexact usage diminishes it, and ambiguous
usage confuses your reader. Select words that state your point
exactly.

The speaker ^implied̶ ̶i̶n̶f̶e̶r̶r̶e̶d̶ that our enrollment had increased significantly this year.

Jennifer spends too much money on video games, ^but̶ ̶a̶n̶d̶ she works hard to earn it. [*And* adds or continues; *but* contrasts. In this case, negative and positive information are contrasted.]

The lecture will focus on ^motivating ̶i̶n̶s̶p̶i̶r̶i̶n̶g̶ athletes. [*Inspiring* is ambiguous in this context because the lecture could be about "how to inspire athletes" or "athletes who are inspiring."]

(2) Connotations

The **connotation** of a word is what the word suggests or implies. *Beach,* for instance, may connote natural beauty, warmth, surf, water sports, fun, sunburn, crowds, or even gritty sandwiches. Context has much to do with the connotations a word evokes; in a treatise on shoreline management, *beach* has scientific, geographic connotations, whereas in a fashion magazine, it evokes images of bathing suits. In addition to being influenced by context, most readers carry with them a wealth of personal associations that can influence how they respond to the words on the page. The challenge for writers is to choose the words that are most likely to evoke the appropriate connotations from their readers.

One of the reasons I am recommending Mr. Krueger for this job is that he is so ^persistent ̶r̶e̶l̶e̶n̶t̶l̶e̶s̶s̶. [*Relentless* has negative connotations that are inappropriate for a recommendation.]

I love the ^aroma ̶o̶d̶o̶r̶ of freshly baked bread. [Many odors are unpleasant; *aroma* sounds more positive, especially in association with food.]

(3) Specific, concrete words

A **general** word is all-inclusive, indefinite, and sweeping in scope. A **specific** word is precise, definite, and limited in scope.

General	Specific	More Specific/Concrete
food	fast food	cheeseburger
entertainment	film	*Titanic*
place	city	Atlanta

An **abstract** word deals with concepts, with ideas, with what cannot be touched, heard, or seen. A **concrete** word signifies particular objects, the practical, and what can be touched, heard, or seen.

Abstract	democracy, loyal, evil, hate, charity
Concrete	mosquito, spotted, crunch, grab

Some writers use too many abstract or general words, leaving their writing vague and lifeless. As you select words to fit your context, you should be as specific and concrete as you can. For example, instead of the word *bad,* consider using a more precise adjective.

bad planks:	rotten, warped, scorched, knotty, termite-ridden
bad children:	rowdy, rude, ungrateful, perverse, spoiled
bad meat:	tough, tainted, overcooked, contaminated

To test whether or not a word is specific, you can ask one or more of these questions about what you want to say: Exactly who? Exactly what? Exactly when? Exactly where? Exactly how? As you study the following examples, notice what a difference specific, concrete words can make in expressing an idea and how specific details can expand or develop it.

Vague	She has kept no reminders of performing in her youth.
Specific	She has kept no sequined costume, no photographs, no fliers or posters from that part of her youth.

—LOUISE ERDRICH

Vague	He realized he was running through the cold night.
Specific	He found himself hurrying over creaking snow through the blackness of a winter night. —LOREN EISELEY

As these examples show, sentences with specific details are often longer than sentences without them. But the need to be specific does not necessarily conflict with the need to be concise. (See chapter 25.) Simply substituting one word for another can often help readers to see, hear, taste, or smell what you are hoping to convey.

I had an accident while trying to catch a fish.

[handwritten corrections: "fell out of the canoe" above "had an accident"; "land a muskie" above "catch a fish"]

Occasionally, a skillful writer can achieve a dramatic effect by mixing concrete and abstract terms, as in the following example.

We inhaled those nice big fluffy fumes of human sweat, urine, effluvia, and sebaceous secretions.   —TOM WOLFE

And all writers use abstract words and generalizations when these are vital to communicating their ideas, as in the following sentence.

At its best, [art] reveals the nobility that coexists in human nature along with flaws and evils, and the beauty and truth it can perceive.

—BARBARA TUCHMAN

Abstract words are exact when they are used to express abstractions—words such as *immortal, inexhaustible, soul, spirit, compassion, sacrifice,* and *endurance.* When you use abstract words and generalizations, make sure you do so deliberately and with good reason.

(4) Figurative language

Commonly found in nonfiction prose as well as in fiction, poetry, and drama, figurative language uses words in an imaginative rather than a literal sense. Simile and metaphor are the chief **figures of speech.** A **simile** is the comparison of dissimilar things using *like* or *as*. A **metaphor** is an implied comparison of dissimilar things not using *like* or *as*.

Similes

He was **like a piece of rare and delicate china** which was always being saved from breaking and finally fell. —ALICE WALKER

The thick blood welled out of him **like red velvet,** but still he did not die. —GEORGE ORWELL

She sat **like a great icon** in the back of the classroom, tranquil, guarded, sealed up, watchful. —REGINALD MCKNIGHT

Metaphors

His **money was a sharp pair of scissors** that snipped rapidly through tangles of red tape. —HISAYE YAMAMOTO

We refuse to believe that **the bank of justice** is bankrupt.
—MARTIN LUTHER KING, JR.

It was gurgling out of her own throat, **a long ribbon of laughter,** like water. —SANDRA CISNEROS [a metaphor and a simile]

Single words are often used metaphorically.

These roses must be **planted** in good soil. [literal]

Keep your life **planted** wherever you can put down the most roots. [metaphorical]

We always **sweep** the leaves off the sidewalk. [literal]

He seems likely to **sweep** her right off her feet. [metaphorical]

Similes and metaphors are especially valuable when they are concrete and point up essential relationships that cannot otherwise be communicated. Similes and metaphors can also be extended throughout a comparison paragraph, but be careful not to mix them. (See **18c.**)

Other common figures of speech include **personification** (attributing to nonhumans characteristics possessed only by humans), **paradox** (a seemingly contradictory statement that actually makes sense when you think about it), and **irony** (a deliberate incongruity between what is stated and what is meant). In addition, experienced writers often enjoy using **overstatement, understatement, images,** and **allusions.** Figures such as these can contribute to lively, memorable writing even if they do not always contribute to exactness. (See **9e.**)

24b Exact word choice requires an understanding of idioms.

An **idiom** is an expression whose meaning is peculiar to the language or differs from the individual meanings of its elements. Be careful to use idiomatic English, not unidiomatic approximations. *She talked down to him* is idiomatic. *She talked under to him* is not. Occasionally, the idiomatic use of prepositions proves difficult. If you do not know which preposition to use with a given word, check the dictionary. For instance, *agree* may be followed by *about, on, to,* or *with.* The choice depends on the context. Writers sometimes have trouble with expressions such as these:

Dealing with Troublesome Idioms

Instead of	Use
abide with	abide by the decision
according with	according to the source

Instead of	Use
bored **of**	bored **by** it
comply **to**	comply **with** rules
conform **of/on**	conform **to/with** standards
differ **to**	differ **with** them
in accordance **to**	in accordance **with** policy
independent **to**	independent **of** his family
happened **on**	happened **by** accident
plan **on**	plan **to** go
superior **than**	superior **to** others
type **of a**	type **of** business

Many idioms—such as *all the same, to mean well, eating crow, raining cats and dogs*—cannot be understood from the individual meanings of their elements. Some such as *turning something over in one's mind* are metaphorical. Such expressions cannot be meaningfully translated word for word into another language. Used every day, they are at the very heart of the English language. As you encounter idioms that are new to you, master their meanings just as you would when learning new words.

24c Fresh expressions are more distinctive than worn-out ones.

Such expressions as *bite the dust, breath of fresh air,* or *smooth as silk* were once striking and effective. Excessive use, however, has drained them of their original force and made them **clichés.** Some **euphemisms** (pleasant-sounding substitutions for more explicit but possibly offensive words) are not only trite but also wordy or awkward—for example, *correctional facility* for *jail* or *pre-owned* for *used.* Many political slogans and the catchy phraseology of advertisements soon become hackneyed. Faddish or trendy expressions such as *whatever, im-*

pacted, paradigm, input, or *be into* (as in "I am into exercising") were so overused that they quickly became clichés.

Nearly every writer uses clichés from time to time because they are so much a part of the language, especially the spoken language. But experienced writers often give a fresh twist to an old saying.

> I seek a narrative, a fiction, to order days like the one I spent several years ago, on a gray June day in Chicago, when I took a roller-coaster ride on the bell curve of my experience. —GAYLE PEM-BERTON [COMPARE frequent references elsewhere to being on "an emotional roller coaster"]

Variations on familiar expressions from literature or the Bible, many of which have become part of everyday language, can often be used effectively in your own writing.

> Now is the summer of my great content. —KATHERINE LANPHER [COMPARE Shakespeare's "Now is the winter of our discontent. . . ."]

Good writers, however, do not rely too heavily on the words of others; they choose their own words to express their ideas.

24d The use of the first and second persons can help writers be exact.

Although there are times when it is inappropriate, the use of *I* when you are writing about personal experiences is both appropriate and natural. It is also the clearest way to distinguish your own views from those of others or to make a direct appeal to readers. However, if you frequently repeat *I feel* or *I think*, your readers may think you don't understand much beyond your own experience.

The second person (you) is a way to connect with readers. It can also be less wordy and more precise than the third-person alternatives.

Chapter
25 Conciseness

Using words economically is fundamental to writing clearly because unnecessary words or phrases distract readers and blur meaning. Good writers know how to make their points concisely. This chapter discusses how to

- avoid redundant and unnecessary words (**25a**),
- combine sentences (**25b**),
- use repetition for emphasis (**25c**), and
- use pronouns and elliptical constructions to eliminate repetition (**25d**).

In some situations, repeating a word or phrase can be useful. (See **26b**, **21e**, and **3d**.) But in most cases, repetition is a sign of inefficiency.

Wordy	In the early part of August, a hurricane was moving threateningly toward Houston.
Concise	In early August, a hurricane threatened Houston.
Repetitious	This excellent baker makes excellent bread.
Concise	This baker makes excellent bread.

25a Every word should count; words or phrases that add nothing to the meaning should be omitted.

(1) Redundancy

Restating a key point in different words can help readers understand it. (See **7c(3)**.) But there is no need to explain the meaning of readily understood terms by using different words that say the same thing or to emphasize a word by rephrasing it. If you do, your work will suffer from redundancy: repetition for no good reason.

Ballerinas auditioned ~~in the tryouts~~ for *The Nutcracker*.

Useless Words in Common Phrases

yellow [in color]	circular [in shape]
at 9:45 a.m. [in the morning]	return/refer [back]
[basic] essentials	rich [and wealthy] nations
bitter [-tasting] salad	small [-size] potatoes
but [though]	to apply [or utilize] rules
connect [up together]	[true] facts
because [of the fact that]	was [more or less] hinting
[really and truly] fearless	by [virtue of] his authority
fans [who were] watching TV	the oil [that exists] in shale

Avoid grammatical redundancy, such as double subjects (*my sister [she] is*), double comparisons ([*more*] *easier than*), and double negatives (*could[n't] hardly*).

(2) Unnecessary words

Beware of empty or vague words such as *area, aspect, element, factor, field, kind, situation, thing,* or *type*. Replace such inexact words with exact ones that say precisely what you mean.

The tax increase involved many ~~factors.~~ complex issues.

If ~~In the event that~~ taxes are raised, ~~expect~~ voters will complaints ~~on the part of the voters~~.

Some One- or Two-Word Replacements for Common Expressions

at all times	**always**
at this point in time	**now**
by means of	**by**
for the purpose of	**for**
in an employment situation	**at work**
in spite of the fact that	**although**
on account of the fact that	**because**
somewhere in the neighborhood of $2,500	**about $2,500**

One exact word can say as much as many inexact ones. (See **24a**.)

spoke in a low and hard-to-hear voice	**mumbled**
persons who really know their particular field	**experts**

(3) Expletives

There followed by a form of *be* is an expletive—a word that signals that the subject will follow the verb. (See **21f**.) Because expletives shift emphasis away from the subject, they can result in unnecessary words. They can also be imprecise because they substitute a form of *be* for a forceful verb.

> ~~There were three~~ _Three_ children _were_ playing in the yard.

The *it* construction is also an expletive when *it* has no word to refer to and is followed by a form of *be*.

> _Learning to ski_ It is easy ~~to learn to ski~~.

The *it* construction is necessary only when there is no logical subject. For example: *It is going to snow.*

25b Combining sentences or simplifying phrases and clauses can eliminate needless words.

Note the differences in emphasis as you study the following examples.

~~The grass was like a carpet. It~~ *A carpet of blue-green grass* covered the whole playing field.

~~The color of the grass was blue green.~~

Some ~~phony~~ unscrupulous brokers are *cheating* ~~taking money and savings from~~ elderly ~~old~~ people *out of their* ~~who need that money because they planned to use it as a retirement~~ pension*s*.

25c Repetition is useful only when it contributes to emphasis, clarity, or coherence. (See also 20b, 21e, and 3d.)

~~Your teacher is unlike my teacher.~~ Your teacher likes teaching better than mine ~~does~~.

We will not rest until we have pursued **every** lead, inspected **every** piece of evidence, and interviewed **every** suspect. [In this case, the repetition of *every* is useful because it emphasizes the writer's determination.]

25d Pronouns and constructions that omit words that will be understood by the reader without being repeated (elliptical constructions) can eliminate needless repetition. (See 16e.)

Instead of repeating a noun or substituting a clumsy synonym, use a pronoun. If the reference is clear (see 16e(2)), several pronouns can refer to the same antecedent.

The hall outside these offices was empty. ~~The hall~~ ^It had dirty floors, and ^its the walls ~~of this corridor~~ were covered with graffiti.

An **elliptical construction** helps the writer of the following example be concise. Sometimes, as an aid to clarity, commas mark omissions that avoid repetition.

My family functioned like a baseball team; my mom was the coach; my brother, the pitcher; and my sister, the shortstop.

As these examples show, parallelism reinforces elliptical constructions. (See chapter **20**.)

Chapter 26
Clarity and Completeness

Clarity in writing depends on more than grammar. Clarity results from critical thinking (1), logical development (2), and exactness of diction (24) at least as much as it does from correct use of grammar. In rapid speech we omit words because we do not hear them. For example, instead of "We had better study hard," a speaker might say, "We better study hard." *Had* must be included in writing, however, to make your meaning clear. This chapter will help you

- use articles, pronouns, conjunctions, and prepositions for clarity (26a);
- include all necessary verbs and auxiliaries in a sentence (26b); and
- complete comparisons (26c) and intensifiers (26d).

26a Articles, pronouns, conjunctions, or prepositions are sometimes necessary for clarity and completeness.

(1) Use of an article (*a, an, the*)

Unless the following sentence is edited, it could mean that either one person or two people are "standing nearby"; it is ambiguous.

A friend and ∧ helper stood nearby.

The indefinite articles *a* and *an* are generally used with singular countable nouns; the definite article *the* is used with singular or plural noncount nouns to indicate a specific person, place, or thing. The article can occasionally be omitted entirely.

(2) Omitted conjunctions or prepositions

Prepositions may sometimes be omitted in speech but never in writing. When your sentence has a compound verb (two verbs), you may need to supply a different preposition for each verb to make your meaning clear.

> We had never tried that type of film before.

> I neither believe in nor approve of those attitudes.

In the following sentence, use a comma when the conjunction *and* is omitted.

> Habitat for Humanity built the house, (**and**) then later painted it. [COMPARE Habitat for Humanity built the house and later painted it. (See **27f(2)**.)]

26b Verbs and auxiliaries that are sometimes omitted in speech are necessary in writing to avoid awkwardness.

The revision eliminates the awkwardness in the following sentence.

> Voter turnout has never been and will never be 100 percent.

Although *is* may not be heard in speech, it is included in writing.

Lamont ˄is strong and very tall.

In sentences such as the following, the second verb is optional.

The storm was fierce and the thunder (**was**) deafening.

26c Complete comparisons are needed to explain meaning if it is not suggested by the context.

He is taller **than his brother.**

Most people think television is more violent **than it used to be.**

Comparisons can be completed by other words or phrases in the sentence, by other sentences in the paragraph, or by the context.

In the next century, people will need more education.

26d The intensifiers *so, such,* and *too* need a completing phrase or clause.

My hair is **so** long **that I must get it cut today.**

Julian has **such** a hearty laugh **that it makes everyone feel good.**

It is just **too** much **for me to try to do.**

Punctuation

Punctuation

Chapter
27 The Comma

Punctuation lends to written language the flexibility that facial expressions, pauses, and variations in voice pitch give to spoken language. For instance, a pause before *Mary* in the first example below makes it clear that the spoken sentence refers to only two people—the sister and a person named Mary Ellen. In the second example, a pause after *Mary* lets us know that the sentence refers to three people—the sister, Mary, and Ellen. In written language, a comma creates this pause.

> When my sister called, Mary Ellen answered.
> When my sister called Mary, Ellen answered.

But pauses are not a reliable guide for comma use because commas are often called for where we do not pause and pauses occur where no comma is called for. Knowing four basic principles about commas works better. This chapter will help you understand that commas

- come before coordinating conjunctions when they link independent clauses (**27a**);
- follow introductory adverbial clauses and, usually, introductory phrases (**27b**);
- separate items in a series (including coordinate adjectives) (**27c**); and
- set off nonrestrictive and other parenthetical elements (**27d**).

27a Commas come before a coordinating conjunction that links independent clauses.

The coordinating conjunctions are *and, but, for, nor, or, so,* and *yet.* An independent clause is a group of words that can stand as a sentence. A comma must come before a coordinating conjunction that links two independent clauses.

INDEPENDENT CLAUSE,	CONJUNCTION	INDEPENDENT CLAUSE.
Subject + predicate,	and but or nor for so yet	subject + predicate.

The minutes would pass, **and** then suddenly Einstein would stop pacing as his face relaxed into a gentle smile.   —BANESH HOFFMANN

Samuel Coleridge-Taylor was an early twentieth-century British composer of African descent who wrote some beautiful symphonies, **but** today few know of his work.

Parents must give their children respect, **or** their children will not respect them.

From one point of view their migration was the fruit of an old prophecy, **for** indeed they emerged from a sunless world.

—N. SCOTT MOMADAY

I have not stopped hoping, **nor** have I stopped believing in the essential goodness of people.

They struggled to be the women society insisted they should be, **so** they often stifled their own creative urges.

The immigrants were officially prohibited from speaking in public, **yet** their silent protest was compelling.

When a sentence contains multiple clauses, a comma comes before each coordinating conjunction.

I chose to follow in the footsteps of my unconventional Aunt Esther, **and** I have never regretted my choice, **but** I think my mother was jealous of Aunt Esther, **and** I fear she never approved of me.

When the clauses are short, the comma can be omitted before *and, but,* or *or,* but not usually before *for, nor, so,* or *yet.* (See page 295.)

I enjoy hiking **and** it keeps me trim.

I trust Joe, for we are old friends.

Sometimes a semicolon instead of a comma separates independent clauses, especially when the second one contains commas or when it reveals a contrast. (See **28a.**)

Most people, according to my mother, skip cleaning in the corners; **but, she used to say,** they don't skip payday.

No comma, however, comes before an *and* that links two verbs (a compound predicate) rather than two clauses.

She **slapped** the hamburger patty onto the grill **and seasoned** it liberally before taking my order. [compound predicate—no comma before *and*]

27b A comma usually follows introductory words, phrases, and clauses.

(1) Introductory clauses

INTRODUCTORY CLAUSE,
INDEPENDENT CLAUSE.

When you write, you make a sound in the reader's head.

—RUSSELL BAKER

Although the safest automobile on the road is expensive, the protection it offers makes the cost worthwhile. [adverbial clause preceding the independent clause]

The comma may be omitted after an introductory clause when the clause is short.

When you sneeze you are responding to a nasal irritant.

A comma is usually unnecessary when the dependent clause follows the independent clause.

My grandmother's name will ensure me citizenship in the tribe **because it's on the Dawes roll.** [*Because,* a subordinating conjunction, introduces an adverbial clause.]

A comma can precede a dependent clause only loosely connected to an independent clause.

My aunt is now retired, **although she was a banker for years.**

(2) Introductory phrases

INTRODUCTORY PHRASE,	
or	subject + predicate.
INTRODUCTORY WORD,	

Prepositional phrases

From our porch, I could not hear what my father was saying, but I could hear my mother's laughter, throaty and rich with joy.

If the comma after an introductory prepositional phrase is not necessary to prevent misreading, it can be omitted.

For safety the university installed call boxes linked directly to campus security.

Other types of phrases

Having traveled nowhere, she believed the rest of the world was like her own small town; **having read little,** she had no sense of how other people think. [participial phrases before both independent clauses; see 12a–b]

The language difference aside, life in Germany doesn't seem much different from life in America. [absolute phrase; see 27d(7)]

Introductory words

Furthermore, the person responsible for damaging university equipment will be fined. [transitional expression; see pages 299–300]

Well, sit down and be quiet. [interjection]

Yes, I bought my tickets yesterday. **No,** I didn't pay cash. [introductory *yes* or *no*]

Commas are not used after phrases that begin inverted sentences. (See **21f**.)

> With the hurricane came the tornadoes. [COMPARE Tornadoes came with the hurricane.]
>
> Of far greater concern than censorship of bad words is censorship of ideas. —DONNA WOOLFOLK CROSS

27c Commas separate parallel items such as those in a series.

A series contains three or more parallel elements. (To be parallel, elements must be grammatically equal. See chapter **20**.) The punctuation of a series depends on its form.

(1) To separate words, phrases, and clauses in a series

> A pet should be affectionate, trusting, obedient, and intelligent. [words in a series]
>
> My job requires me to start work at 7 a.m., to drive to three different towns every day, and to carry heavy repair equipment upstairs. [phrases in a series]
>
> My idea of a great vacation spot is one where no telephone rings, someone else fixes me great food, and I sit on the porch in the cool shade all day and read mystery novels. [clauses in a series]

If items in a series contain internal commas, you can make the meaning clear by separating the items with semicolons. (See **28b**.)

> The main reasons I decided to replace my old car were that my fiancé, who is 6 feet 5 inches tall, couldn't sit in it; that I had over 100,000 miles on it; and that it needed a new transmission.

For special emphasis, writers sometimes use commas to slow the pace when coordinating conjunctions link all the items in a series.

We cannot put it off for a month, or a week, or even a day.

(2) To separate coordinate adjectives

Coordinate adjectives are two or more adjectives that modify the same noun or pronoun. One test for coordinate adjectives is to switch them; another is to put *and* between them. If the meaning does not change, the adjectives are coordinate. Commas separate coordinate adjectives not linked by a coordinating conjunction.

It is a **waiting, silent, limp** room.   —EUDORA WELTY   [*Waiting, silent,* and *limp* all modify *room.* COMPARE It is a silent, limp waiting room.]

Walking along the **rushing, shallow** creek, I slipped on a rock and sank above my boot tops into a **small, still** pool. [*Rushing* and *shallow* modify *creek,* and *small* and *still* modify *pool.*]

27d Commas set off nonrestrictive and other parenthetical elements, as well as contrasted elements, items in dates, and so on.

Nonrestrictive clauses or phrases give nonessential information about a noun or pronoun. They can be omitted without changing the meaning. To set off a nonrestrictive word or word group, use two commas, unless the element is placed at the beginning or end of the sentence.

Restrictive clauses or phrases follow and limit the words they modify. They are essential to the clear identification of the word or words they refer to.

(1) Nonrestrictive clauses or phrases used as modifiers

Clauses or phrases that *describe* rather than limit the meaning of the noun they modify are nonrestrictive. Set off by commas, they are nonessential parenthetical elements that may be omitted. Clauses that *limit* the noun are restrictive. Not set off by commas, they identify the noun or pronoun they modify by telling which one (or ones) and are essential elements that may not be omitted. In the first example below, "my sister" identifies the person the rest of the sentence is describing. As a result, any additional information serves only to describe "my sister." "Any sister," however, could be any woman who has a sibling, not just the writer's sister, and so needs a modifier that limits it to a specific person—a person who is a sister and who forgets birthdays.

	Nonrestrictive	Restrictive or Essential
Clauses	**My sister**, *who forgot my birthday*, is quite selfish.	**Any sister** *who forgets birthdays* is quite selfish.
	Mr. Jackson, *who won the teaching award*, lives next door.	**The man** *who won the teaching award* lives next door.
Phrases	**Our** new car, *covered in mud*, looks worn out.	**The** new car *covered in mud* looks worn out.

Sometimes only the omission or use of commas indicates whether a modifier is restrictive or nonrestrictive and thus signals the writer's exact meaning.

The party opposed taxes which would be a burden to working Americans. [opposition to levying taxes of a certain kind]

> The party opposed taxes, which would be a burden to working Americans. [opposition to levying taxes of any kind, all of which would be a burden to working Americans]

Although traditionally writers have used *that* at the beginning of restrictive clauses, *which* has become acceptable if it does not cause confusion.

> I like to drive a car that [or which] has fast acceleration and nimble handling.

(2) Nonrestrictive appositives

Appositives can supply additional but nonessential details about a noun or pronoun (nonrestrictive), or else they limit the meaning of a noun or pronoun by indicating which one is meant (restrictive).

Nonrestrictive	Restrictive or Essential
Even Zeke Thornbush, **my friend,** let me down.	Even **my friend** Zeke Thornbush let me down.
The ringed planet, **Saturn,** can be seen at dawn.	The planet **Saturn** can be seen at dawn.

Abbreviations of titles or degrees after names are treated as nonrestrictive appositives: "Was the card from Ann Evans, Ph.D., or from A. H. Evans, M.D.?"

(3) Contrasted elements

> Human beings, **unlike oysters,** frequently reveal their emotions.
> —GEORGE F. WILL

In sentences where contrasted elements are introduced by *not* and *but,* some writers put a comma before *but,* whereas others do not. Generally, the comma before *but* emphasizes the contrast.

> Today the Black Hills are being invaded again, not for gold but for uranium. —PETER MATTHIESSEN

(4) Geographical names, items in dates, and addresses

> **Nashville, Tennessee,** is the largest country and western music center in the United States.
>
> I had to write to **Ms. Melanie Hobson, 2873 Central Avenue, Orange Park, FL 32065.** [no comma between the state abbreviation and the ZIP code]
>
> Hunter applied for the job on **Wednesday, June 7, 2000,** but turned it down on June 12 because it paid only minimum wage.
>
> OR
>
> Hunter applied for the job on Wednesday, 7 June and turned it down on Monday, 12 June because it paid only minimum wage. [Commas are omitted when the date precedes the month.]

(5) Parenthetical expressions

> Language, **then,** sets the tone of our society. —EDWIN NEWMAN

When they cause little or no pause in reading, expressions such as *also, too, of course, perhaps, at least, therefore,* and *likewise* need not be set off by commas.

> My awareness of the absurd has perhaps grown in recent years.

(6) Mild interjections and words used in direct address

> **Ah,** that's my idea of a good meal. [interjection]
>
> Now is the time, **my friend,** to stop smoking. [direct address]

(7) Absolute phrases

An absolute phrase is a part of a sentence that is not grammatically connected to any other part.

> **His temper being what it is,** I don't want a confrontation.
>
> She was gazing out the window, **her breathing growing slower and slower.**

27e   Commas are occasionally needed for ease in reading.

Without commas the following sentences would confuse the reader, if only temporarily.

> Still, water must be transported to dry areas. [COMPARE Still water . . .]
>
> The day before, I had talked with her on the phone. [COMPARE I had talked with her . . . the day before.]
>
> The earth breathes, in a certain sense.   —LEWIS THOMAS   [COMPARE The earth breathes in moisture.]

Sometimes a comma replaces a clearly understood word or group of words.

> Scholars often see the humor in mistakes; pedants, never.

27f   Unnecessary (or misplaced) commas send false signals that can confuse a reader.

Unnecessary commas

- often separate the main sentence elements (27f(1)),
- are used improperly with a coordinating conjunction (27f(2)),
- set off words that are not parenthetical (27f(3)),

- set off restrictive elements (27f(4)), and
- are used improperly in a series (27f(5)).

(1) Not between the subject and the verb or the verb and its object

Although speakers often pause after the subject or the object of a sentence, that pause should not be reflected by a comma.

Most older students⊙must hold a job in addition to going to school. [separation of the subject (*students*) and verb (*must hold*)]

The lawyer said⊙that I could appeal the speeding ticket. [separation of the verb (*said*) and the direct object (a noun clause: *that I could . . .*)]

(2) Not after coordinating conjunctions (see chapter 14 and 27a)

It is incorrect to use a comma after a coordinating conjunction (*and, but, for, nor, or, so, yet*). Writers also sometimes put an unnecessary comma before a coordinating conjunction that does not link independent clauses.

For three decades the Surgeon General's office has warned us about the dangers of smoking but⊙millions of people still smoke. [separation of the conjunction (*but*) and the subject of the clause (*millions of people*)]

I fed the dog⊙and put it out for the night. [separation of compound verbs (*fed* and *put out*)]

(3) After clearly parenthetical words and short phrases

Parenthetical words and phrases are those that are nonessential—such as asides or interpolations.

Martha was born⊙in Miami in 1976. [The phrase, *in Miami*, modifies *born*, an integral part of the sentence.]

Perhaps⊙ the valve is not correctly calibrated. [*Perhaps* is not a parenthetical element.]

(4) Not to set off restrictive (necessary) clauses, phrases, or appositives (see 27d)

A restrictive clause, phrase, or appositive (27d(2)) is essential to the meaning of the sentence.

Everyone⊙ who owns an automobile⊙ needs to have collision insurance. [The *who* clause is essential; people who do not have cars do not need collision insurance.]

With strains of bagpipes in the background, crowds watched two men⊙ carrying lances charge each other on horseback. [The men carrying lances were being watched, not just any two men.]

(5) Not before the first item of a series or after the last (including a series of adjectives modifying the same noun—coordinate adjectives)

Field trips were required in a few courses, such as⊙ botany, geology, and sociology. [No comma is needed before the first item of the series (*botany*).]

I've always wanted a low-slung, fast, elegant⊙ convertible. [No comma is needed after the last item in the series (*elegant*).]

Chapter

28 The Semicolon

A stronger mark of punctuation than the comma, the semicolon connects sentence elements that are grammatically equal such as two independent clauses (see **12b**). This chapter can help you understand that semicolons

- link closely related independent clauses (**28a**),
- separate parts of a sentence containing internal commas by acting as a stronger mark than the comma (**28b**), and
- do not connect independent clauses with phrases or dependent clauses (**28c**).

Mary said she was hungry; Hugh thought she wanted to go out to dinner. [closely related clauses]

Watching stupid, sentimental, dull soap operas; eating junk food like french fries, cheeseburgers, and milkshakes; and just doing nothing are my favorite vices. [parts containing internal commas]

28a Semicolons connect independent clauses not linked by a coordinating conjunction.

Two or more related sentences (or independent clauses) can be linked by a semicolon, connected by a comma and one of the coordinating conjunctions (*and, but, for, nor, or, so, yet*), or punctuated as separate sentences.

Many Web sites are interesting; some are inaccurate.

Many Web sites are interesting, **but** some are inaccurate.

Many Web sites are interesting. Some are inaccurate.

Many Web sites are interesting; **however,** some are inaccurate.

Semicolons indicate a close connection between ideas, conjunctions indicate a more distant connection, and periods separate them.

Sometimes a semicolon (instead of the usual comma) comes before a coordinating conjunction when a writer wants to emphasize the contrast between the two ideas being joined. (See 27a, page 403.)

> Politicians may refrain from negative campaigning for a time; but when the race gets close, they can't seem to resist trying to dredge up personal dirt to use on their opponents.

Occasionally, a comma separates short, very closely related main clauses.

> I am thrilled by a symphony, I ignore a film score; I respond to the form, I don't notice music that lacks a structure. [A semicolon is used between pairs of independent clauses joined by commas.]

When placed between independent clauses, a semicolon comes before words such as *for example, however, on the contrary, therefore* (conjunctive adverbs). (See 14b and the list on page 299.)

> Some french fries are greasy; **however,** others are not. I like them any way you fix them.

28b Semicolons separate elements that themselves contain commas.

> The chief attorney for a major manufacturer was accused of several felonies, which included concealing evidence that the company knew there was a lethal defect in one of its products; persuading an employee to lie about the callous, profit-driven refusal to fix the defect; and actually shredding important, irreplaceable legal documents.

28c Semicolons do not connect parts that are grammatically unequal, such as phrases and clauses.

Semicolons do not connect clauses with phrases. (See 12a–b.)

Needing them to provide summer shade; we planted two of the largest trees we could afford.

Semicolons do not connect a main clause with a subordinate clause.

I learned that he would not graduate this term; which really surprised me.

Chapter
29   The Apostrophe

Apostrophes are part of the words they are used in, whereas other punctuation marks follow the words they are used with. This chapter discusses how apostrophes

- show possession (except with personal pronouns) (**29a**);
- mark omissions in contractions (**29b**);
- form certain plurals (**29c**); but not others, and
- do not show the possessive form of personal pronouns (**29d**).

29a   Apostrophes show possession—ownership— for nouns and some indefinite pronouns (*everyone, somebody*).

The possessive case shows ownership, and it is marked by an apostrophe. (See **29a(2)**.)

Al's pie   someone's car

A possessive can follow the word it explains (modifies).

Is that new computer Ana's or Kim's?

A grammar checker does not find most apostrophe errors, but it is good at finding missing apostrophes in contractions such as *can't* or *don't*.

---

(1) With singular nouns (including people's names), indefinite pronouns, and acronyms

the dean's office   NASA's goal   anyone's computer

(2) With plural nouns (including people's names) ending in *-s*

the boys' game   the babies' toys   the Joneses' house

Plurals that do not end in -s add the apostrophe and -s.

men's lives   women's cars   children's swing set

(3) To show joint ownership or to make a compound noun possessive

Olga and Nadia's house [COMPARE Olga and Nadia's houses—they jointly own more than one house.]

her mother-in-law's telephone

Walter Bryan Jr.'s letter [To avoid confusion, no comma follows *Jr.'s,* although *Jr.* is usually set off by commas; see **27d(2)**.]

(4) To show individual ownership

Tamiko's and Sam's apartments [different apartments]

(5) Before gerunds (see 12a(3)) and to show time relationships or an academic degree

Lucy's having to be there seemed unnecessary.

an hour's delay   in a week's time   bachelor's degree

Proper names of organizations and geographical locations are not consistent in using the apostrophe or the apostrophe and -s. Follow local usage.

Devil's Island   Devils Tower   Devil Mountain

29b The apostrophe marks omissions in contractions and numbers.

don't   they'll   class of '98

Many instructors do not permit contractions in college writing, so you can safely write out the two words and omit contractions altogether: *do not, they will.*

29c The apostrophe and *-s* form the plurals of letters, numbers, and words referred to as words.

The apostrophe and *-s* are used to make the plural of a letter of the alphabet or an abbreviation followed by a period.

his *p's* and *q's*   Ibid.'s   Ph.D.'s

To prevent confusion, an *'s* can also be used to show the plural of capital letters and of words referred to as words.

too many *A's*   all of the *if's* and *and's*

If there is no possibility of confusion, either *'s* or *-s* forms such plurals as the following.

the 1990's OR the 1990s   her *and's* OR her *ands*
his *7's* OR his *7s*   the *&'s* OR the *&s*

Who's is the contraction for *who is. Whose* is the possessive form of the relative pronoun *who.*

Who's [Who is] responsible? **Whose** responsibility is it?

29d Personal pronouns and plural nouns that are not possessive do not take an apostrophe.

Each personal pronoun (*I, we, you, he, she, it, they*) has its own form to show possession (*my, mine, our, ours, your, yours, his, her, hers, its, their, theirs*).

A friend of **theirs** knows a cousin of **yours.**

An apostrophe is not used with *-s* to indicate plurals of words that are not possessive case.

The **Smiths** are home.   Idaho **potatoes** are on sale.

Do not confuse *it's* with *its*. *It's* is a contraction for *it is*. *Its* is the possessive form of *it*. Whenever you write *it's*, you should be able to substitute *it is*.

Its motor is small.   **It's** [it is] a small motor.

Chapter
30   Quotation Marks

Quotation marks are always used in pairs. The first mark indicates the beginning of the quotation, and the second indicates the end. Any other marks associated with the quotation follow the rules explained in this chapter. After studying this chapter, you will have a better understanding of

- direct quotations (**30a**),
- long quotations set in indented blocks (**30b**),
- certain titles (**30c**),
- words used in a special sense (**30d**),
- overuse of quotation marks (**30e**), and
- the conventions of quotation marks (**30f**).

30a   Quotation marks set off most quotations, dialogue, and thoughts.

Double quotation marks set off direct quotations, but not indirect ones. Single quotation marks enclose a quotation within a quotation.

(1) Direct quotations

"People are trapped in history," writes James Baldwin, "and history is trapped in them."

(2) Indirect quotations

James Baldwin claims that people cannot escape history and that history cannot exist without people.

(3) Quotations within quotations

"Then Elena said 'get out of my life,' " Martin complained.
[See page 423 for how to punctuate a quotation within a
quotation presented as an indented block.]

British English and some other languages reverse
the use of single (') and double (") quotation marks. For
college and professional writing within the United States,
honor the American convention. (See 30f.)

---

(4) Dialogue

Dialogue is directly quoted conversation. When quoting conversation, write what each person says, no matter how short, as
if it were a separate paragraph.

When quoting more than one paragraph by a single speaker,
put quotation marks at the beginning of each new paragraph.
However, use only one set of closing quotation marks, at the
end of the last paragraph.

(5) Thoughts

Double quotation marks set off thoughts as if they were stated.

"I won't make that mistake again," I thought.

30b Long quotations are indented.

Although short quotations are run into the text, long ones are
indented. In this case the indentation shows that you are quoting, so quotation marks are not used. (See 7f(2), page 185.)

(1) Prose

When using the MLA style of documentation (see 7e), set off any quotation consisting of more than four lines by indenting all lines one inch (or ten spaces). When using the American Psychological Association (APA) style (see 7h), set off quotations of forty words or more by indenting all lines five to seven spaces (one-half inch). When using either MLA or APA style, double-space the lines in the block.

In MLA style, do not indent the first line of a single quoted paragraph or less. Indent each first line of two or more paragraphs three spaces. In APA style, indent the first line of the second and subsequent paragraphs five to seven spaces.

A colon may introduce a long quotation that is not an integral part of the structure of the preceding sentence. Otherwise, use the punctuation that sentence calls for, even if the result is no punctuation before the blocked quotation. Use internal quotation marks only if they appear in the original. Place the page number on which the quotation is found in parentheses after the final period (parenthetical citation).

(2) Poetry

Except for very special emphasis, enclose a quotation of three (or fewer) lines of poetry in quotation marks and run it into the text. Use a slash with a space on each side to show line divisions. (See 31h.)

> In "The Collar," George Herbert, frustrated because his faith seems to have no immediate rewards, exclaims, "Sure there was wine / Before my sighs did dry it; there was corn / Before my tears did drown it."

Passages of more than three lines should be set off—double-spaced and indented one inch (or ten spaces). If unusual spacing is part of the poem, reproduce the spacing as nearly as possible.

30c Quotation marks enclose the titles of short works such as stories, essays, poems, songs, episodes of a radio or television series, articles in periodicals, and subdivisions of books.

Lon Otto's *Cover Me* contains such wonderful stories as "Winners" and "How I Got Rid of That Stump." [short stories]

"Nani" is my favorite of the poems by Alberto Ríos that we studied this semester. [short poem—see 34a for titles of long poems]

Did you read William Gibson's "Disneyland with the Death Penalty" when it appeared in *Wired*? [article in a periodical]

Use double quotation marks to enclose the title of a short work appearing in a longer italicized (underlined) title. Use single marks for such a title within a longer title enclosed in double quotation marks.

"Cynicism in Hardy's 'Ah, Are You Digging on My Grave?' "

30d Used sparingly, quotation marks may enclose words intended in a special or ironic sense.

And I do mean good and evil, not "adjustment and deviance," the gutless language that so often characterizes modern discussions of psychological topics.   —CAROL TAVRIS

Quotation marks can be used in definitions. (See 34e.)

Ploy means "a strategy used to gain an advantage."

30e Quotation marks are not needed to call attention to clichés or to a *yes* or a *no* or to highlight dubious usage.

A good debater does not beat around the bush. [cliché]

I have to learn to say no to people who ask me to do more than I should.

A wimp can't say no to anyone. [Neither *wimp,* a slang term, nor *no* is set off with quotation marks.]

30f Follow American printing conventions for using various marks of punctuation with quoted material.

(1) Commas and periods

Generally speaking, commas go inside closing quotation marks; so do periods if the quotation ends the sentence.

"Lou," she said, "let's go someplace after class." [comma and period inside the quotation marks]

The period goes at the end of the sentence if other words follow the end of the quotation.

"I don't know why my CD player doesn't work," she said.

(2) Semicolons and colons

Semicolons and colons always go outside the quotation marks.

She spoke of "the gothic tale"; I immediately thought of "The Dunwich Horror": H. P. Lovecraft's masterpiece is the epitome of "gothic."

(3) Question marks, exclamation points, and dashes

When a question mark, an exclamation point, or a dash is part of the quoted matter, it goes inside the quotation marks. When it is not, it goes outside.

Inside the quotation marks:

> Pilate asked, "What is truth?"
>
> Gordon replied, "No way!"
>
> "Achievement—success!—" states Heather Evans, "has become a national obsession."
>
> Why do children keep asking "Why?" [a question within a question—one question mark inside the quotation marks]

Outside the quotation marks:

> What is the meaning of the term "half-truth"?
>
> Stop whistling "All I Do Is Dream of You"!
>
> She exclaimed, "I'm surprised at you!"—understandable under the circumstances.

When a quotation containing one of these marks ends your own sentence, you do not add an additional end mark either inside or outside the quotation marks.

Chapter
31
The Period and Other Marks

Periods, question marks, exclamation points, colons, dashes, parentheses, brackets, slashes, and ellipsis points are important in writing and in transferring meaning from spoken to written language.

This chapter will help you understand how to use

- end punctuation—the period (**31a**), the question mark (**31b**), and the exclamation point (**31c**);
- the colon (**31d**);
- the dash (**31e**), parentheses (**31f**), brackets (**31g**), the slash (**31h**); and
- ellipsis points (**31i**).

The MLA (Modern Language Association) and APA (American Psychological Association) style manuals state specifically that only one space follows all punctuation marks.

31a Periods punctuate certain sentences and abbreviations.

(1) After a declarative or a mildly imperative sentence

We are first and foremost fellow human beings. [declarative]

Respect your heritage. [mild imperative]

(2) After some abbreviations

Dr.   Jr.   a.m.   p.m.   vs.   etc.   et al.

Periods are not used with all abbreviations (for example, *MVP, mph, FM*).

Only one period follows an abbreviation that ends a sentence.

The study was performed by Ben Werthman et al.

31b The question mark follows direct (but not indirect) questions.

A command is sometimes stated as a question and is followed by a question mark.

Would you pass the salt?

An indirect question is phrased as a statement and so ends with a period.

What in the world is Jennifer doing? [direct question]

They want to know what Jennifer is doing. [indirect question]

Declarative sentences sometimes contain direct questions.

When the question comes up, Why don't you invest in the stock market? we answer that we live on a budget.

A question mark inside parentheses shows that the writer is not sure whether the preceding word, figure, or date is correct.

Chaucer was born in 1340(?) and died in 1400.

Do not punctuate an indirect question with a question mark.

She asked him if he would go.

31c An exclamation point can be used after a word or group of words that is emphatic or shows strong feeling.

Wow! Amazing! That was the best movie I've ever seen!

Use the exclamation point sparingly.

31d The colon calls attention to what follows, and it also separates time, scriptural references, and titles and subtitles.

A colon generally signals that what follows is important. Leave only one space after a colon.

(1) To direct attention to an explanation or summary, a series, or a quotation

I am always seeking the answer to the eternal question: How can we be joined to another person—spouse, parent, child—yet still remain ourselves?

The colon can introduce a second independent clause that explains or expands the first.

For I had no brain tumor, no eyestrain, no high blood pressure, nothing wrong with me at all: I simply had migraine headaches, and migraine headaches were, as everyone who did not have them knew, imaginary.   —JOAN DIDION

Style manuals are fairly consistent on whether to capitalize the first word of a passage that follows a colon (see **33d**). All style manuals agree that after a colon you should capitalize the first letter of a rule or principle or of a quoted sentence. MLA and *The*

Chicago Manual of Style permit the use of a lowercase letter when other material follows a colon; APA also permits the use of a lowercase letter unless what follows the colon is a complete sentence.

Be especially careful not to use an unnecessary colon between a verb and its complement or object, between a preposition and its object, or after *such as.*

> The winners were: Asa, Vanna, and Jack.
>
> Many vegetarians do not eat dairy products, such as: butter and cheese.

(2) To separate figures in time references as well as titles and subtitles

> We are to be there by 11:30 a.m.
>
> I just read *Women's Ways of Knowing: The Development of Self, Voice, and Mind.*

Many writers prefer to use a colon in scriptural references: He quoted from Psalms 3:5. However, MLA recommends periods (Psalms 3.5), and recent biblical scholarship follows this practice as well.

(3) After the salutation of a business letter

> Dear Dr. D'Angelo: Dear Faustine:

31e The dash marks a break in thought, sets off a parenthetical element for emphasis or clarity, and sets off an introductory series.

In handwriting indicate a dash by an unbroken line the length of two hyphens—approximately one-eighth of an inch; on a typewriter, by typing two hyphens with no spaces; and on a keyboard, by typing two hyphens, which most word processing programs convert automatically to an em dash (—).

Use dashes sparingly, not as easy or automatic substitutes for commas, semicolons, or end marks.

(1) To mark a sudden break in thought, an abrupt change in tone, or faltering speech

When we were in first grade, my friend Charlotte finally learned to read every page in her primer——by gluing all of them together.

I know who she is, Mrs.——Mrs.——Mrs. Somebody——the Mayor of Gilpin——or Springtown.

(2) To set off a parenthetical element for emphasis or (if it contains commas) for clarity

Those deep feelings of friendship that are so difficult to express—— feelings of appreciation, of understanding, of love——are really the feelings we should tell our friends about most directly.

(3) After an introductory list or series

"Keen, calculating, perspicacious, acute and astute——I was all of these." —MAX SCHULMAN

31f Parentheses set off nonessential matter and enclose numerals or letters used for lists.

Scores on the Scholastic Aptitude Test (SAT) have been declining for some years.

Bernard Shaw once demonstrated that, by following the rules (up to a point), we could spell fish this way: ghoti. —JOHN IRVING

In general, a sound argument contains (1) a clear statement of its point placed near the beginning and (2) a refutation of opposing positions, usually right after the point statement.

In the next example the entire sentence is parenthetical. (See 33d.)

If we refuse to talk "like a lady," we are ridiculed and criticized for being unfeminine. ("She thinks like a man" is, at best, a left-handed compliment.)   —ROBIN LAKOFF

Dashes, parentheses, and commas are all used to set off parenthetical matter, but they express varying degrees of emphasis. Dashes set off parenthetical elements sharply and usually emphasize them. Parentheses usually deemphasize the elements they enclose. Commas separate elements, usually without emphasizing them.

31g Brackets set off insertions (such as *sic*) in or alterations to quoted matter (including many ellipses) and replace parentheses within parentheses. (See 30a(3).)

The *Home Herald* printed the beginning of the mayor's speech, "My dear fiends [*sic*] and fellow citizens." [A bracketed *sic*—meaning "thus"—tells the reader that the error appears in the original.]

Not every expert agrees. (See, for example, Katie Hafner and Matthew Lyon's *Where Wizards Stay Up Late* [New York: Simon, 1996].)

[I]f the network was ever going to become more than a test bed [. . .], word of its potential had to spread.   —KATIE HAFNER and MATTHEW LYON   [The first pair of brackets indicates the *I* is changed from a lowercase letter; the second pair encloses an ellipsis showing that a word or words have been omitted.]

31h The slash marks line divisions in quoted poetry and indicates that either of two terms is applicable.

Between terms, there are no spaces before or after a slash, but a space is placed before and after a slash used between lines of poetry.

> I noticed that there is yet another book out on writer/critic John Ciardi.

> Wallace Stevens refers to the listener who, "nothing himself, beholds / Nothing that is not there and the nothing that is."

Extensive use of the slash to indicate that either of two terms is applicable (as in *and/or, he/she*) can make writing choppy. You can use *or* instead of the slash.

31i Ellipsis points (three equally spaced periods) mark an omission from a quoted passage or a reflective pause or hesitation.

(1) To mark an omission within a quoted passage

The *MLA Style Manual*—but not the *Publication Manual of the American Psychological Association*—recommends enclosing ellipsis points in brackets to distinguish those showing omitted material from those used by the author. (See 31g.) In any case, make sure your omission does not change the meaning of the material you quote.

Original   To bring rowing to minorities, it's important to first understand why they aren't rowing. The first clue is that not long ago programs spent as much energy keeping minorities out of rowing as they now expend to attract them. —TINA FISHER FORDE

Omission within a quoted sentence

> Noting that "programs spent [. . .] energy keeping minorities out of rowing," Tina Fisher Forde explains one reason for the small numbers of minorities in rowing.

Omission at the beginning or end of a quoted sentence

Neither ellipsis points nor capitals are used at the beginning of a quotation, whether it is run into the text or set off in a block.

An omission that coincides with the end of your sentence requires a period in addition to the three bracketed ellipsis points. Put a space between the last word quoted and the bracket and then include the three spaced ellipsis points. Close the bracket and place the period immediately after it. With a parenthetical reference, the period comes after the second parenthesis instead.

> Tina Fisher Forde claims that in the past rowing programs worked hard at "keeping minorities out of rowing [. . .]."
>
> OR rowing [. . .]" (19).

If the quoted material ends with a question mark or exclamation point, three bracketed ellipsis points are added and the mark is placed immediately after the closing bracket.

To indicate the omission of a full line or more in quoted poetry, use spaced periods covering the length of either the line above it or the omitted line.

> She sang beyond the genius of the sea.
> [. . . . .]
> The song and water were not medleyed sound
> Even if what she sang was what she heard,
> Since what she sang was uttered word by word.
>
> —WALLACE STEVENS

(2) To mark a reflective pause or hesitation.

> Love, like other emotions, has causes . . . and consequences.
>
> —LAWRENCE CASLER

Mechanics

Mechanics

Chapter

32

Spelling, the Spell Checker, and Hyphenation

This chapter explains how to improve your spelling and how to use hyphens. It covers in detail

- using a spell checker (**32a**),
- spelling words according to pronunciation (**32b**),
- spelling words that sound alike (**32c**),
- using affixes (prefixes and suffixes) correctly (**32d–e**),
- dealing with *ei* and *ie* (**32f**), and
- using hyphenation to link and divide words (**32g**).

Spelling problems are highly visible, and misspellings may make a reader doubt whether the writer can present information correctly. Therefore, always proofread to detect misspellings or typographic errors. (See **3g**.)

One way to improve your spelling is to record the words you have misspelled and study them. Another way is to develop your own tricks to help you remember. For example, you might remember the spelling of *separate* by reminding yourself that it has *a rat* in it.

Most spelling errors occur

- when pronunciation is a problem (**32b**),
- when words sound alike (**32c**),
- when affixes are attached (**32d–e**), and
- when words contain *ei/ie* (**32f**).

If you have trouble with spelling, consult your dictionary. Watch out for restrictive labels such as *British* or *chiefly British* and use the American form.

| **American** | theater | fertilize | color | connection |
| **British** | theatre | fertilise | colour | connexion |

If your dictionary lists two unlabeled alternatives, either form is correct—for example, *fulfill* or *fulfil, symbolic* or *symbolical.* The first option listed is usually the more common form.

32a Spell checkers can be valuable tools, but they must be used with caution.

Some people often feel that they no longer need to worry about spelling because computers have spell checkers to correct errors. Although a spell checker can be helpful, it does not solve all spelling problems. For example, the computer cannot tell when you confuse such words as *principal* and *principle* because it cannot know which meaning is called for.

In addition, there are times when you will be writing in-class papers or essay exams and a spell checker will not be available. A basic knowledge of spelling can help you avoid making a poor impression.

THE TRUTH ABOUT SPELL CHECKERS

A spell checker will not catch

- typographic errors when the error makes a word (such as *was* for *saw*).
- misspellings such as *could of* or *would of* for *could have* or *would have* (those that result from mistaking words that are not stressed in speech).
- misspellings that result from using the wrong member of a pair of words (homophones) that sound alike (such as *their/there*), although it will sometimes flag such words to question your usage. When that happens, look the word up in the dictionary (again) to be sure. Spell checkers often give incorrect advice.
- words that are correctly spelled but wrongly used such as *affect* for *effect.* As with homophones, spell checkers will occasionally flag

such words, but you are much safer doing your own checking. You can set the search-and-replace function of your word processor to look for each word and then make sure you have used it correctly.

A spell checker will usually catch

- a letter dropped or added when a prefix is added.
- misspellings of irregular words or those that change the vowel of the root word when a suffix is added, but you will have to watch carefully to catch those the spell checker misses.
- words that are not in its dictionary. Either it will not tell you how to spell them, or it will suggest erroneous alternatives.

32b Spelling often does not reflect pronunciation.

Many words in English are not spelled as they are pronounced. One trick you might use is to be aware of how the word would sound if it were pronounced as it is spelled. Following is a list of such words with the trouble spots boldfaced.

accident**all**y	Fe**b**ruary	nuc**lear**
athlete	gene**r**ally	**per**spire
can**di**date	gover**n**ment	Realtor
congra**tu**lations	mod**er**n	stren**gth**

It is sometimes helpful to think of the spelling of the root word as a guide to correct spelling.

confidence, confide	exultation, exult
different, differ	indomitable, dominate

CAUTION Words such as *have, and,* and *than* are often not stressed in speech and are thus misspelled. A spell checker will not catch these misspellings.

I would ~~of~~ rather had fish ~~then~~ soup ~~an~~ salad.
(have) *(than)* *(and)*

32c The meanings of words that sound alike are determined by the spelling.

Words such as *sole* and *soul* are homophones: they sound alike but have different meanings and spellings.

(1) Contractions and possessive pronouns

In contractions, an apostrophe indicates an omitted letter. In possessive pronouns, there is no apostrophe.

Contraction	Possessive
It's my turn next.	Each group waits **its** turn.
You're next.	**Your** turn is next.

(See **29b** and **29d**.)

(2) Single words and two-word phrases

He wore **everyday** clothes.	He wears them **every day.**
Maybe we will go.	We **may be** going.

CAUTION *A lot* and *all right* are still spelled as two words; *alot* and *alright* are considered incorrect, although *alright* is often used in newspapers and magazines. (See the *Glossary of Usage*.)

(3) Singular nouns ending in *-nce* and plural nouns ending in *-nts*

Assistance is available.	I have two **assistants.**
For **instance,** Jack can go.	They arrived **instants** ago.
My **patience** is frayed.	Some **patients** waited for hours.

The following list contains words that sound exactly alike (*break/brake*) and ones that are similar in sound, especially in rapid speech (*believe/belief*). The spell checker cannot identify words that are correctly spelled but wrongly used. If you are unsure about the difference in meaning between any pair of words, consult the *Glossary of Usage*, the *Index*, or your dictionary.

Words Whose Spellings Are Frequently Confused

accept, except

access, excess

advice, advise

affect, effect

aisles, isles

alley, ally

already, all ready

altar, alter

altogether, all together

always, all ways

amoral, immoral

angel, angle

ask, ax

assistance, assistants

baring, barring, bearing

began, begin

believe, belief

board, bored

break, brake

breath, breathe

buy, by, bye

capital, capitol

censor, censure, sensor

choose, chose

cite, site, sight

clothes, cloths

coarse, course

complement, compliment

conscience, conscious

council, counsel

cursor, curser

dairy, diary

decent, descent, dissent

desert, dessert

device, devise

discreet, discrete

dyeing, dying

elicit, illicit

emigrate, immigrate

envelop, envelope

fair, fare

faze, phase

fine, find

formerly, formally

forth, fourth

forward, foreword

gorilla, guerrilla

have, of

hear, here

heard, herd

heroin, heroine

hole, whole

holy, wholly

horse, hoarse

human, humane

its, it's

later, latter	raise, rise (See **17f**.)
lay, lie (See **17f**.)	respectfully, respectively
lead, led	right, rite, write
lessen, lesson	road, rode
lightning, lightening	sat, set (See **17f**.)
lose, loose	sense, since
marital, martial	shown, shone
maybe, may be	stationary, stationery
minor, miner	straight, strait
moral, morale	than, then
of, off	their, there, they're,
passed, past	there're
patience, patients	threw, through, thorough
peace, piece	throne, thrown
personal, personnel	to, too, two
plain, plane	tract, track
pray, prey	waist, waste
precede, proceed	weak, week
presence, presents	weather, whether
principle, principal	were, wear, where, we're
prophecy, prophesy	which, witch
purpose, propose	who's, whose
quiet, quit, quite	your, you're

32d Adding a prefix to a base word changes the meaning.

Prefixes are added to the beginning of the base word, called the
root.

necessary, **un**necessary   moral, **im**moral

 No letter is added or dropped when a prefix is added. This type
of misspelling is usually detected by a spell checker.

32e Adding a suffix may change the spelling of the base word.

resist, resist**ant**   beauty, beaut**iful**

Spelling, however, is irregular and follows certain conventions.

(1) Dropping or retaining a final *-e*

A word ending in an unpronounced *e* drops the final *e* before a suffix beginning with a vowel.

bride, brid**al**   combine, combin**ation**

A word ending in an unpronounced *e* retains the final *e* before a suffix beginning with a consonant.

entire, entire**ly**   rude, rude**ness**

Some exceptions are, *duly, ninth, truly, wholly.*

To keep the /s/ sound in *ce* or the /j/ sound in *ge*, keep the final *e* before *-able* or *-ous.*

courag**eous**   manag**eable**   notic**eable**

(2) Doubling a final consonant

Double the final consonant before a suffix beginning with a vowel if (a) the consonant ends a one-syllable word or a stressed syllable and (b) the consonant is preceded by a single vowel.

drop, dro**pp**ing   BUT   droop, drooping
admit, admi**tt**ed   BUT   picket, picketed

(3) Changing or retaining a final *-y*

Change the *y* to *i* before suffixes—except *-ing.*

defy: def**ies**, def**ied**, def**iance**   BUT   defy**ing**

Most verbs ending in *y* preceded by a vowel do not change the *y* before *-s* or *-ed: stay, stays, stayed.* Similarly, nouns like *joys* or *days* retain the *y* before *-s.* The following spelling irregularities are especially troublesome: *lays, laid; pays, paid; says, said.*

(4) Retaining a final *-l* before *-ly*

cool, cool**ly**   real, real**ly**   usual, usual**ly**

(5) Adding *-s* or *-es* to form the plural of nouns

scientist**s**   sister**s**-in-law [chief word pluralized]

toy**s**   the Smith**s** [proper names]

For nouns ending in an *f* or *fe,* change the ending to *ve* before adding *-s* when the sound of the plural changes from *f* to *v: thief, thieves; life, lives;* BUT *roof, roofs.*

For nouns ending in *s, z, ch, sh,* or *x,* add *-es* when the plural adds another syllable.

box, box**es**   peach, peach**es**   the Rodriguez**es**

Nouns ending in *y* preceded by a consonant add *-es* after changing the *y* to *i.*

company, compan**ies**   ninety, ninet**ies**

Usage varies for nouns ending in *o* preceded by a consonant. Consult a dictionary if you have a question.

echo**es**	hero**es**	potato**es**	veto**es** [*-es* only]
auto**s**	memo**s**	pimento**s**	pro**s** [*-s* only]

Certain irregular nouns do not add *-s* or *-es* to form the plural.

Singular	woman	goose	sheep	child
Plural	women	gee**se**	sheep	child**ren**

Words derived from other languages generally form their plurals as they did in their original languages. If you are uncertain about how to make any word plural, look in the dictionary.

Singular	criterion	alumnus, -a	analysis	datum	species
Plural	criteria	alumni, -ae	analyses	data	species

32f *Ei* and *ie* are often confused.

When the sound is /i/ (as in *me*), write *ie* except after *c,* in which case write *ei.*

chief   priest   yield

BUT after *c* conceit   perceive   receive

When the sound is other than /i/, you should usually write *ei.*

eight   foreign   heir   rein   their   weight

Some exceptions include *either, neither, friend,* and *species.*

32g Hyphens can link or divide words.

Hyphens link, or make a compound of, two or more words and divide words at the end of a line.

(1) Linking two or more words to form a compound

Nouns   We planted forget-me-nots and Johnny-jump-ups.

Verbs   She speed-read the paper. I double-checked.

Some compounds are listed in the dictionary with hyphens (*eye-opener*), others are written as two words (*eye chart*), and still others are written as one word (*eyewitness*). When in doubt, consult your dictionary.

Hyphenate two or more words serving as a single adjective before a noun.

a well-built house [COMPARE a house that is well built]

In a series, hyphens can carry over from one item to the next.

eighteenth- and nineteenth-century houses

Omit the hyphen in the following cases:

- after an adverb ending in *-ly* (*quickly frozen foods*) and
- in chemical terms (*sodium chloride solution*).

Hyphenate spelled-out fractions and compound numbers from *twenty-one* to *ninety-nine* (or *twenty-first* to *ninety-ninth*).

one-eighth   eighty-four   twenty-third

Also hyphenate combinations of figures and letters (*mid-1990s*), as well as nine-digit ZIP codes (*Dallas, TX 75392-0041*).

Hyphenate to avoid ambiguity.

re-sign the petition [COMPARE resign the position]

In addition, hyphenate between a prefix and a capital letter and between a noun and the suffix *-elect*.

anti-American   President-elect

Otherwise, in general, do not hyphenate prefixes or suffixes.

(2) Hyphens at the ends of lines

If you must divide a word at the end of a line, use a hyphen to separate syllables. However, remember that not every division between syllables is an appropriate place for dividing a word:

- Take care not to divide abbreviations, initials, capitalized acronyms, or one-syllable words.
- Do not create one-letter syllables by putting the first or last letter of a word at the end or beginning of a line or put the last two letters of a word at the beginning of a line.
- Divide most words between consonants but hyphenated words only at the hyphen.

For further guidance, check your dictionary.

Chapter
33 Capitals

This chapter offers guidelines to help you know when and how

- to capitalize proper names (**33a**),
- to use capitals for titles of persons (**33b**),
- to capitalize words in titles of works (**33c**),
- to capitalize the first word of directly quoted speech (**33d**), and
- to avoid unnecessary capitalization (**33e**).

If you have a special problem, consult a good, recent dictionary (see **23a**).

When capitalizing a word is optional, be consistent.

sunbelt OR Sunbelt   a.m. OR A.M.

33a Proper names are capitalized and so, usually, are their abbreviations and acronyms.

Common nouns like *college* and *street* are capitalized only when they are essential parts of proper names.

(1) Names, nicknames, and trademarks

Zora Neale Hurston   Buffalo Bill   Scotch tape

(2) Names of peoples and their languages

African Americans   Asians   English   Urdu
Blacks, Whites OR blacks, whites [Whichever you choose, be consistent.]

(3) Geographical names

China   Mississippi River
Ellis Island   Lincoln Memorial

(4) Names of organizations, government agencies, institutions, and companies

B'nai B'rith   National Endowment for the Arts
International Red Cross   Howard University
Internal Revenue Service   Chicago Cubs

(5) Names for days of the week, months, and holidays

Wednesday   August   Thanksgiving

The names of the seasons—spring, summer, fall, winter—are not capitalized.

(6) Historical documents, periods, events, and movements

Declaration of Independence   Gulf War
Stone Age   Impressionism

(7) Names of religions and of their adherents, holy days, holy books, and words denoting the Supreme Being

Christian, Hindu, Muslim, Jew
Bible, Book of Mormon, Koran, Talmud
Easter, Ramadan, Yom Kippur
Allah, Buddha, God, Vishnu, Yahweh

(8) Personifications

Then into the room walked Death. [COMPARE His death shocked everyone.]

Her heart belonged to Envy. [COMPARE She frequently experienced envy.]

(See also page 387.)

(9) Words derived from proper names

Americanize [verb]   Marxism [noun]   Orwellian [adjective]

(10) Abbreviations and acronyms or shortened forms of capitalized words

AMEX, AT&T, B.A., CBS, CST, JFK, NFL, OPEC, UNESCO, YMCA [All of these are derived from the initial letters of capitalized word groups.]

(See also chapter **35** and **31a(2)**.)

33b Titles that precede the name of a person are capitalized but not those that follow it or stand alone.

Uncle Roy   Roy, my uncle

President Lincoln   the president of the United States

Words referring to family relationships are usually capitalized when the words substitute for proper names.

Tell Mother I'll write soon. [COMPARE My mother wants me to write.]

33c The first, last, and all major words in titles are capitalized. (See 34a and 30c.)

In the style favored by the Modern Language Association (MLA) and in that recommended by the *Chicago Manual of Style* (*CMS*), all words in titles and subtitles are capitalized, except articles, coordinating conjunctions, prepositions, and the *to* in infinitives (unless they are the first or last word). The articles are *a, an,* and *the;* the coordinating conjunctions are *and, but, for, nor, or, so,* and *yet.* MLA style favors lowercasing all prepositions, including long prepositions such as *before, between,* and *through,* which formerly were capitalized. APA style requires capitalizing any word that has four or more letters, including prepositions.

Men Are from Mars, Women Are from Venus [MLA and *CMS*]
Men Are From Mars, Women Are From Venus [APA]

33d The first word of every sentence (or unit written as a sentence) and of directly quoted speech is capitalized.

Oh, really! Do you want to become more efficient? Not right now.
Beth got out of the car and shouted, "Home at last!"

33e Unnecessary capitals are distracting.

(1) Common nouns

Do not capitalize common nouns preceded by the indefinite articles *a* and *an* or by such modifiers as *every* or *several*.

a speech course in theater and television [COMPARE Speech 324: Theater and Television]

a university, several high schools [COMPARE University of Michigan, Hickman High School]

(2) Emphasis

Occasionally, a common noun is capitalized for emphasis or clarity.

The motivation of many politicians is Power.

If you overuse this strategy, however, it will not achieve its purpose. There are better ways to achieve emphasis. (See chapter **21**.)

Style Sheet for Capitalization

Capitals	No Capitals
the South	driving south
Southerners [geographical regions]	the southern regions [compass points]
Revolutionary War	an eighteenth-century war
a Chihuahua [a breed of dog named after a state in Mexico]	a poodle [a breed of dog]
a Ford tractor	a farm tractor
Washington State University	a state university
Declaration of Independence	a declaration of independence
German, Italian, Japanese	a language course
the PTA [OR the P.T.A.]	an organization for parents and teachers

Parkinson's disease [a disease named for a person]	flu, asthma, leukemia
the U.S. Army	a peacetime army
two Democratic candidates [a political party]	democratic procedures [refers to a form of government]
May	spring
Memorial Day	a holiday
Dr. Katherine Kadohata	every doctor, my doctor

Chapter
34   Italics

Italics are a typesetting convention. A word processing program allows you to follow the conventions of professional typesetters who use italics in the following ways. Italics identify or indicate

- the titles of separate publications (**34a**),
- foreign words (**34b**),
- the names of legal cases (**34c**),
- the names of ships and satellites (**34d**), and
- words used primarily as illustrations and algebraic expressions or statistical symbols (**34e**).

In handwritten or typewritten papers, you can indicate italics by underlining.

It was on *60 Minutes.*   It was on <u>60 Minutes</u>.

34a Italics identify the titles of separate works. (See 30c and 33c.)

A separate work is one published (or produced) as a whole rather than as part of a larger published work. A newspaper, for example, is a separate publication, but an editorial in that newspaper is not. Different conventions are used for indicating the title of the newspaper and the title of the editorial. (See **30c**.)

Have you seen Russell Baker's "Disturbers of the Peace" in today's *New York Times*?

Books	*The Bluest Eye*	*A World Lit Only by Fire*
Magazines	*Wired*	*National Geographic*
Newspapers	*USA Today*	*Wall Street Journal*
Plays, films	*Othello*	*The Thin Red Line*
Television and radio shows	*Biography*	*Texaco Presents the Metropolitan Opera*
Recordings	*Hard Day's Night*	*Great Verdi Overtures*
Works of art	*Mona Lisa*	*David*
Long poems	*Paradise Lost*	*The Divine Comedy*
Comic strips	*Peanuts*	*Doonesbury*
Genera, species	*Homo sapiens*	*Rosa setigera*
Software programs	*Photoshop*	*WordPerfect*

The titles of major historical documents or religious texts are not italicized and do not take quotation marks.

The Magna Carta marked a turning point in English history.

The Bible, which is a sacred text like the Koran or the Torah, begins with the Book of Genesis.

The title at the top of your paper or report (unless it is also the title of a book or includes the title of a book) should not be italicized. (See **33c**.)

34b **Italics identify foreign words and phrases that occur in English sentences.**

I tell her I know Chinese. "*Beyeh fa-foon*," I say. "*Shee-veh, Ji nu*," meaning "Stop acting crazy. Rice gruel, Soy sauce." —GISH JEN

Countless words from other languages have become part of English vocabulary and are therefore not italicized.

karate (Japanese)   cliché (French)   patio (Spanish)

34c Italics identify the names of legal cases.

Andrews v. City of Philadelphia   *Roe v. Wade*

34d Italics identify the names of specific ships, satellites, and spacecraft.

U.S.S. Enterprise   the space shuttle *Challenger*

The names of trains and the names of a general class or a trademark are not italicized.

34e Italics indicate words, letters, or figures spoken of as such or used as illustrations, statistical symbols, or the variables in algebraic expressions.

I had hoped to earn an *A* for that course. $c = r^2$

34f Used sparingly, italics occasionally show emphasis.

These *are* the right files. [making it clear that these files are, indeed, the correct ones]

If they take offense, then that's *their* problem.

Chapter

35

Abbreviations, Acronyms, and Numbers

An abbreviation is a shortened version of a word or phrase: *dept.* (department). An acronym is formed by the initial letters of a series of words or from the combination of syllables of other words: *AIDS* (**a**cquired **i**mmuno**d**eficiency **s**yndrome). Abbreviations are usually marked with periods. Acronyms are not.

This chapter will help you learn

- how and when to abbreviate (35a–e),
- when to explain an acronym (35f), and
- how to decide if you should spell out a number or use numerals (35g–h).

35a **Designations such as *Ms., Mr., Mrs., Dr.,* and *St.* appear before a proper name, and those such as *Jr., Sr.,* and *II* after.**

Ms. Gretel Lopez	P. T. Lawrence, III
Dr. Sonya Allen	Mark Ngo, Sr.
St. Paul	Erika C. Scheurer, Ph.D.

Avoid redundant designations.

Dr. Carol Ballou OR Carol Ballou, M.D. [NOT Dr. Carol Ballou, M.D.]

Most abbreviations form plurals by adding *-s* alone, without an apostrophe. Exceptions are made when adding an *-s* would create a different abbreviation: *Mr., Mrs.* When this is the case, consult a dictionary.

Use abbreviations for job titles (such as *Prof., Sen., Capt.,* or *Rev.*) only at the beginning of someone's name.

35b The names of streets, cities, states, countries, continents, months, and days of the week are usually written out in full.

To make sentences easy to read, write out in full the names that appear within them.

> On a Tuesday in September, we drove ninety-nine miles to Minneapolis, Minnesota; the next day we flew to Los Angeles, where we stayed in a hotel on Wilshire Boulevard.

35c Abbreviations are used for addresses in correspondence.

Although words like *Street, Avenue, Road, Company,* and *Corporation* are usually written out when they appear in sentences, they are abbreviated in the address for a letter (see **10c**) or other correspondence. Similarly, the names of states are also abbreviated when they are part of an address. No period follows the postal abbreviation for a state.

Sentence	Derson Manufacturing is located on Madison Street.
Address	Derson Manufacturing 200 Madison St. Watertown, MN 55388

35d Abbreviations are used in bibliographies and other citations of research.

When used within a sentence, words such as *volume, chapter,* and *page* are written out in full.

> I read the introductory chapter and pages 82–89 in the first volume of the committee's report.

In bibliographies, footnotes, and endnotes (see chapter 7), the following abbreviations are used.

abr.	abridged, abridgment
app.	appendix
Apr.	April
Assn.	Association
Aug.	August
bull.	bulletin
c.	circa, about (for example, c. 1960)
CD	compact disc
CD-ROM	compact disc read-only memory
ch., chs.	chapter, chapters
comp.	compiled by, compiler
cont.	contents OR continued
Dec.	December
dept.	department
dir.	directed by, director
diss.	dissertation
DVD	digital videodisc
ed., eds.	edited by OR editor(s) OR edition(s)
et al.	*et alii, et aliae* (and others)
Feb.	February
fig.	figure

ftp	file transfer protocol
fwd.	foreword, foreword by
govt.	government
GPO	Government Printing Office
HR	House of Representatives
html	hypertext markup language
http	hypertext transfer protocol
illus.	illustrated by, illustrator, illustration
inc.	incorporated OR including
Inst.	Institute, Institution
intl.	international
introd.	introduction, introduced by
Jan.	January
Mar.	March
MB	megabyte
MOO	multiuser domain, object-oriented
ms., mss.	manuscript, manuscripts
n, nn	note, notes (used immediately after page number: 6n3)
natl.	national
n.d.	no date [of publication]
no., nos.	number [of issue], numbers
Nov.	November
n.p.	no place [of publication] OR no publisher
n. pag.	no pagination
Oct.	October
P	Press (used in documentation; see *U*)
p., pp.	page, pages
pref.	preface, preface by
pseud.	pseudonym

pt., pts.	part, parts
rept.	reported by, report
rev.	revision, revised, revised by OR review, reviewed by
rpt.	reprinted, reprint
sec., secs.	section, sections
Sept.	September
ser.	series
Soc.	Society
supp.	supplement
trans.	translated by, translator, translation
U	University (used in documentation; Wesleyan UP OR U of California P)
vol., vols.	volume, volumes (omitted before volume numbers unless the reference would be unclear)
www	World Wide Web

35e Certain abbreviations are acceptable within sentences.

Some abbreviations are acceptable within sentences because they have come to function as the full equivalent of words.

(1) Clipped forms

Because it functions as a word, a clipped form does not end with a period. Some clipped forms such as *rep* (representative), *exec* (executive), or *info* (information) are too informal for use in college writing. Others—such as *exam, lab,* and *math*—are becoming acceptable because they have been used so frequently that they no longer seem like abbreviations.

(2) Time period and zone

82 B.C. [OR B.C.E.]   A.D. 95 [OR 95 C.E.]
for before Christ [OR   for *anno Domini,* in the year of
before the common era]   our Lord [OR the common era]

7:40 a.m. [OR A.M.]   4:52 EST [OR E.S.T.]
for *ante meridiem,* before noon   for eastern standard time

Words designating units of time, such as *minute* or *month,* are written out when they appear in sentences. They can be abbreviated in tables or charts.

min.   mo.   yr.

(3) The United States

The abbreviation for the United States (U.S.) can be used as an adjective.

the U.S. Navy, the U.S. economy [COMPARE The United States continues to enjoy a strong economy.]

(4) Names of individuals

Writers use initials in the names of individuals who are commonly referred to by their initials.

FDR   JFK   E. B. White

In most cases, however, first and last names should be written out in full.

Phyllis D. Miller

(5) Expressions in Latin

So that you can use these abbreviations correctly, the English equivalent is provided here in brackets.

cf. [compare]	et al. [and others]	i.e. [that is]
e.g. [for example]	etc. [and so forth]	vs. OR v. [versus]

35f Acronyms are usually spelled out the first time they are used.

Some acronyms have been used so frequently that they are likely to be recognized without explanation.

CBS	NASA	NFL	YMCA

In most cases, however, you should identify an acronym the first time you use it.

FEMA (the Federal Emergency Management Administration) was criticized for its slow response to the victims of Hurricane Andrew.

OR

The Federal Emergency Management Administration (FEMA) was criticized. . . .

By spelling out acronyms the first time you use them, you help your audience to follow your discussion.

35g Numbers are written in different ways.

When you use numbers infrequently in a piece of writing, you can spell out those that can be expressed in one or two words and use figures for the others. When you use numbers frequently, spell out those from one to nine and use figures for all others.

Always	over three inches
But	three-quarters of an inch OR .75 inches

Always after 124 days
But after thirty-three days OR after 33 days

In a discussion of related items containing both single- and double- or triple-digit numbers, use figures for all numbers.

Lana worked **7** hours last week, but Julio worked **22.**

If a sentence begins with a number, spell out the number.

Two hundred twenty-five contestants competed in the talent show.

Note that *and* is not used in this case.

35h Some numbers follow special usages.

(1) Time of day

4 p.m. OR 4:00 p.m. OR four o'clock in the afternoon
9:30 a.m. OR half-past nine in the morning

(2) Dates

November 8, 1962 OR 8 November 1962 [NOT November 8th, 1962]
the fifties OR the 1950s
the fourteenth century
in 1362
from 1998 to 2001 OR 1998–2001

Many languages invert the numbers for the month and the day, writing **18/9/01** for *September 18, 2001.* In American practice, the month precedes the day: **9/18/01.**

(3) Addresses

25 Arrow Drive, Apartment 1 OR 25 Arrow Dr., Apt. 1
21 Second Street
459 East 35 Street OR 459 East 35th Street

(4) Identification numbers

Channel 10   Edward III   Interstate 40   Room 222

(5) Pages and other divisions of books and plays

page 15   chapter 8   part 2
in act 2, scene 1 OR in Act II, Scene I

(6) Decimals and percentages

a 2.5 average   12 percent   0.853 metric tons

(7) Large round numbers

forty million dollars OR $40 million OR $40,000,000

(8) Legal or commercial writing

The lawyer's fee will exceed two million (2,000,000) dollars.
OR
The lawyer's fee will exceed two million dollars ($2,000,000).

Glossaries

Glossary of Usage

The following short glossary covers the most common usage problems. It also distinguishes between written English and conversational English. An expression that may be acceptable in spoken English or in a letter to a friend is labeled **colloquial** or **informal** and is usually not acceptable in college or professional writing. College writing is sometimes referred to as "edited American English" or "academic discourse." The following labels are used in this glossary.

College and professional writing	Words or phrases listed in dictionaries without special usage labels; appropriate in college or business writing.
Conversational	Words or phrases that dictionaries label *informal, slang,* or *colloquial;* although often acceptable in spoken language, not generally appropriate in college writing.
Unacceptable	Words or phrases labeled in dictionaries as *archaic, illiterate, nonstandard, obsolete, substandard;* generally not accepted in college writing.

You may also wish to consult **32c** for a list of words that sound alike but have different meanings.

accept, except   *Accept* means "to receive"; *except* means "to exclude": I **accept** your apology. All **except** Joe will go.

advice, advise   *Advice* is a noun, and *advise* is a verb: I accept your **advice.** Please **advise** me of the situation.

affect, effect   The verb *affect* means "to influence" or "to touch the emotions." The noun *effect* means "result of an action or antecedent": Smoking **affects** the heart. His tears **affected** her deeply. Drugs have side **effects.** The **effect** on sales was good. When used as a verb, *effect* means "to produce" or "to cause": The medicine **effected** a complete cure.

aggravate   Widely used for "annoy" or "irritate." Many writers, however, restrict the meaning of *aggravate* to "intensify, make worse": Noises **aggravate** a headache.

ain't   Unacceptable in writing unless used in dialogue or for humorous effect.

allusion, illusion   An *allusion* is a casual or indirect reference. An *illusion* is a false idea or an unreal image: The **allusion** was to Shakespeare's *Twelfth Night.* His idea of college is an **illusion.**

alot   A misspelling of the overused and nonspecific phrase *a lot.*

already, all ready   *Already* means "before or by the time specified." *All ready* means "completely prepared": She is **already** in the car. The picnic supplies are **all ready** for you.

alright   Not yet a generally accepted spelling of *all right,* although it is becoming more common in journalistic writing.

altogether, all together   *Altogether* means "wholly, thoroughly." *All together* means "in a group": That book is **altogether** too difficult, unless the class reads it **all together.**

among, between   These prepositions are used with plural objects (including collective nouns). As a rule, use *among* with objects denoting three or more (a group), and use *between* with those denoting only two: danced **among** the flowers, whispering **among** themselves; reading **between** the lines, just **between** you and me.

amount of, number of   Use *amount of* with a singular noncount noun: The **amount of** rain varies. Use *number of* with a plural count noun: The **number of** errors was excessive. See **number** and **noun** in the **Glossary of Terms.**

and/or   This combination is appropriate in professional writing but acceptable in college writing only when the context calls for both *and* and *or* as well as either one singly: To write a comparison/contrast essay, examine the points of similarity **and/or** difference between two stated things.

anxious   Not to be used as a synonym for *eager.*

anyone, any one; everyone, every one   Distinguish between each one-word and two-word compound. *Anyone* means "any person at all"; *any one* refers to one of a group. Similarly, *everyone* means "all," and *every one* refers to each one in a group: Was **anyone** hurt? Was **any one** of you hurt? **Everyone** should attend. **Every one** of them should attend.

anyways, anywheres   Unacceptable for *anyway, anywhere.*

apt, liable, likely   *Apt* is generally accepted and now used interchangeably with *liable* and *likely* before an infinitive. *Liable* is generally limited to situations that have an undesirable outcome: He is not **likely** to get sick. He is **liable** to get sick. (See **liable, likely**.) He is **apt** to get sick.

as   1. As a conjunction, *as* expresses sameness of degree, quantity, or manner: **As** scholars have noted . . . OR Do **as** I do. As a preposition, *as* expresses equivalence: I think of Tom **as** my brother. [Tom = brother] Use *like* to express similarity: Tom is **like** a brother.
   2. Use *if, that,* or *whether* instead of *as* after such verbs as *feel, know, say,* or *see:* I do not know **whether** my adviser is right.
   3. In subordinate clauses, use *because* to introduce a causal relationship and *while* to introduce a time relationship: **Because** it was raining, we watched TV. **While** it was raining, we watched TV.

assure, ensure, insure   *Assure* means "to state with confidence." *Ensure* and *insure* are sometimes used interchangeably to mean "make certain." *Insure* has the further meaning of "to protect against loss": Marlon **assured** me that he would vote for my ticket. I **ensured** (or **insured**) that Vincent had his tickets before I left home. Bing **insured** her car against theft.

as to   Imprecise; use the clearer word *about:* He wasn't certain **about** the time.

at   Unacceptable in college writing when *at* follows *where,* even with intervening words. We did not know where the museum was **at**.

awful   Unacceptable for the often overused adverb *awfully:* She is **awfully** intelligent.

awhile, a while   *Awhile,* an adverb, is not used as the object of a preposition: We rested **awhile**. [COMPARE We rested for **a while**.]

bad Unacceptable as an adverb: Bill danced **badly.** Acceptable as a subject complement after sense verbs such as *feel, look, smell.* I feel **bad** when I have a cold. See **15a.**

being as, being that Wordy and imprecise; use *since, because.*

beside, besides Always a preposition, *beside* usually means "next to," sometimes "apart from": The chair was **beside** the table. As a preposition, *besides* means "in addition to" or "other than": She has many books **besides** those on the table. As an adverb, *besides* means "also" or "moreover": The library has a fine collection of books; **besides,** it has a number of valuable manuscripts.

better Unacceptable for *had better:* We **had better** run the spell check. See **had better.**

between See **among, between.**

biannual, biennial *Biannual* means "twice in one year," whereas *biennial* means "every two years": An equinox is a **biannual** event. The state legislature's meetings are **biennial** rather than annual.

bring, take Both words describe the same action but from different standpoints. Someone *brings* something *to* the speaker's location, whereas someone else *takes* something *away* from the speaker's location: **Bring** your book when you come to class. I **take** my notes home with my book.

busted Unacceptable as the past tense of *burst.*

but what, but that Conversational after expressions of doubt such as "no doubt" or "did not know." Use *that:* I do not doubt **that** they are correct.

can, may *Can* refers to ability, and *may* refers to permission: I **can** [am able to] drive fifty miles an hour, but I **may** not [am not permitted to] exceed the speed limit.

can't hardly, can't scarcely Unacceptable for *can hardly, can scarcely.*

capital, capitol A *capital* is a governing city; it also means "funds." As a modifier, *capital* means "chief" or "principal." A *capitol* is a statehouse; the *Capitol* is the U.S. congressional building in Washington, D.C.

censor, censure   *Censor* (verb) means "to remove or suppress because of immoral or otherwise objectionable ideas": Do you think a movie ratings board should **censor** films that have too much sex and violence? A *censor* (noun) is a person who suppresses those ideas. *Censure* (verb) means "to blame or criticize"; a *censure* (noun) is an expression of disapproval or blame. The senate **censured** Joseph McCarthy.

center around   Conversational for "to be focused on" or for "to center on."

chairman, chairperson, chair   *Chairman* is misused as a generic term. *Chairperson* or *chair* is generally preferred as the generic term.

cite, site, sight   *Cite* means "to mention." *Site* is a locale. *Sight* is a view or the ability to see: Be sure to **cite** your sources in your paper. The president visited the disaster **site**. What a tragic **sight!**

compare to, compare with   *Compare to* means "regard as similar," and *compare with* means "examine to discover similarities or differences." The instructor **compared** the diagram **to** the finished product. The student **compared** the first draft **with** the second.

complement, compliment   *Complement* means "to complete" or "to supply needs"; *compliment* means "to express praise." *Complimentary* means "given free," as in "**complimentary** tickets": Their personalities **complement** each other. Betsy **complimented** Jim on his award.

comprise, compose   *Comprise* means "to contain." *Compose* means "to make up": The collection **comprises** many volumes. That collection **is composed** of medieval manuscripts.

consensus of opinion   Redundant. Omit "of opinion."

consequently, subsequently   *Consequently* means "as a result of"; *subsequently* means "following": The catcher missed the ball; **consequently,** the other team scored. **Subsequently,** they won the game.

contact   Although often used in professional writing, this usage is considered imprecise in college writing; use *telephone, see, talk to, write to,* or the like.

continual, continuous   *Continual* means "recurring at regular intervals": He coughed **continually.** *Continuous* means "recurring without interruption": He talked **continuously.**

convince, persuade   *Convince* refers to a change of opinion or belief, whereas *persuade* refers to motivation to act: What does it take to **convince** you that you sing beautifully? I must **persuade** you to stop smoking.

council, counsel   Homonyms; *council* is a noun meaning "an advisory or decision-making group." *Counsel* as a verb means "to give advice," and as a noun, "a legal adviser."

criteria, criterion   *Criteria* is a plural noun meaning "a set of standards for judgment." The singular form is *criterion.*

different than, different from   Both are widely used, although *different from* is generally preferred in college writing.

disinterested, uninterested   *Disinterested* means "impartial" or "lacking prejudice": a *disinterested* referee. *Uninterested* means "indifferent, lacking interest": A **disinterested** observer will give a fair opinion. An **uninterested** observer may fall asleep.

don't   Unacceptable when used for *doesn't:* My father **doesn't** dance.

drug   Unacceptable as the past tense of *dragged.*

due to   Usually avoided in college writing when used as a preposition in place of *because* or *on account of:* **Because of** holiday traffic, we arrived an hour late.

effect   See **affect, effect.**

e.g.   Abbreviation from Latin *exempli gratia,* meaning "for example." Replace with the English equivalent *for example* or *for instance.* Do not confuse with **i.e.**

elicit, illicit   *Elicit* means "to draw forth." *Illicit* means "unlawful": It is **illicit** to **elicit** public funds for your private use.

emigrate from, immigrate to   The prefix *e-* (a variant of *ex-*) means "out of." To *emigrate* is to go out of one's own country to settle in another. The prefix *im-* (a variant of *in-*) means "into." To *immigrate* is to come into a different country to settle. The corresponding adjective or noun forms are *emigrant* and *immigrant:* The Ulster Scots **emigrated from** Scotland to Ireland and then **immigrated to** the southern United States.

eminent, imminent *Eminent* means "distinguished"; *imminent* means "about to happen": Maria Hughes is an **eminent** scholar. The storm is **imminent.**

ensure See **assure, ensure, insure.**

enthused Conversational usage, not accepted in college writing. Use *enthusiastic.*

especially, specially *Especially* means "outstandingly"; *specially* means "for a particular purpose, specifically": This is an **especially** nice party. I bought this tape **specially** for the occasion.

-ess A female suffix now considered sexist, therefore unacceptable. Use *poet, author, actor,* and *waiter* or *server* instead of *poetess, authoress, actress,* and *waitress.*

etc. From the Latin *et cetera* meaning "and other things." In college writing, substitute *and so on* or *and so forth.* Because *etc.* means "and other things," *and etc.* is redundant.

every day, everyday As two words, *every day* is an adjective and a noun meaning "daily," but as one word, *everyday* is an adjective meaning "mundane," or "ordinary": It is an **every day** occurrence. These are **everyday** problems.

everyone, every one See **anyone, any one.**

explicit, implicit *Explicit* means "expressed directly or precisely." *Implicit* means "implied or expressed indirectly": The instructions were **explicit.** There was an **implicit** suggestion in her lecture.

farther, further Generally, *farther* refers to geographic distance: six miles **farther.** *Further* is used as a synonym for *additional* in more abstract references: **further** delay, **further** proof.

fewer, less *Fewer* refers to people or objects that can be counted; *less* refers to amounts that can be observed or to abstract nouns: **fewer** pencils, **less** milk, **less** support.

field Usually wordy or imprecise when used to refer to an academic or scientific discipline: We want to study ~~the field of~~ medicine. ~~My field is~~ I study feminist rhetoric.

firstly, secondly In college writing, use *first, second* instead.

former, latter *Former* refers to the first of two; *latter* to the second of two. If three or more items are mentioned, use *first* and *last:* John and Ian are both British; the **former** is from England, and the **latter** is from Scotland.

fun Conversational when used as an adjective. Use *fun* as a noun in college writing. We were having ~~a fun visit~~.

get Useful in many idioms but not appropriate in college writing in expressions such as the following: The baby's whining ~~got to an-noyed~~ me. The puppy ~~got~~ became fat. I'm going to ~~get~~ take re-venge on you for that.

good, well *Good* is an adjective frequently misused as an adverb; *well* is an adverb: He dances **well.** He had a **good** time. *Well* in the sense of "in good health" may be used as a subject complement interchangeably with *good* in such expressions as "Pedro doesn't feel **well** (or **good**)."

great Overworked for more precise words such as *skillful, good, clever, enthusiastic,* or *very well.*

had ought (meaning "ought to") Omit the verb *had:* We **ought to** go home.

half a, a half, a half a Use *half of a, half a,* or *a half.*

hanged, hung *Hanged* refers specifically to "put to death by hang-ing": She was **hanged** at dawn. *Hung* is the usual past participle: He had **hung** the picture.

he Used inappropriately as a generic term for both men and women. See **16d(1)** and **23d(1).**

hisself Use *himself.*

hopefully Means "with hope." Used inappropriately for *I hope* or *it is hoped.*

i.e. Abbreviation for the Latin *id est,* meaning "that is." Use *that is* instead. Do not confuse with **e.g.**

if, whether Use *if* to mean "in the event that"; *whether* suggests al-ternatives: I can't go **if** you drive; **whether** I go depends on who is driving.

illusion See **allusion, illusion.**

imminent See **eminent, imminent.**

impact Jargon when used to mean "have an effect": The new tax ~~impacts~~ affects everyone.

implement Jargon when used to mean "accomplish": We ~~implemented~~ accomplished our goals.

implicit See **explicit, implicit.**

imply, infer *Imply* means "suggest without actually stating," and *infer* means "draw a conclusion based on evidence": He **implied** that he was angry, but I **inferred** that he was frightened.

in, into *In* points to location, *into* to movement or a change in condition: We were **in** Atlanta. The prisoners were herded **into** a cell.

ingenious, ingenuous *Ingenious* means "creative or shrewd." *Ingenuous* means "innocent or unworldly": Terry's **ingenious** plan worked without complication. The criminal's **ingenuous** smile was misleading.

in regards to Unacceptable for *in regard to.*

irregardless Use *regardless.*

its, it's *Its* is a possessive pronoun, as in "The dog buried **its** bone." *It's* is a contraction of *it is,* as in "**It's** a beautiful day."

kind, sort, type Used interchangeably. Singular forms are modified by *this* or *that,* plural forms by *these* or *those:* **This kind** (**sort, type**) of argument is unacceptable. **These kinds** (**sorts, types**) of arguments are unacceptable.

lay, lie Use *lay* (*laid, laying*) in the sense of "put" or "place." Use *lie* (*lay, lain, lying*) in the sense of "rest" or "recline." *Lay* takes an object (to **lay** something), whereas *lie* does not. See also **17f.**

| *Lay*—to put or place | He had **laid** the book on the table. | The man was **laying** the carpet. |
| *Lie*—to recline | He had **lain** down to take a nap. | The cat was **lying** on the bed. |

learn Unacceptable for *teach, instruct, inform:* He **taught** me bowling.

leave Unacceptable for *let* in the sense of allowing: **Let** [NOT leave] him have the hammer.

lend, loan *Lend* is a verb meaning "to give temporarily." *Loan* is a noun meaning "something borrowed." In college writing, do not use loan as a verb: The banks **lend** money for mortgages. Most of us have student **loans** to repay.

less See **fewer, less.**

liable, likely *Liable* usually means "exposed" or "responsible" in an undesirable sense. *Likely* means "probably," "destined," or "susceptible": If you wreck the car, you are **liable** for damages. With her brains, she is **likely** to succeed.

like Although *like* is widely used as a conjunction in spoken English, *as, as if,* and *as though* are preferred for college English.

literally Often misused as an intensifier, *literally* means "actually" or "exactly as stated": I was ~~literally~~ **nearly** frozen after I shoveled snow for an hour.

lose, loose *Lose* is a verb: did **lose,** will **lose.** *Loose* is chiefly an adjective: a **loose** belt.

lots Conversational for *many, much.*

mankind Considered inappropriate because it excludes women. Use *humanity, human race.*

may be, maybe *May be* is a verb phrase; *maybe* is an adverb: The rumor **may be** true. **Maybe** the rumor is true.

may, can See **can, may.**

media, medium *Media* is plural: Some people think the **media** have sometimes created the news in addition to reporting it. *Medium* is singular: The newspaper is one **medium** that people seem to trust.

most Use *almost* in expressions such as "almost everyone," "almost all." Use *most* only as a superlative: **most** writers.

myself Use only when preceded by an antecedent in the same sentence: Li and **I** went swimming. BUT **I** made **myself** go swimming.

nothing like, nowhere near In college writing, use *not nearly:* My car is ~~nowhere near~~ **not nearly** as old as yours.

nowheres Unacceptable for *nowhere.*

number As subjects, *a number* is generally plural and *the number* is singular. Make sure that the verb agrees with the subject: **A number** of possibilities **are** open. **The number** of possibilities **is** limited. See also **amount of, number of.**

of Often mistaken for the sound of the unstressed *have:* "They must ~~of~~ **have** [OR would **have**, could **have**, might **have**, ought to **have**, may **have**, should **have**, would **have**] gone home."

off of Use *off* in phrases such as "walked off ~~of~~ the field."

OK, O.K., okay Conversational usage. All three are acceptable spellings. It is usually better to replace *OK* with a more specific word.

on account of Use the less wordy *because:* I went home ~~on account of being~~ **because I was** tired.

parameter Overused and imprecise for *boundary, perimeter.*

passed, past *Passed* is the past tense of the verb *pass. Past* as a noun or adjective refers to a former time: We **passed** them in the street. Don't worry about **past** mistakes.

people, persons In college writing, use *people* to refer to a general group, *person* to refer to an individual or group of individuals: A lot of **people** were at the concert last night. They will admit only one **person** at a time.

phenomena Plural form of *phenomenon.*

plus Acceptable as a preposition. Weak when used instead of the co-ordinating conjunction *and.* I telephoned ~~plus~~ **and** I sent flowers.

precede, proceed To *precede* is to "go ahead of"; to *proceed* is to "go forward": His song will **precede** the fight scene. He will **proceed** with the song.

prejudice, prejudiced Use *prejudice,* a noun, when the word is the subject or an object; use *prejudiced,* an adjective, when the word modifies a noun or serves as a complement: **Prejudiced** people often are unaware of their **prejudices. Prejudice** is ugly in all its forms. She is not **prejudiced.**

principal, principle   The adjective or noun *principal* means "chief" or "chief official." The noun may also mean "capital." The noun *principle* means "fundamental truth": The **principal** factor in the salary decision was his belief in the **principle** of sexual equality.

proceed   See **precede, proceed.**

raise, rear   See **rear, raise.**

raise, rise   Use *raise* (*raised, raising*) in the sense of "to lift or cause to move upward, to bring up or increase." Use *rise* (*rose, risen, rising*) in the sense of "to get up, to move or extend upward, ascend." *Raise* (a transitive verb) takes an object; *rise* (an intransitive verb) does not. See **17f.**

> *Raise*—to lift   Retailers **raised** prices.
>
> *Rise*—to ascend   Retail prices **rose** sharply.

rarely ever   Use either *rarely* alone or *hardly ever:* He **rarely ever** (or **hardly ever**) goes to the library.

real, really   Use *real* as an adjective, *really* as an adverb. *Real* is often misused in expressions such as the following, where it is an adverb modifying the adjective *beautiful:* It is a **real really** beautiful day.

rear, raise   *Rear* is preferred when speaking of bringing up children.

refer back   Redundant. Use *refer.*

regard, regarding, regards   Use *in regard to, with regard to,* or *regarding.*

relation, relationship   In college writing, use *relation* when linking things, *relationship* when linking people: We studied the **relation** between language and social change. My best friend and I were concerned about our **relationship.**

respectfully, respectively   *Respectfully* means "showing respect"; *respectively* means "in the order designated": We always treated Ms. Bender **respectfully.** I tried out a Chevy, a Ford, and a Plymouth, **respectively.**

sensuous, sensual   *Sensuous* refers to gratification of the senses in response to art, music, nature, and so on; *sensual* refers to gratification of the physical senses: Titian's paintings are very **sensuous.** A fine dinner can be a **sensual** experience.

shall, will   Traditionally *shall* was used with *I* or *we* to express future tense, and *will* was used with the other personal pronouns, but *shall* has almost disappeared in contemporary American English. *Shall* is still used in legal writing to convey obligation.

should, would   *Should* expresses obligation or condition: Students **should** not be rude in class. *Would* expresses wishes or habitual actions: If you **would** drive me to the library in Cedarville, I **would** have new books to read.

sit, set   Use *sit* in the sense of "to be seated" and *set* in the sense of "to place something." *Set,* a transitive verb, takes an object. *Sit,* an intransitive verb, does not. See **17f.**

Sit—to be seated   Jonathon **sat** under the tree.

Set—to place something   Maria **set** the cookies on the table.

so   Overused as an intensifier; use a more precise modifier: She was ~~so~~ **intensely** focused.

some   Conversational and vague when used as a substitute for such words as *remarkable, memorable:* She was ~~some~~ **a remarkable** athlete.

sometime, sometimes, some time   *Sometime* is an adverb meaning "at an unspecified time"; *sometimes* is an adverb meaning "at times"; *some time* is an adjective-noun pair meaning "a span of time": Let's go to the movies **sometime. Sometimes** we go to the movies. They agreed to allow **some time** to pass before going to the movies together again.

sort, sort of   See **kind, sort** and **kind of a, sort of a.**

stationary, stationery   *Stationary* means "in a fixed position"; *stationery* means "writing paper and envelopes."

supposed to, used to   In college writing, be sure to include the frequently unsounded *-d* at the end of these expressions.

sure   Conversational when used as an adverb. Use *certainly* or *undoubtedly:* I ~~sure~~ **certainly** like your new hat.

take See **bring, take.**

than, then Use *than* in comparisons: She is taller **than** I am. Use *then* in statements relating to time: I stopped and **then** I looked both ways.

that, which *That* has traditionally been used with a restrictive clause: The cup **that** is on the table is full [distinguishes a specific cup that is full]. *Which* has traditionally been used with a nonrestrictive clause: The cup, **which** is on the table, is full ["which is on the table" gives nonessential information]. Increasingly, however, writers are using these interchangeably, and the distinction between them is becoming blurred. (See **27d**.)

their, there, they're, there're *Their* is the possessive form of *they; there* is ordinarily an adverb or an expletive; *they're* is a contraction of *they are; there're* is a contraction of *there are:* **There** is no explanation for **their** behavior. **They're** making trouble **there** on the ball field. **There're** no tickets left.

theirself, theirselves Use *themselves.*

them Unacceptable when used as an adjective; use *those* or *these* instead: ~~them~~ those apples.

then Sometimes incorrectly used for *than.* Unlike *then, than* does not relate to time: He's a better skater ~~then~~ **than** his brother.

this here, that there, these here, them there Redundant; use *this, that, these, those.*

thusly Use *thus.*

to, too Distinguish the preposition *to* from the adverb *too:* When the weather is **too** hot to play ball, they go **to** the movies.

try and Conversational for *try to:* I will try ~~and~~ **to** see him today.

unique Because *unique* means "one of a kind," it is illogical to use *unique* with a comparative, as in *very unique.* Do not confuse with *unusual.*

uninterested See **disinterested.**

usage Not a substitute for *use of. Usage* refers to a customary practice and most often refers to language; *use of* refers to the employment of something: English teachers are concerned about verb **usage.** We had the **use of** the cabin for a week.

use to Should be *used to.*

utilize Often pretentious; *use* is preferred.

wait on Unacceptable as a substitute for *wait for.*

ways Unacceptable for *way* when referring to distance: It's a long ~~ways~~ **way** from home.

well See **good, well.**

where Conversational as a substitute for *that:* I saw on TV ~~where~~ **that** she had been elected.

where . . . at, where . . . to Omit the superfluous *at, to:* **Where** is the library ~~at~~? **Where** are you moving ~~to~~?

which When referring to persons, use *who* or *that.* See **that, which.**

who, which, that *Who* refers to persons, *which,* to things. *That* generally refers to things but may refer to groups of people.

who, whom *Who* is used as the subject or subject complement in a clause, *whom* is used as an object: **Who** gave the money to **whom**?

whose, who's *Whose* indicates possession: **Whose** book is this? The mountain **whose** summit is over twelve thousand feet was difficult to climb. *Who's* is the contraction of *who is:* **Who's** going to the movie?

with regards to See **regard, regarding, regards.**

your, you're *Your* is the possessive of *you:* in **your** house. *You're* is a contraction of *you are:* **You're** gaining strength. See also **its, it's.**

Glossary of Terms

This glossary presents brief explanations of frequently used terms. Consult the index for references to further discussion of most of the terms and for a number of terms not listed.

absolute phrase   A grammatically unconnected part of a sentence—generally a noun or pronoun followed by a participle (and sometimes modifiers): We will have a cookout, **weather permitting** [noun + present participle]. See **12a(6)**, **19a**, and **22b(4)**. See also **phrase** and **sentence modifier.**

abstract noun   A noun that expresses qualities, concepts, and emotions that cannot be perceived through the senses: truth, justice, fear, future. See **24a(3)**.

acronym   A word formed by combining the initial letters of a series of words: laser—*l*ight *a*mplification by *s*timulated *e*mission of *ra*diation.

active voice   The form of a verb indicating that the grammatical subject carries out the action: Emily *sliced* the ham. See chapter **17** and **21d(1)**. See also **passive voice, verb,** and **voice.**

adjective   The part of speech modifying a noun or a pronoun: *shy, sleepy, attractive, famous, historic.* Adjective-making suffixes are *-al, -able, -ant, -ative, -ic, -ish, -less, -ous, -y. Limiting adjectives* restrict the meaning of the words they modify: *that* pie, *its* leaves. *Descriptive adjectives* name a quality of a noun, including degrees of comparison: *red* shirt, *bigger* planes. *Proper adjectives* are derived from proper nouns: *Spanish* rice. See **33a**. Two or more adjectives separated by a comma, instead of by a coordinating conjunction, are referred to as *coordinate adjectives:* a *brisk, cold* walk. See **27c(2)**. *Interrogative adjectives* are used to ask questions: *Whose* book is it? See also **degree** and **predicate adjective.**

adjectival clause   A subordinate clause used as an adjective: people *who bite their fingernails.* See **12b(2)**, **27d**, and **15e(3)**. See also **clause.**

adjectival phrase   A phrase used as an adjective: The woman *carrying the large notebook* is my sister. See **12a(3–5)**. See also **phrase**.

adverb   The part of speech modifying a verb, an adjective, or another adverb: *rapidly* approached, *too* bitter, *very graciously* accepted. An adverb may also modify a verbal, a phrase or clause, or the rest of the sentence: *Usually,* an artist does her best work when she is focusing *entirely* on the task at hand. The adverb-making suffix is *-ly:* the adjective *rare* becomes the adverb *rarely.*

adverbial clause   A subordinate clause used as an adverb to indicate time, place, cause, condition, concession, comparison, purpose, or result: *Although he is usually quiet* [concession], everyone listens to him *when he speaks* [time], *because he makes good suggestions* [cause]. See **12b(2)**, **27b(1)**, and **22b(1)**. See also **clause** and **conditional clause**.

adverbial conjunction   See **conjunctive adverb**.

adverbial phrase   A phrase used as an adverb to indicate time, place, cause, condition, concession, comparison, purpose, or result. See **12a(3–4)**, and **(6)** and **19a(2)**. See also **adverbial clause.**

agreement   The correspondence in number and person of a subject and verb (*the dog barks, dogs bark*) or in number and gender of a pronoun and its antecedent (the *team* boarded *its* bus, the *members* carrying *their* bags). See **16d** and **17e**.

allusion   A brief, unexplained reference to a work or to a person, place, event, or thing that the writer expects the reader to be familiar with. See **9a(1)**.

analogy   A rhetorical device using the features of something familiar (and often concrete) to explain something unfamiliar (and often abstract), or similarities between things that are not usually associated.

analysis   A separation of a whole into its constituent parts; for example, separating a literary work into its elements for study.

antecedent   A word or group of words that a pronoun refers to. *Pets* can be polite or rude, like *their* trainers. See **16e**.

antonym   A word that means the opposite of another: *follow* is the antonym for *lead*.

APA   American Psychological Association. See **7h–i**.

appeal   The means of persuasion in argumentative writing; relies on reason, authority, and/or emotion.

appositive   A noun or noun phrase placed near another to identify, explain, or supplement its meaning. See **27d(2)**, **19a(3)**, **22b(4)**, and **22c(3)**.

argument   Writing that uses various rhetorical strategies and appeals to convince the reader of the truth or falsity of a given proposition or thesis. See **appeal** and **thesis.**

article   *The* (definite article)*, a,* or *an* (indefinite articles) used as adjectives before nouns: *the* cups, *a* cup, *an* extra cup. See **26a**.

audience   The person or persons for whom the writing is intended. See **1g(2)**.

auxiliary   A form of *be, have,* or *will* that combines with a verb to indicate voice, tense, or mood: *was* going, *had* gone. Modals such as *will, would,* and *may* are also considered auxiliaries. See chapter **17** and **26b**.

balanced sentence   A sentence with grammatically equal structures.

bibliography   A list of books, articles, essays, or other material, usually on a particular subject.

brainstorming   A method of generating ideas about a subject; involves listing ideas as they occur in a session of intensive thinking about the subject. See **2a**.

case   The form or position of a noun or pronoun that shows its use or relation to other words in a sentence. The three cases in English are the *subjective* (or nominative), which is usually the subject of a sentence; the *possessive* (or genitive), which indicates ownership; and the *objective* (or accusative), which functions as the object of a verb or preposition. See chapter **16** and **29a**.

cause and effect   A rhetorical strategy by which a writer seeks to explain why something happened or what the results of a particular event or condition were or will be. See **2e(4)**.

CD-ROM Acronym for *Compact Disk-Read Only Memory.* CD-ROMs store large amounts of information—as much as 300,000 pages.

citation Notation (usually parenthetical) in a paper that refers to a source. See **7e(1)** and **7h(1)**.

chronological order The arrangement of events in a time sequence (usually the order in which they occurred).

claim A conclusion that a writer expects readers to accept. A claim should be supported by accurate and representative source material. See chapter **5**.

classification and division A rhetorical strategy in which a writer sorts elements into categories (*classification*) or breaks a topic down into its constituent parts to show how they are related (*division*). See **2e(6)**.

clause A sequence of related words within a sentence. A clause has both a subject and a predicate and functions either as an independent unit (*independent clause*) or as a dependent unit (*subordinate clause,* used as an adverb, an adjective, or a noun). See **12b** and chapter **19**. See also **sentence.**

cliché An expression that may once have been fresh and effective but that has become trite and worn out with overuse. See **24c**.

coherence The principle that all the parts of a piece of writing should stick together, one sentence leading to the next, each idea evolving from the previous one. See **15e–f** and **3c**.

collaborative writing A method of writing involving a cooperative effort between two or more persons.

collective noun A noun singular in form that denotes a group: *flock, jury, band, public, committee.* See **17e(8)**.

colloquialism A word or phrase characteristic of informal speech. "He's *grumpy*" is a colloquial expression describing an irritable person. See **23b(1)**.

comma splice, comma fault A punctuation error in which two independent clauses are joined by a comma with no coordinating conjunction. See chapter **14**. Patricia went to the game, **and** her brother stayed home.

common gender   A term applied to words that can refer to either sex (*parent, instructor, salesperson, people, anyone*). See **23d**.

common noun   A noun referring to any or all members of a class or group (*woman, city, apple, holiday*) rather than to a specific member (*Susan B. Anthony, Las Vegas, Winesap, New Year's Day*). See **noun.**

comparative degree   See **degree.**

comparison and contrast   A rhetorical strategy in which the writer examines similarities and/or differences between two ideas or objects. See **2e(5)**.

complement   A word or words used to complete the sense of a verb. The term usually refers to a subject complement, an object complement, or the complement of a verb like *be.* See **11c**.

complex sentence   A sentence containing one independent clause and at least one subordinate clause: *My neighbor noticed a stranger* [independent clause] *who looked suspicious* [subordinate clause]. See **12c(3)**, chapter **19**, and **22c(1)**. See also **clause.**

compound-complex sentence   A sentence containing at least two independent clauses and one or more subordinate clauses: *When the lights went out* [subordinate clause], *there was no flashlight at hand* [independent clause], *so we sat outside and gazed at the stars* [independent clause]. See **12c(4)**. See also **clause.**

compound sentence   A sentence containing at least two independent clauses and no subordinate clause: *The water supply was dwindling* [independent clause], *so rationing became mandatory* [independent clause]. See **12c(2)**, **27a**, and **28a**. See also **clause.**

concession   Agreeing with a point made by your opponent in response to your own argument.

conclusion   A sentence, paragraph, or group of paragraphs that brings a piece of writing to a satisfying close. See **3b(2)**.

concrete noun   Concrete nouns refer to things that can be experienced through the senses: *cologne, sunset, onions, thorns.* COMPARE **abstract noun.**

conjugation   A set or table of the inflected forms of a verb that indicates tense, person, number, voice, and mood. See chapter **17**, pages 329–32.

conjunction A part of speech (such as *and* or *although*) used to connect words, phrases, clauses, or sentences. *Coordinating conjunctions* (*and, but, or, nor, for, so, yet*) connect and relate words and word groups of equal grammatical rank: Color-blind people can usually see blue, *but* they may confuse red with green *or* with yellow. See **12b(3)** and chapter **20**. See also **correlatives.** *Subordinating conjunctions* (such as *although, if, when*—see the list on pages 286–87) mark a dependent clause and connect it with a main clause: *When* Frank sulks, he acts *as if* he were deaf. See chapter **19**.

conjunctive adverb A word (*however, therefore, nevertheless*) that serves not only as an adverb but also as a connective. See **14b**, **28a**, and **3d**.

connotation The suggested or implied meaning of a word through the associations it evokes in the reader's mind. See **24a(2)**. See also **denotation.**

consonant A class of speech sounds represented in English by any letter other than *a, e, i, o,* or *u.*

context The surrounding information that helps give a particular word, sentence, or paragraph its meaning: *cabinet* means "a group of leaders" in a political context and "a place for storage" in a building context. *Context* also refers to circumstances surrounding the composition of a piece of writing—the occasion, the purpose, the audience, and what the writer and reader already understand about the topic. See **1g**.

contraction Condensing two words into one by adding an apostrophe to replace the omitted letter or letters: *aren't, don't.*

controlling idea The central idea of a paragraph or essay, often expressed in the paragraph's **topic sentence** or the essay's **thesis** statement. See **3c(1)** and **2b**.

coordinating conjunction One of seven connectives: *and, but, for, or, nor, so, yet.* See **12b(3)**, **27a**, chapter **19**, and chapter **20**. See also **conjunction.**

coordination The use of grammatically equivalent constructions to link ideas, usually (but not always) those of equal weight. See **27c(2)**, **19b**, and chapter **20**.

correlatives   One of five pairs of connectives used to link equivalent constructions: *both . . . and; either . . . or; neither . . . nor; not only . . . but also; whether . . . or.* See **20c**.

count, noncount nouns   Count nouns are individual, countable entities; cannot be viewed as a mass (*word, finger, remark*). Noncount nouns are a mass or a continuum (*hope, water*). See **11c** and **noun.**

credibility   The reliability of a person or evidence. See **5d** and **1f**.

critical thinking/reading/writing   The ability to analyze and synthesize ideas: to distinguish between fact and opinion, to recognize the importance of evidence and logic, to evaluate for credibility, and to avoid common fallacies. See chapter **5**.

cumulative sentence   A sentence in which the subject and predicate come first, followed by modifiers. (Also called a loose sentence.) See **21b**.

dangling modifier   A word or phrase that does not clearly refer to another word or word group in the sentence. See **15f**.

declension   A set or table of inflected forms of nouns or pronouns. See the examples on page 311.

deduction   A form of logical reasoning that begins with a generalization (*premise*), relates a specific fact to that generalization, and forms a *conclusion* that fits both. See **5h(2)**. COMPARE **induction.**

definition   A brief explanation of the meaning of a word, as in a dictionary. Also, an extended piece of writing, employing a variety of rhetorical strategies, to explain what something is or means. See **2e(7)**.

degree   The form of an adverb or adjective that indicates relative quality, quantity, or manner. The three degrees are *positive,* a quality of a single element; *comparative,* between two elements; and *superlative,* among three or more elements: *good, better, best; fast, faster, fastest.* See **15c**.

demonstratives   Four words that point out (*this, that, these, those*).

denotation   The literal meaning of a word as commonly defined. See **24a(1)**. See also **connotation.**

dependent clause A subordinate clause. See **clause.**

description A rhetorical strategy using details perceivable by the senses to portray a scene, object, performance, and so on. See **2e(2).**

determiner A word (such as *a, an, the, my, their*) that signals the approach of a noun: **the** newly mown *hay.*

development The elaboration of an idea through organized discussion filled with examples, details, and other information. See **2d.**

diction The writer's choice of exact, idiomatic, and fresh words, as well as appropriate levels of usage. See chapters **23** and **24.**

direct address A name or descriptive term (set off by commas) designating the one or ones spoken to: Play it again, *Sam.*

direct discourse See **direct quotation.**

direct object A noun (or noun clause) naming *whom* or *what* after an active verb: Emily sliced the *ham.* See **11c(2).** See also **object.**

direct quotation A repetition of the exact spoken or written words of others: "Where an opinion is general," writes Jane Austen, "it is usually correct." See **30a** and **7d.**

double negative The nonstandard combination of two negatives, which has a negative meaning: We ca*n't* do *nothing* about the weather. See **15g.**

draft, drafting A working version of a piece of writing. The process of putting ideas into writing so they can be revised and edited. See **2e–f.**

edited American English (EAE) The term adopted by the National Council of Teachers of English for the academic and business style expected in most college writing.

editing Reworking sentences for clarity, sense, and conformity to conventional rules of spelling, punctuation, mechanics, grammar, and sentence structure.

electronic mail See **e-mail.**

ellipsis Three spaced periods that indicate material omitted from a quotation. See **31i.**

elliptical construction   The omission of an element essential to the grammar but not to the intended meaning: Cats are cleaner than pigs [are].

e-mail   Electronic mail; transfers messages over a communications network, mainly the Internet.

ethos   Can be translated as "arguing honorably" and is employed when you tell others the truth and treat them with respect. See pages 94 –95, **logos,** and **pathos.**

euphemism   An indirect or "nice" expression used instead of a more direct one: *correctional facility* instead of *jail.* See **24c.**

evidence   Facts, statistics, examples, testimony, sensory details, and so on that support generalizations.

example   Any fact, anecdote, reference, or the like used to illustrate an idea. See **2d.**

expletive   Signals a transformation in sentence structure without a change of meaning, i.e. *there* shifts subject-verb order (*There* were over four thousand runners in the marathon.); *it* transforms the main clause into a subordinate clause (It is apparent that the plane is late.). See **17e(5).**

fallacy   A false argument or incorrect reasoning. See **5i.**

faulty predication   The use of a predicate that does not logically be-long with a given subject: One superstition is **involves** a black cat. See **18d.**

figurative language   The use of words in an imaginative rather than a literal sense. See **24a(4).**

focus   The narrowing of a subject to a manageable size; also the sharpening of the writer's view of the subject. See **2a–c.**

fragment   A group of words that begins with a capital letter and ends with a period but that lacks a subject, a predicate, or both. See chapter **13.**

freewriting   A method of finding a writing topic by composing for a specified length of time without stopping to reflect, reread, or correct errors.

function words Words (such as prepositions, conjunctions, auxiliaries, and articles) that indicate the functions of other words in a sentence and the grammatical relations between them.

fused sentence Two or more sentences run together, with no punctuation or conjunctions to separate them. Also called a run-on sentence. Unacceptable in college and professional writing. See chapter **14**.

gender The grammatical distinction that labels nouns or pronouns as masculine, feminine, or neuter. In English, grammatical gender usually corresponds to natural gender.

general/specific, generalization *General* words are all-embracing, indefinite, sweeping in scope: *food. Specific* words are precise, explicit, limited in scope: *spaghetti carbonara.* The same is true of *general* and *specific* ideas.

generalization In argument, a conclusion drawn from facts and/or other evidence. Often used loosely to refer to statements that are too broad, indefinite, or sweeping in scope.

gerund A verbal that ends in *-ing* and functions as a noun. *Riding* a bike is good exercise.

grammar The system of rules by which words are arranged into the structures meaningful in a language.

graphics Images or pictures that can be displayed in a document.

hardware In computer terminology, the tangible components of the computer system such as the keyboard, the monitor, and the components inside the system box.

helping verb A verb that combines with another verb to indicate voice, tense, or mood. See **17a**, **auxiliary,** and **modal.**

historical present A tense used to describe events in literature or history that are permanently preserved in the present: The tragedy *is* that Iago *deceives* Othello. See **17c(1)** and **9a**.

homophones Words that have the same sound and sometimes the same spelling but that differ in meaning (*their, there,* and *they're* or *capital* meaning "funds" and *capital* meaning "government city"). See **32c**.

hyperbole An intentional overstatement made for rhetorical effect. See **9e**. COMPARE **understatement.**

idiom A fixed expression (within a language) whose meaning cannot be deduced from its elements: *put up a fight; to mean well.* See **24b**.

illustration In writing, the use of specific details to give substance and interest to a subject. See **2d**.

imperative mood See **mood.**

inclusive language The use of language in such a way that no group of people is ignored, insulted, or condescended to. It is an answer to sexist, racist, and classist language. See **23d**.

independent clause See **clause.**

indicative mood See **mood.**

indirect discourse Information paraphrased or summarized from a source and, with attribution, integrated into a writer's own sentence.

indirect object A word (or words) naming the one (or ones) indirectly affected by the action of the verb: Emily sliced *me* some ham. See **object.**

indirect question A question phrased as a statement, usually a subordinate clause: We can ask *whether Milton's blindness was the result of glaucoma,* but we cannot be sure. See **31b**.

indirect quotation A report of the written or spoken words of another without using the exact words of the speaker or writer: The registrar said *that the bank returned my tuition check.* COMPARE **direct quotation.**

induction A form of logical reasoning that begins with evidence and interprets it to form a conclusion. See **5h**. COMPARE **deduction.**

infinitive Usually made up of the word *to* plus the present form of a verb (called the *stem* of the infinitive). Infinitives are used chiefly as nouns, less frequently as adjectives or adverbs. Lashanda wanted *to continue* the debate.

infinitive phrase A phrase that employs the infinitive form of the verb: *to go to the store, to run the race.* See **phrase.**

inflection   A change in the form of a word to show a specific meaning or grammatical function: **verb:** *talk, talks, talked;* **noun:** *dog, dogs, dog's, dogs';* **pronoun:** *he, him, his; they, them, their, theirs;* **adjective:** *thin, thinner, thinnest;* **adverb:** *rapidly, more rapidly, most rapidly.*

intensifier   A modifier used for emphasis: *very* excited, *certainly* pleased. See **qualifier.**

intensive/reflexive pronoun   The *-self* pronouns (such as *myself, himself, themselves*). The *intensive* is used for emphasis: The teenagers *themselves* had the best idea. The *reflexive* is used as an object of a verb, verbal, or preposition: He blames *himself.*

interjection   A word (one of the eight parts of speech) expressing a simple exclamation: *Hey! Oops!* (See **31c**.)

interrogative   A word such as *which, whose,* or *why* used to ask a question: *Which* is the more expensive?

intransitive verb   A verb (such as *appear* or *belong*) that does not take an object: Sarah *ran* fast. See chapter **17**. See also **verb** and **transitive verb.**

invention   The process of using strategies to generate ideas for writing. See **2a** and **2e**.

inversion   A change in the usual word order of a sentence: Into the valley of death rode the six hundred. See **21f**.

irony   A deliberate inconsistency between what is stated and what is meant. Irony can be verbal or situational. See **24a(4)**.

irregular verb   A verb that is not inflected in the usual way—that is, by the addition of *-d* or *-ed* to the present form to create the past tense and past participle.

jargon   Technical slang, appropriate as a shortcut to communication when the audience is knowledgeable about the topic and the terms. See **23b(6)**.

journal   A special-interest periodical. Also a notebook in which a writer records personal thoughts and experiences.

justification Inserting spaces between words so that every line is the same length and makes the right or left margin, or both margins, straight.

linking verb A verb that relates the subject complement to the subject, e.g. *become, seem, appear, feel, look, taste, smell, sound* and forms of the verb *be:* She *is* a writer. The bread *looks* burned. See **17a**.

listing An informal way of gathering ideas about a writing topic in which a writer lists ideas about the subject. See pages 31–32.

logic The presentation of ideas that shows a clear, predictable, and structured relation among those ideas. See chapters **18** and **5**.

logos The logical use of language in effective arguments. See pages 94–95, **ethos,** and **pathos.**

loose sentence See **cumulative sentence.**

main idea The part of the paragraph or paper to which all the other ideas relate. See **2b**, **topic sentence,** and **thesis.**

metaphor An imaginative comparison between dissimilar things without using *like* or *as.* See **24a(4)** and **9e.**

misplaced modifier A descriptive or qualifying word (modifier) placed in an awkward position, usually far away from what it modifies: I read that there was a big fire *in yesterday's newspaper.* I read in yesterday's newspaper that there was a big fire. [Place the modifier after the verb *read.*] See **15e.**

mixed construction A garbled sentence that is the result of an unintentional shift from one grammatical pattern to another. See **18c(2)**.

mixed metaphor A construction that confuses two or more metaphors: He was *playing with fire* and got in *over his head.* See **18c(1)**.

MLA Modern Language Association. See **7e–f.**

modal A helping verb (not conjugated) that shows ability (*can, could*); permission or possibility (*may, might*); determination, promise, or intention (*shall, should; will, would*); obligation (*ought*); or necessity (*must*).

modifier A word or word group that describes, limits, or qualifies another. See chapter **15**.

mood The way a speaker or writer regards an assertion—that is, as a declarative statement or a question (*indicative* mood); as a command or request (*imperative*); or as a supposition, hypothesis, recommendation, or condition contrary to fact (*subjunctive*). See **17d(2)**.

narration A rhetorical strategy that recounts a sequence of events, usually in chronological order. See **2e(1)**.

netiquette Guidelines for proper behavior in e-mail correspondence, chat rooms, and so on.

nominalization The practice of using nouns instead of active verbs: She *made a list* of the schedule changes. [COMPARE She *listed* the schedule changes.]

nonrestrictive Nonessential to the identification of the word or words referred to. My best friend, *Pauline,* understands me. See **27d**.

nonstandard Speech forms that are common in colloquial writing but that should be avoided in college and business writing. See **23b(4)**.

noun A part of speech that names a person, place, thing, idea, animal, quality, or action: *Mary, America, apples, justice, goose, strength, departure, NASA, breakthrough, buddy system, sister-in-law.* Noun-making suffixes are *-ance, -ation, -ence, -ism, -ity, -ment, -ness, -ship.* Verbs such as *relax* or *depend* become the nouns *relaxation* or *dependence;* adjectives such as *kind* or *rigid* become the nouns *kindness* or *rigidity.* A noun usually changes form to indicate the plural and the possessive case, as in *man, men; man's, men's.*

noun clause A subordinate clause used as a noun. See **12b**. See also **clause**.

number The inflectional form of a word that identifies it as singular (one) or plural (more than one): *river–rivers, this–those, he sees–they see.* See **17e** and **32e**.

object A noun or noun substitute governed by an active verb, a verbal, or a preposition. See **11c(2–3)** and **12a(4)**. Bill hit the **ball**

[direct object]. She likes to grow **flowers** [object of a verbal]. I gave **him** the keys [indirect object]. They play ball in the **park** [object of a preposition].

object complement   A word that helps complete the meaning of such verbs as *make, paint, elect, name.* An object complement refers to or modifies the direct object: They painted the cellar door *blue.* See **11c(3)** and **15a.** See also **complement.**

overgeneralization   Lacking specificity. See **general/specific, generalization.**

paradox   A statement that seems contradictory but that may actually be true. See **9e.**

parallelism   The use of corresponding grammatically equal elements in sentences and paragraphs. See chapter **20.**

paraphrase   A sentence-by-sentence restatement of the ideas in a passage, using different words. See **7c(3).**

parenthetical element   Nonessential words, phrases, clauses, or sentences (such as an aside) usually set off by commas but often by dashes or parentheses. See **27d, 31e(2),** and **31f.**

participle   A verb form that may function as part of a verb phrase (was *thinking,* had *determined*) or as a modifier (a *determined* effort; the couple, *thinking* about their past). Participles may take objects, complements, and modifiers: The stagehand *carrying the trunk* fell over the threshold. [The participle *carrying* takes the object *trunk;* the whole participial phrase modifies *stagehand.*] See **17b(3)** and **15f.**

particle   A word like *across, away, down, for, in, off, out, up, with* combined with a verb to form idiomatic usages in which the combination has the force of a single-word verb: The authorities refused to *put up* with him.

parts of speech   The classes into which words may be grouped according to their form changes and grammatical relations.

passive voice   The form of the verb showing that its subject is not the agent performing the action of the verb but is rather the goal of that action: The ham *was sliced* by Emily. See chapter **17** and **21d(1).** See also **active voice.**

pathos The use of language in effective arguments to stir the feelings of an audience. See pages 94–95, **ethos,** and **logos.**

perfect tenses The tenses formed by the addition of a form of *have* and showing complex time relations in completing the action of the verb (the present perfect—*have/has eaten;* the past perfect—*had eaten;* and the future perfect—*will/shall have eaten*).

periodic sentence A sentence in which the main idea comes last. See **21b**. COMPARE **cumulative sentence.**

person The form of pronouns and verbs denoting or indicating whether one is speaking (*I am*—first person), is spoken to (*you are*—second person), or spoken about (*he is*—third person). See **17e** and **18e**.

personal pronoun Any one of a group of pronouns—*I, we, you, he, she, it, they,* and their inflected forms—referring to the one (or ones) speaking, spoken to, or spoken about. See chapter **16**.

personification The attributing of human characteristics to nonhuman things (animals, objects, ideas): "That night wind was breathing across me through the spokes of the wheel." —WALLACE STEGNER. See **9e**.

persuasive writing A form of writing intended chiefly to change the reader's opinions or attitudes or to arouse the reader to action. See **1g(1)**.

phrasal verb A unit consisting of a verb plus one or two uninflected words like *after, in, up, off,* or *out* (see **particle**) and having the force of a single-word verb: We *ran out* on them.

phrase A sequence of grammatically related words without a subject and/or a predicate. See **12a** and **13a**. See also **verbal.**

plagiarism Using another writer's words or ideas without acknowledging the source. Akin to theft, plagiarism has serious consequences and should always be avoided. See **7d**.

plural More than one. COMPARE **singular.**

point of view The vantage point from which the topic is viewed. See **18e**. It also refers to the stance a writer takes—objective or impartial (third person), directive (second person), or personal (first person).

positive See **degree.**

predicate A basic grammatical division of a sentence. A predicate is the part of the sentence comprising what is said about the subject. The *complete predicate* consists of the main verb and its auxiliaries (the *simple predicate*) and any complements and modifiers: We *chased the dog all around our grandmother's farm.*

predicate adjective The adjective following a linking verb and modifying the subject. The bread tastes *sweet.* See **15a** and **linking verb.**

predicate noun A noun used as a subject complement: Bromides are *sedatives.* See **11c(3)**. See also **linking verb.**

prefix An added syllable or group of syllables (such as *in-, dis-, un-, pro-*) placed before a word to form a new word: *adequate–inadequate.* A prefix ordinarily changes the meaning.

premise An assumption or a proposition on which an argument or explanation is based. In logic, premises are either major (general) or minor (specific); when combined correctly, they lead to a conclusion. See **5h(2)**. See also **syllogism.**

preposition A part of speech that links and relates a noun or noun substitute to another word in the sentence: The dancers leapt *across* the stage. See page 282 for a list of prepositions.

prepositional phrase A preposition with its object and any modifiers: *in the hall, between you and me, for the new van.*

prewriting The initial stage of the writing process, concerned primarily with planning.

primary source In research or bibliographies, the source that provides firsthand facts.

process analysis A rhetorical strategy either to instruct the reader how to perform a procedure or to explain how something occurs. See **2e(3)**.

progressive verb A verb phrase consisting of a present participle (ending in *-ing*) used with a form of *be* and denoting continuous action: *is attacking, will be eating.*

pronoun   A part of speech that takes the position of nouns and functions as nouns do. See chapter **16** and **17e.**

proofreading   Checking the final draft of a paper to eliminate typographic, spelling, punctuation, and documentation errors. See **4d** and **3g.**

proper adjective   See **adjective.**

proper noun   See **noun.**

purpose   A writer's reason for writing. The purpose for nonfiction writing may be predominantly expressive, expository, or persuasive, though all three aims are likely to be present in some measure. See **1g.**

qualifier   Any modifier that describes or limits: *Sometimes* movies are *too* gory to watch. See **intensifier.**

quotation   The exact words of another person repeated or copied. See **30a** and **7c(2).**

redundant   Needlessly repetitious, unnecessary.

referential writing   Writing whose chief aim is to clarify, explain, or evaluate a subject in order to inform or instruct the reader. Also called expository or informative writing. See **1g.**

reflexive pronoun   See **pronoun.**

refutation   Introducing reasons why others may believe differently and then explaining why these reasons are not convincing. See page 96.

regular verb   A verb that forms its past tense and past participle by adding *-d* or *-ed* to the present form (or the stem of the infinitive): *love, loved.* See chapter **17.**

relative clause   An adjectival clause introduced by a relative pronoun: the programs *that provide services.*

relative pronoun   A noun substitute (*who, whom, whose, that, which, what, whoever, whomever, whichever, whatever*) used to introduce subordinate clauses: He has an aunt **who** *is a principal* [adjectival clause introduced by the relative pronoun *who*]. See chapter **16.**

restrictive   A word, phrase, or clause that limits the word referred to by imposing conditions or by confining the word to a particular group or to a specific item or individual: Every student *who cheats* will be removed from the class. [The restrictive clause *who cheats* imposes conditions on—restricts—the meaning of *every student.* Only those students *who cheat* will be removed.] See **27d**. See also **nonrestrictive.**

revision   Part of the writing process. Writers revise by rereading and rethinking a piece of writing to see where they need to add, delete, move, replace, reshape, and even completely recast ideas.

rhetoric   The art of using language effectively. (See chapter **4** and **1g**.)

rhetorical question   A question posed for effect without expectation of a reply: Who can tell what will happen?

rhetorical situation   The relationship between the writer, the audience, and the context that determines the appropriate approach for a particular piece of writing.

run-on sentence   See **fused sentence.**

secondary source   A source that analyzes or interprets **primary source** material.

sentence   A grammatically independent unit of expression. A simple sentence contains a subject and a predicate. Sentences are classified according to structure (simple, complex, compound, and compound-complex) and purpose (declaratory, interrogatory, imperative, and exclamatory). See chapter **11**.

sentence modifier   An adverb or adverb substitute that modifies the rest of the sentence, not a specific word or word group in it: *Yes,* the plane arrived on time.

sexist language   Language that arbitrarily excludes one sex or the other or that arbitrarily assigns stereotypical roles to one sex or the other. See **16d(1)**, **23d**, and **inclusive language.**

simile   The comparison of two dissimilar things using *like* or *as.* Frank is as trustworthy *as a snake.* See **24a(4)** and **9e**.

simple tenses   The tenses that refer to present, past, and future time.

singular   One. See **number**. COMPARE **plural**.

slang   The casual vocabulary of specific groups or cultures. See **23b**.

software   Computer programs that enable the user to perform specific tasks.

split infinitive   The often awkward separation of the parts of an infinitive by at least one adverb: *to* quietly *go*. See **infinitive.**

squinting modifier   An ambiguous modifier that can refer to either a preceding or a following word: Eating *often* makes her sick. See **15e(4)**.

standard American English   See **edited American English.**

style   An author's choice and arrangement of words, sentence structures, and ideas, as well as less definable characteristics such as rhythm and euphony. See chapter **21**.

subject   A basic grammatical division of a sentence. The subject is a noun or noun substitute about which something is asserted or asked in the predicate. The *complete subject* consists of the *simple subject* and the words associated with it: *The woman in the gray trench coat* asked for information. The term may also refer to the main idea of a piece of writing.

subject complement   A word or words that complete the meaning of a linking verb and that modify or refer to the subject: The old car looked *shabby* [predicate adjective]. The old car was *an eyesore* [predicate noun]. See **11c(3)**, **15a**, and **16b**. See also **linking verb.**

subjunctive mood   See **mood.**

subordinate clause   See **clause.**

subordinating conjunction   See **conjunction.**

subordination   The use of dependent structures (phrases, subordinate clauses) that are lower in grammatical rank than independent ones (simple sentences, main clauses). See chapter **19**.

suffix   An added sound, syllable, or group of syllables placed after a word to form a new word, to change the meaning of a word, or to indicate grammatical function: *light, lighted, lightest, lightly.*

summary   A concise restatement briefer than the original. See **7c(4)**.

superlative degree   See **degree.**

syllogism   A three-part form of deductive reasoning. See **5h(2)**.

synonym   A word that has a meaning similar to that of another word.

syntax   Sentence structure; the grammatical arrangement of words, phrases, and clauses.

synthesis   Inductive reasoning whereby a writer begins with a number of instances (facts or observations) and uses them to draw a general conclusion. See **5h(1)**.

tag question   A question attached to the end of a related statement and set off by a comma: She's coming, *isn't she?* See **14a**.

tense   The form of the verb that denotes time. Inflection of single-word verbs (*pay, paid*) and the use of auxiliaries (*am paid, was paid, will pay*) indicate tense. See **17c**.

thesis   The central point or main idea of an essay. See **2b**.

tone   The writer's attitude toward the subject and the audience, usually conveyed through diction and sentence structure.

topic   The specific, narrowed idea of a paper. See **subject.**

topic sentence   A statement of the central thought of a paragraph, which, though often at the beginning, may appear anywhere in it. Some paragraphs may not have a topic sentence, although the main idea is clearly suggested.

transitions   Words, phrases, sentences, or paragraphs that relate ideas and provide coherence by linking sentences, paragraphs, and larger units of writing. Transitions may be expressions or structural features a writer uses. See **3d**.

transitive verb   A type of verb that takes an object. They *danced* the polka. See **verb** and **intransitive verb.**

truth   In deductive reasoning, the veracity of the premises. If the premises are true, the conclusion is true. An argument may be true but invalid if the relation between the premises is invalid. See **5h(2)**. See also **validity.**

understatement Intentional underemphasis for effect, usually ironic. See **9e**. See also **hyperbole**.

unity All the elements in an essay or paragraph contributing to developing a single idea or thesis. See **3c(2)** and **2b**.

URL Abbreviation for *Uniform Resource Locator,* which identifies an Internet address, including the domain name and often a specific file to be accessed. For example, the URL for the Harcourt Web site includes the indicator that it is on the World Wide Web (http://www), the domain name (harcourtcollege), and the domain (com), all separated by periods: ⟨http://www.harcourtcollege.com⟩.

validity The structural coherence of a deductive argument. An argument is valid when the premises of a syllogism are correctly related to form a conclusion. Validity does not, however, actually refer to the truthfulness of an argument's premises. See **5h(2)**. COMPARE **truth.**

verb A part of speech denoting action, occurrence, or existence (state of being). Verbs are words such as *notify* or *write*. Verb-making suffixes are *-ize* and *-ify: terror,* a noun, becomes *terrorize, terrify,* verbs. See **11b** and chapter **17**. See also **inflection, mood, voice, transitive verb,** and **intransitive verb.**

verbal A word that has the nature of a verb as well as being used as a noun, an adjective, or an adverb. Infinitives, participles, and gerunds are verbals. See **gerund, infinitive,** and **participle.** See also **12a(3)**.

voice The form of a verb that indicates whether or not the subject performs the action denoted by the verb. See **17d**, **active voice,** and **passive voice.**

vowel A speech sound represented in written English by *a, e, i, o, u,* and sometimes *y.*

word order The arrangement of words in sentences. Because of lost inflections, modern English depends heavily on word order to convey meaning: Nancy gave Henry $14,000. Henry gave Nancy $14,000. Tony had built a garage. Tony had a garage built.

World Wide Web (www) A system of Internet servers that store documents, called *Web pages,* formatted in a special computer language (html). See pages 127–30.

Copyrights and Acknowledgments

Index

Numbers and letters in color refer to chapters and sections in the handbook; other numbers refer to pages.

English as a World Language Index

Entries in this index identify topics basic to ESL usage. Numbers and letters in color refer to chapters and sections in the handbook; other numbers refer to pages.